THE LEAP

THE LEAP

A Memoir of Love and Madness
in the Internet Gold Rush

Tom Ashbrook

HOUGHTON MIFFLIN COMPANY
Boston • New York 2000

For information about permission to reproduce selections from
this book, write to Permissions, Houghton Mifflin Company,
215 Park Avenue South, New York, New York 10003.

Library of Congress Cataloging-in-Publication Data

Ashbrook, Tom.
The leap : a memoir of love and madness in the Internet
gold rush / Tom Ashbrook.
    p.   cm.
ISBN 0-395-83934-3   BT 25. ∞|13.73 7|∞
1. Internet industry — United States. 2. New business
enterprises — United States. 3. Ashbrook, Tom.
4. Businessmen — United States — Biography. I. Title.
HD9696.8.U62 A84 2000
658.8′4—dc21 [B] 99-059162

Printed in the United States of America

Book design by Robert Overholtzer

QUM 10 9 8 7 6 5 4 3 2 1

నా భార్యకు

always

Therefore take no thought, saying, What shall we eat? or, What shall we drink? or, Wherewithal shall we be clothed?

— Matthew 6:31

Contents

that drove down dark roads where the dead had lain. Oh, Danielle, I am too far from home.

Then Jesus off the little page, like a friend, like a taunt: "Is not the life more than meat, and the body more than raiment?" I was reading, he was saying, we were moving. In a crumbling hotel room, in a fever in the dark, he moves with grace so focused I become a silent mirror.

On this long day I have seen bones and darkness wrapped in beauty. I have driven out of Rwanda to Bukavu, where Belgian masters left château after château on the equator and hatred in each stone and vine. I have seen the villages with every third house destroyed, and sullen bloodshot boys with dull exhausted knives and guns, and wide boneyards still soft to touch. I have seen truckloads of dull-eyed peasants wandering in dread through sweet green hills and the grimacing joy of old friends finding one another quite unexpectedly alive.

"The Internet will change everything except human nature," I hear Rolly murmuring. Somewhere in the hotel's dark rafters an ancient air conditioner kicks to life, sending one sharp, cold stream down through the swamp of heat. And I am sweating and shivering and turning.

Maybe I'm too old for this. Maybe this is too old for me, for anyone, a creaking, pointless trick of history too bloody, too endless. Who said I had to see firsthand? Who said there was no other way?

So I will think of everything, and think of change. I will take stock and move. I can't sleep anyway. It's too damned hot and cold.

— *from Africa notes, January 1995*

was four days into Africa when the jet lag caught up with me, when everything caught up with me. Standing naked in my boots at 2 A.M., sweating and wired and doing raggedy tai chi to make the night pass. Reading Jesus from Gideon's little Bible and thinking about the girl from Bujumbura and machetes and machine guns and time and the Internet.

Please fasten your seat belt firm and low, a little voice advised at thirty-nine. Instead, I was quietly slipping free. I was ready for a change, for rebirth, for a new skin and tang. I wasn't sure how it would come or what it would be, but I had to have it. Deep in a career, in a life, I was unbuckling, eyeing the exits, ready to walk on the wing.

That night in Bukavu, dreaming wide awake and turning, I saw everything. I saw Jesus and the girl and old John Peng all moving with me, soft, intense, in unison. "Combing the mane of the wild horse," like John Peng taught. Turning like slow motion kung fu kings. Breathing steady, eyes deep and cool, leaning in and out like tai chi masters.

"The white crane stretches its wing," John Peng would say, and we would stretch side-by-side in smooth duet, far from cares and close to happiness.

"I will help you," the girl from Bujumbura whispered at the airport in Rwanda. I was the American reporter, arriving late at night and lost. She was tall and very fine, a Tutsi, and close in the taxi

Chapter 1

Unbuckling

EVERYTHING.

That word was in the water lately. It was in the air. It was *ubiq-uitous.*

Everything to win. Everything to lose. Have everything. Risk everything. Walk away from everything.

And, of course, everything changing. The way we thought and felt and dreamed. Our expectations. The economy. The century. My marriage. The news business. Me. Everything.

It had been almost fifteen years since I first walked into the *Boston Globe* on a bright winter morning with shoes full of snow and a couple of scribbled names in my pocket. The *Globe* was a temple to me then, with its big presses and its brassy editorial voice. It had colorful characters and idealism and prestige and power. It hired me, and it held out the possibility of changing the world. I loved it.

Now things were changing, all right. But the paper didn't seem to have much to do with it, and neither did I. It was the economy, stupid. It was technology I barely understood. And some kind of new world, humming through the telephone lines, that we couldn't touch but was all around us. Changing everything, they said. Everything.

I had always been a heat seeker, but somehow the heat had slipped away from my corner. I was a top editor at the paper now, but what were we editing? And when we went out to report and write, who was honestly panting to read the stuff? We held a management retreat to look into the future, and a somber professor told us that tumbleweeds would blow through the pressroom within a decade. Nobody would bother to pull the last paper from the presses. Nobody would care to read it. When we all laughed, Ted Leonsis, the burly tough guy who would soon be president of America Online, flushed and growled into his microphone from the podium.

We had a simple choice, he said. "Digitize or die."

And I didn't know what he meant.

I would lie awake in bed with Danielle, her leg thrown over mine, and ramble in the night, when the boys were tucked in and she was diving for sleep and rest to face another day of work. I never knew how much she heard. My rant was almost always the same. I don't know where I'm going, I would say to the dark. I'm working for an outfit that pours ink onto wood pulp and sells yesterday's news. We're writing stories I'm not sure anyone cares about. I'm not even sure they're the right stories. I'm not sure anymore, I would say, about anything.

"Uh-huh," she would murmur.

I'm restless, Danielle, I would say. I'm crawling out of my skin. You know, at work, people actually sit in the cafeteria and debate whether newspapers will last long enough for us to retire. Maybe I'm paranoid. But the whole place is starting to smell of dinosaur. I didn't get into this business to be a minor priest in a dying religion, Danielle. I got in because it had gusto and life. Because it felt big and urgent and true. And now I don't know. I don't know if I've still got the passion for this. If it's worth it. Everything's changing. It's not what I came for anymore.

And she would sleep. And I would not. And I wondered what that meant, too.

Danielle was pregnant again. It was her third time, not counting the false starts, and this time we knew it was a girl. It had been eight years since Ben had come, twelve since Dylan. This pregnancy was an indulgence, but we weren't ready to be finished with kids.

We looked at it this way:

If I got promoted to a fabulous career at the paper, this third baby would be the icing on the cake, the lucky jewel in the crown. It could happen. And this would be the lucky child who got the extra trips to Disney World, the fancy skiing lessons, the long summers on the Cape.

And if the career just chugged along, well, that would have to be its own reward, and this child would be our alternate joy. She would be our fresh stake in the simple life, in soccer games and school concerts and silly dancing on winter nights in the living room.

"And what if I just go nuts and throw everything over?" I asked Danielle one Sunday afternoon as we walked around the neighborhood lake. "You know, try something crazy. Something new."

At the water's edge, a fat brown duck fought with two seagulls for a crust of bread. I wished our house were on this lake, with a great, wide lawn and fine veranda and the summer splashing of happy children and us around to hear it.

"You won't throw everything over," she said, pulling my hand onto her budding stomach. She was beautiful. She was sensible. She had known me for a long time.

"Not everything," she said.

Then a promotion passed me by. The next rung on the ladder was suddenly far away. The pull of the chase for the top had kept me with the program. Now I had taken a slap. It didn't mean I had to bolt. I could sit tight. Or I could jump to another paper. But here, suddenly, was a moment to do some completely fresh mapping. Here was a time to look honestly at myself and the world, to acknowledge how much I was chafing, how urgently I needed to make some big decisions.

And there was something else. My old college pal Rolly Rouse had been calling with a stream of wild ideas lately. I couldn't get used to hearing his voice again. In my mind's eye Rolly was still a skinny kid with a long ponytail and an unplugged electric guitar, racing through Jimi Hendrix riffs in 1973, our freshman year at Yale. We had shared a suite of rooms and some sweet, goofy growing up. I could still see young Stone Phillips, already anchorman-handsome, rolling on our floor in tears of laughter, reciting Kant while we lit farts with a match. And David Levitt, now a software wizard for Bill Gates's old partner Paul Allen, wrapping on a boa constrictor and dancing free and naked under his banana curl Afro. And Danny Schneider, an attorney in New York now and my dearest pal, grinning his beautiful idiot Buddha grin at the whole show.

But intense, hyperkinetic, driven Rolly Rouse on my phone? Now? This I would not have predicted. For years we had barely kept up. I knew he had gone on to study architecture and engineering and to do something with energy and housing. I knew he was married, to Carole, and that they had a young daughter. And that was about it until we happened to move into houses a mile apart and ran into each other at the local liquor store in Newton, our leafy suburb on the western edge of Boston.

Rolly was as high-strung and cerebral as ever — a "brainiac," my kids would say. At first the reaquaintance made me jumpy. His rate of idea production per second seemed almost crazed. At any moment he would cut loose on lessons of history and economic cycles and patterns in time, on Peter Drucker and George Gilder and technology waves and the finer points of inflation adjustment. Everything.

Danielle would roll her eyes and flee. I was charmed. My world of reporters and editors and deadlines was full of quick takes and deep irony and carefully veiled inner lives. We had our passions, but they tended to be well armored and held in reserve. Rolly was different. Twenty years after college, his personal world was still charged right out front with clenched-fist conviction and a dukes-up passion for big ideas. He wore everything on his sleeve — heart, brain, obsessions. He would talk and talk with complete and sincere absorption in his subject, whatever it happened to be, and I would wait for the cynical disavowal or ironic cocked eyebrow that never came. This was strangely refreshing.

We saw each other occasionally for a beer and conversation, and now he was on the phone almost every day. Talking about "new media." Talking about the Internet. Talking about maybe starting a new company — maybe with me.

How could we do that? He had a mortgage. I had a mortgage. We had no money worth mentioning. We had car payments and insurance bills and credit cards with all-American balances. We had lives already and kids to feed!

But I always returned his calls. They were too interesting to ignore. And I was too restless not to listen.

For a while, John Peng saved me from the itch. He showed up like a perfect gift, like oxygen, wisdom, and calm.

I met him early one morning on the big field near our house. I was out walking our tall yellow lab, Sadie, as I did every morning. The field was dog central for the neighborhood. When Sadie was a pup, I had always socialized with the neighbors rounding the field, jogging along in twos and threes or mobbed up for a stroll while our dogs tumbled and yelped. I had loved the fresh air and early morning sky and the easy puppy care chatter of feeding schedules and chewed shoes.

But now Sadie was a few years older and less frenetic, and I often walked alone with her, tossing her sticks and thinking. Work was weighing on me. Money, too. And time. There wasn't enough of it, and the little we had was slipping by. I was hopeless at office politics. The paycheck was good but never enough. The kids were growing up too fast, and the hours we worked seemed only to get longer. Danielle and I weren't laughing the way we used to laugh. Passion, even communication beyond the car pool schedule, had to wait in line with everything else. Life was a mess of compromises that I was tired of making.

I stopped noticing the morning sky. I started talking to Sadie more than usual, and one morning had to admit flat out that I was talking to myself, muttering vague complaints and bits of combative conversation like an old man on a bus station bench. I was living the two-car, six-figure, green suburb American dream — and muttering to myself like a bag lady in the rain. I was scaring the dog.

Then John Peng appeared. The first time I saw him, it was as if I had stumbled into a misplaced clip of exotic film. The neighborhood field was a familiar zone of soccer balls and L. L. Bean jackets and well-fed hounds with names like Brewster and Benson. Neighbors walked their dogs and rushed off to jobs as psychiatrists and lawyers and architects and software programmers. They had different degrees but one class: striving suburban strapped. Nobody felt secure, but everyone tried to act it.

On this morning, on a low hill in a corner of the field, I saw a dignified Chinese man slowly removing a dark blue jacket, folding it, and placing it carefully on the grass. With an old athlete's ease, he moved to a sunny spot at the center of the hilltop and began what was clearly a deeply familiar routine of stretching and deep breathing. By the time I had rounded the field again, he was doing tai chi.

I couldn't stop staring. Danielle and I had spent almost ten years in Asia, a good chunk of that time in Hong Kong, where for several hours every morning the parks were lined with people moving through the smooth ballet of tai chi. It looked like underwater martial arts, with its slow, meditative mix of balance and motion, retreat and attack. I had always wanted to learn but had never found the right opportunity.

Within a few weeks John Peng had become both my teacher and my friend. I didn't make new friends much anymore. Certainly not seventy-five-year-old friends from Harbin, in the far north of China. He was visiting his son, a mathematician in Boston. He was my good luck.

John Peng was a man of action, with clear, dark eyes and a striking strength of bearing. In our third conversation, I asked if he would teach me tai chi. He agreed, glad for the company, I think. The next morning he met me on the low hilltop with a handwritten list, in English and Chinese, of the first twenty-four basic moves I would need to learn, and we began.

We met every day, on fine mornings and in rain and in snow. I was awkward. He was patient, moving side-by-side with me, working to convey the significance of each motion. He was insistent that my learning be more than physical. Tai chi, he said, was about the mind and spirit.

"Comb the mane of wild horse," he would call out in his halting English and dignified Chinese on our first mornings, starting me through the sequence of movements that added up to simple tai chi.

"No thinking," he would say when we paused. "Only moving. Breathing. Be focused but free of mind. Be full of energy, but calm. Be full of power but never rigid."

Could he possibly know, I wondered, how well and truly I wanted to take his advice? Maybe he did. Morning after morning, month af-

ter month, we worked on that hillside, repeating and refining and repeating until even Sadie knew the routines by heart and would dance
with a stick in her mouth as we approached the end, eager to move
on and play fetch.

I was never a more willing student. I wanted more than anything
to be full of energy but calm, full of power but fluid. To be focused.
To breathe like a bodhisattva. To be free.

"Grasp the peacock's tail," John Peng would say, and I would follow his smooth, embracing gesture across the wet morning grass.

"Move with cloud hands," he would say, and we would move
slowly sideways, palms turning softly before our faces, minds floating free.

"Pick up needle from bottom of sea," he would say, and I would
bend close to the ground, exhaling cares and finding depth.

Silently, after the first weeks, we would repeat the slow routine
three times, start to finish. When the concentration was good and
the effort was complete, I left the field exhilarated, aware and alive in
every breath and fingertip. The colors came back to the morning sky,
to the trees and grass, to everything.

One morning after a year of mornings, John Peng told me he was
going back to China, that the time had come for him to see his other
children and grandchildren. He told me he had first started doing tai
chi at the same age I was now, and that he had never stopped, and
that it had never failed him through many difficulties. He advised
me to do the same and invited me to come and do tai chi with him
along the Sunghua River in China. Then we practiced together one
last time, immersed in a common prayer of motion and breathing
and awareness.

I knew I had been given a gift. John Peng's tai chi had reawakened
me. It had opened my eyes to the pleasure and power of a focused
spirit.

Which was good.

But it wasn't enough.

"You won't throw everything over," she said.

"Not everything."

She said it with a confidence shadowed by an old fear, and with some reason. We had led a charmed life, people said, and I guessed they were right. Things had come easily, but I was the one who believed in the charm. I was the Illinois farmboy raised in the warm embrace of small churches and "Kumbayah" campfires, raised to believe that the world was full of warm hearts and helping hands and endless possibilities that only required full-throated pursuit. Danielle was not so sure on any of those points.

We had been sweethearts since we were sixteen. I was a tall, bookish kid, raised baling hay and herding sheep and dreaming of the big world. She was a first breeze from that world, the honey-skinned immigrant daughter of a French father and German mother, exotic in our prairie town, writing fevered teenage poetry and grappling with America, grappling with me. Biologically, we were a happy head-on collision. In other ways, we seriously mistook each other. I saw Euroexotica in a gentle, brown-haired girl whose charmingly accented family had suffered war and dislocation and wanted stability in America. She saw American bedrock in a blue-jeaned native son who was locked and loaded with relentless American dreams. We were not what we each first perceived. It would be interesting.

The year we met, in the summer that Watergate tumbled out, she watched me catch a ride on a hog truck from Peoria to Philadelphia, go to work in Washington's political disintegration, and get caught up in riots in Miami, when National Guardsmen and antiwar protesters fought in the streets over Richard Nixon's nomination to a doomed reelection.

When the Alaskan oil pipeline boom was on, she waved me north, twice, to work as a roustabout and dynamiter and come back longhaired in the muscled pride of youth, battered hard hat and caribou antlers off the tundra thrown over my Kerouac backpack.

When Eastern mysticism was the rage we headed out together, to India for a year, still just kids, to study Telugu and the Vedas, to wander through the Himalayas and dance along the Bay of Bengal, knowing everything and knowing nothing.

As a boy, one of my dreams had been to somehow hock our modest family farm and buy my hometown newspaper, the *Bloomington Pantagraph.* In the early '80s, when prices for farmland were at a historic low and prices for newspapers at a historic high, the de

Young family, who owned the *San Francisco Chronicle,* bought the *Pantagraph* for tens of millions of dollars.

The de Youngs didn't know me from a bump on a log, from a boy on a tractor. Neither did the local sellers. But I watched the transaction with a private sense of humiliation. My naive dream had been utterly laughable. There was no printing press out there with my name on it and probably would never be. So I kept moving.

When Mao died and China opened, Danielle and I made our base in Hong Kong to start careers in journalism and education, me as a green reporter at the *South China Morning Post,* she as a teacher for the United Nations, helping the waves of refugees that were sailing out of Vietnam.

When Asia exploded with wealth in the late '80s we were back again, now for the *Boston Globe,* starting a family in Tokyo and watching Japan's economic bubble grow, with fresh-off-the-boat Ferraris purring through the narrow, golden streets of the city.

We came home as the Berlin Wall came down, me to guide foreign news coverage from Boston at the end of the Cold War, she to become a young associate dean at MIT. We thought we were settling down, but it wasn't that simple.

People in my family had never had corporate jobs before my generation. They were farmers and forest rangers and schemers, always on the margins of the celebrated mainstream economy and its impositions. I could still remember that my father had a copy of *The Organization Man* under his nightstand when I was a boy, but I would bet he never got through it. I had never expected a corporate job either. Journalism had been my dodge. Now here I was, a newsroom manager in a large media company with an increasingly corporate feel. I had proven I could climb a corporate ladder, but was that what I had started out to do? I didn't think so.

My old friend Jonathan Kaufman, a reporter for the *Wall Street Journal,* used to accuse me of being a serial adventurer, of requiring a life-shifting thrill every few years, the way a vampire needs blood. Maybe he was right. When life is charmed, why not keep rolling the dice? Danielle probably could have told me why. She had her own view of life's odds and dangers. But I didn't want to hear it. I was on a hot clock, and I was restless. Yes, this time things were different.

We had a lot to lose, with real careers and kids and commitments. But there had to be a way to keep life fresh and free. Surely there was a way.

I remembered castrating lambs in the long-ago spring with my grandfather. We had a nifty tool like a long pliers that reached over their nappy little sacks and pinched the narrow tubes behind their nuts until they snapped. The lambs ran off as if nothing had happened. But of course it had.

"And what if we didn't have this nice tool?" our beloved old Swede asked me, standing in the barn as we sent the last lamb out the door, out into the pasture where Danielle and I would be married ten years later.

When I looked blank, he pushed his worn hat back and told me how when he was a boy the old shepherds would take a lamb's fuzzy scrotum right in their teeth, find the tubes, and bite down firm till they could feel them pop. That way you knew for sure the job was done, he said. And you didn't need fancy tools.

I made a face.

"Aw, that's nothing," he laughed, eyes twinkling. "Listen, Tom. I'll tell you something. You get in close enough to anything, and you really mean business, you'll be surprised at the things you can do."

Yessir, I nodded. And I got in close to a lot of things.

The flight from Brussels to Rwanda was seven easy hours, with clear skies all the way. The earth rolled under our little jet like a perfect promotion for *National Geographic*: alps, sea, desert, jungle. From 30,000 feet, it all looked as clean and virgin as the day it was made.

In seat 7A, I dropped a file of notes and clippings into my old gray shoulder bag. I had picked up that bag years before in a jammed Hong Kong alleyway. I had carried her on hundreds of trips through places in boom or in trouble, packed with the simple tools of the correspondent's trade. In India and Moscow and Nicaragua and Tokyo and Tibet she had been my portable note file, the rough sling for my laptop, my stashbox of rumpled press credentials, my lumpy pillow, my companion. Her zippers stuck. Her worn pocket corners were full of strange small coins and odd phone numbers and dust from all over. I was stupidly loyal to that bag, sentimental the way you might be about a favorite saddle or an old baseball cap. Or maybe an old career. Now we were on the road again, and I was testing.

This spring's itinerary was all laid out in her side pocket. Rwanda. Zaire. Somalia. The Balkans. Even with stopovers in London and Paris, it was a nasty lineup, by design. I had taken a few years off the road to work as an editor at the newspaper. I was cocky. My climb through the newsroom ranks was very fast. For a moment it seemed just possible that I might be running the whole show before lunchtime. But it didn't work out that way, and I was bailing out of the race for the top.

This was my first season back in the field. I didn't want to ease into it. I wanted destinations that would put my nose right back in the hard spots. I had always loved the news business, with its deadlines and drama. But I was hitting the age when journalists ask themselves if they really want to spend the rest of their lives chronicling other people's passions. There was still a newsroom to be run, and I would have a hand in that, but I was suffocating there. I needed to be out, maybe farther than I knew, to see if the old joy would still meet me. And it was there, but it was changed and so was I. I was judging in a new way. What I saw was sorrowful and moving, but it looked older than news should be, as if the world were living all at once across so many centuries that flight was time travel, and I was headed back when I wanted to go forward, to find the world's new energy, and my own. The past would be with us always, present and consequential and demanding. But I didn't have always. I had now. Forgive me, I thought, walking through the gutted streets of Mogadishu and Vukovar and graveyards on the equator. For a while I may need a different vista.

And there was a candidate. They called it the Internet, and it was supposed to be the new frontier. It was young and fresh and knew nothing of genocide and war. My pal David Levitt had been talking about it by different names for years, since his early days at MIT. I barely understood it, but I did understand "new frontier." That had a ring to it. I thought about it one blazing afternoon when a Somali gunman laid the business end of his grenade launcher against my neck at about the same moment that my kids were heading off to school on another continent. He was General Aidid's man, at the shell-pocked edge of General Aidid's godforsaken bit of turf. But what difference did that make?

I needed a change.

The baby came right on schedule. She was beautiful from her first wrinkled, blue, and mucky moment, straight out of the womb, to the drying table, to her mother's arms. She bellowed like a little sailor and we cried, Danielle and I, like we always cried, and I felt the familiar, primal rush of emotion. I would die for this child. I would kill for this child. And most of all, I would live, really live, for this child.

We named her Lauren Ingrid, an American name teamed with a middle nod to family Germans and Swedes. Danielle had vetoed India, my first choice, as too colonial and odd, and who could care now that she was here. Her hair was jet black and stood straight up, as if she carried an electric charge. Her tiny face beamed with instant self-possession. Her brothers, Dylan and Ben, huddled happily around their mother and new sister on the hospital bed, and I saw my whole family right there, young and trusting and vulnerable.

From the middle of the tableau, exhausted and serene, Danielle's deep green eyes stared straight into mine. I had known those lovely level eyes for a long time. I couldn't hide much from them. They saw. And they spoke. And right then they were speaking bigtime.

I'm counting on you, her eyes said as she cradled our tiny new daughter. Do you understand that?

I got it — loud and clear. I always had. I had always delivered. Not riches, not mansions. But a full fridge and good pay. Now I'd been with one employer, and doing well, for more than a dozen years. If that wasn't steady, I didn't know what was.

But I was twitching, and she knew it. She knew my rhythm. And now it had a reason. A big wave to ride and a hole to watch out for. Despite every near-giveaway and marketing trick the *Globe*'s inventive circulation department could come up with, the paper was losing readers. So was nearly every other major newspaper in the United States. I didn't have the same old confidence in the institution that cut my paycheck. For that matter, the whole brick-and-mortar economy seemed to be shouting the same message we saw on the flood of mutual fund fliers that fattened our daily pile of junk mail: past performance is no guarantee of future returns.

Brick-and-mortar. I had just begun to hear the phrase used, and used derisively. Brick-and-mortar as distinct from online, from electronic, from digital. Brick-and-mortar meant factories and warehouses and stores — and printing presses. It meant any commercial asset that was physical, heavy, solid, depreciating — as opposed to the world that was electronic, light, untouchable. For thousands of years, wealth and power had been measured by brick-and-mortar. Now, brick-and-mortar was suddenly the butt of jokes. It was the past. Zipping electrons were the future. Brick-and-mortar was a burden, a ball and chain. It was the old economy. It was history. And its past performance was no guarantee of future returns. Damn straight, I'd tell myself, proud to imagine that I was no slave to habit or fear. Every boomer and under with six ounces of awareness ought to be asking him- or herself right now how they were going to make it when the rain came, when their corner of the old economy met its maker. The scythe of time. The new economy.

Yessir, I would spout when the kids were in bed and I was brooding and pacing. It's all changing, and I for one am not going to be caught flat-footed. Not me. No way. I would not be frozen by dumb fear and some pitiful need to gulp the next paycheck. I would walk away.

"But to what? What is your alternative?" Danielle would gently ask, looking up from a stack of bills and the checkbook (which to my great relief she ran). She had heard me rant many times before, then calmly packed me off to work or the kids' soccer games or maybe Africa, and I would cool off and get back into our routine. My outbursts were coming more often now. And each time, those green eyes would level in for just an instant, for a quick reading, just checking the bullshit meter, deciding there was nothing unmanageable to worry about. Not yet anyway.

Now she was taking her reading again, locking eyes from the big hospital bed, her long hair pushed back and spilling over one shoulder of her dressing gown, her children gathered around her, our new

daughter perfect and helpless in her arms. I have just given you another child, her eyes said. You wanted a daughter, and I have given
you a daughter. She was still exhausted from the delivery. I could see
it in the economy of her movements — nothing wasted, nothing
quick. Even her eyes moved at a slow, gentle roll, taking in her sons,
her daughter, me, the moment, defining the intimate universe of our
family.

We are counting on you, her eyes said.

I stepped close to the bed and leaned down to put my forehead on
hers, my arms around the boys. Yes, I thought. I'm here for you. Always. With everything I have. Everything.

But what does that mean I should do? I wondered in the car on
the way home, while Dylan and Ben laughed and tussled in the
backseat. Dig in or move on? Fight on with the paper or get the
hell out?

And if, just if, I left the paper — hell, maybe leave newspapers entirely — what about Danielle's question?

What exactly was the alternative?

I wasn't sure. It would probably never happen. But I was starting
to see a slim little path. I was keeping dangerous company.

Rolly Rouse was the only person I knew who stopped breathing
when he talked.

It wasn't that he breathed less. He didn't breathe at all, for long,
long stretches. There wasn't time. And there wasn't leftover brain capacity for mundane chores like firing up the lungs. When Rolly
talked, he thought, and when he thought, his brain was like a great
furnace that sucked up all the oxygen in his body, sometimes all the
oxygen in a room. They say humans use only ten percent of their
mental capacity. Rolly surely used more, much more. When he got
into high gear, which is where he spent most of his time, he used so
much of his brain that he couldn't breathe.

For a long time I didn't know this. We were spending more and
more time together, after work, on weekends, over lunch. I was looking for new ideas and inspiration, and Rolly was a blazing idea factory. He was medium height and weight, with the big shoulders of a

former school athlete now set above a hint of middle-age paunch. His skin still had its youthful translucence and his face its fine features. His fingers were lean and deliberate — what you'd expect in an architect or fine craftsman. The ponytail of his college days was years gone, but his brown hair was still on the long side, and he still wore the full Sundance Kid mustache, slightly drooping at the corners, that gave him, at first glance, a jaunty wayfarer's look. But he was not a jaunty guy. With a monumental effort, he could laugh and slap backs and play the hail-fellow. But his pale eyes always blazed under long, thin lids and a swept-back pair of hawkish eyebrows. And when he talked, not breathing, those eyes began to bulge, and in his passion and intensity and oxygen deprivation and rising flush, you could see a touch of Mongol warrior. If this guy rode into your village on horseback, you hoped he was on your side.

Conversation with Rolly was not for the faint of heart. There were no throwaway lines, no casual, uncommitted riffs. Every statement was linked to a sincerely held idea, and every idea was linked to a hundred more equally impassioned ideas, and each of those to a thousand more, and every single one joined in a vast, deliberate mental matrix that Rolly's mind never stopped tending and updating and rearranging and testing. It was a full and amazingly detailed worldview and fact catalogue and logic engine behind those bulging eyes.

Way back in college I had already thought of Rolly's interior life as unusually intricate, conscious, crystalline. Xanadu. A grand and mindful intellectual project in all the ways that my inner music was simply sensual and wild. Now, twenty years later, I realized to my astonishment that his intellectual project, the great crystal palace in his mind, had never stopped growing, had never even slowed down. It had doubled up and doubled up like compounding interest behind those pale, fired-up eyes. And it was still growing, like that fifty-ton mushroom unearthed in Michigan, like the expanding universe, like Xanadu on steroids.

For precious chunks of nearly every day I checked out of deliberate thought — singing out loud, savoring a sunset or a pretty smile, rolling on the floor with the kids. Just a happy, dumb animal. Rolly never checked out. He couldn't. He was too desperately committed to the project within. It was his pride and his prison.

In social settings I would watch as some unsuspecting soul cradling a glass of wine stepped into Rolly's perimeter, exchanged pleasantries for a moment, then made a casual remark that held the slightest, uncrafted, unintended hook of a serious idea. Rolly would turn, the hook would go in, and the palace within would be engaged. His poor chatmate had no idea what she was in for, and Rolly had no way of disengaging. It was the old pig and python story. Once he bit on an idea, even a mere notion, he had to go all the way with its consideration. All the way to hidden assumptions and nineteenth-century antecedents and Renaissance parallels and the base behavior patterns of our Neanderthal ancestors. Every idea that hit the perimeter had to be processed and tested and integrated or rejected or finally, very rarely, laughed off. There was no reverse gear and no neutral.

Some people ran. Some played through. I loved it. It was just the amazement I was looking for, just the fresh prism and challenge and, maybe, the brewing vat for a change of life. And once I understood that he wasn't breathing, that the flush and desperate edge had a simple physiological explanation, it was even relaxing to engage his realm, a relief from the ordinary chatter that poured out of the radio and the TV and half of what I read. It was invigorating.

Rolly, Carole, and Kendra lived just ten or twelve blocks from us, in a bungalow on the other side of the town center, on a quiet street that nestled up against wooded reservation land. The house was homey — with a steep roof, perched on a hillside with a big green and white awning that shaded its front porch in the summertime. Rolly and I sat there in the summer of 1994 and talked and talked. The subject was usually new media — the CD-ROMs and online services that were beginning to change the way information was moved and shared. The goal of our conversations wasn't clear, but we were each looking for something that maybe the other had.

When I had headed off to Hong Kong in 1977, Rolly had thrown himself into the innovative end of the energy business. Those were still the years of energy crisis, and Rolly had become a leader in passive solar design, working out of the Massachusetts Energy Office. In the mid-'80s, he joined Citizens Conservation Corporation, a subsidiary of the innovative oil company Citizens Energy run by Bobby Kennedy's son Joe.

By the mid-'90s, Rolly had left Citizens, where he had been chief operating officer, and launched a successful consulting business using sophisticated software to help multifamily property owners update their buildings to maximize market value and profitability. He was making good money, building a great reputation — and crawling out of his skin — not so much with boredom as with a sense that this could not be what life was all about.

We sat on his shaded porch one late afternoon in July as Rolly described how he had opened a notepad at a suffocatingly dull energy conference in 1991 and begun making a list of major trends he saw unfolding in the world, then mapping them against what he was doing with his life.

There was no match. And he began to dream.

He loved homes, beautifully designed homes that created environments where people could find joy and thrive. He loved traditional homes, not the boxy cookie-cutter homes of postwar modernism but the soaring, celebratory, character-filled homes of the Victorian era. He saw that a lot of other people were gravitating toward such homes, too. People wanted to live, he joked, "in the home they wished their grandparents had had." Not the dark, cloistered, and usually modest home of reality but an open, gracious, sun-filled version of that traditional home with all the modern conveniences. The home of people's dreams.

He told me how he had shared his vision with an old friend, Katherine Ahern, in early 1994. Katherine was an artist working as a real estate assessor who could never quite decide how to define her own path in life, where the focus of her career should be. She had listened closely as Rolly poured out his obsession.

"She just stared at me while I went on," said Rolly, solemnly describing the epiphany he had had that day. "And when I was finished, she put it right to me. She said, 'Look, Rolly, I don't know what I want to do with my life, and I desperately wish I did. You know what you want to do with yours, and you're not doing it!'"

So he had begun to push his ideas out into the world. He talked with Buz and Shawn Laughlin, friends in Wellesley who were a talented filmmaking and editing couple as well as serial home renovators; they had repeatedly bought old homes, turned them into showplaces, sold them at a good profit, and moved into ever-grander old homes. He had talked with Megan Gadd, a ski resort heiress with a great eye for design. And to Tom Timko, an old pal in high-tech marketing. And of course to Carole, his wife, who oversaw the management of thousands of units of public housing for the State of Massachusetts. And to a few others, including me.

It was getting late, and I needed to install an air conditioner at home for Danielle and the baby. Rolly and I kept talking as we drove to a warehouse store, picked up a window unit, and took it to my place. We had talked before about homes and new media and the opportunity there. We had talked about home design and the difficulties people faced in getting the homes they really wanted. But this conversation was more concrete. Rolly was beginning to decribe the outlines of a business, a business he wanted to call BuildingBlocks.

He had written down some ideas, he said, and wanted me to take them home and think about them and tell him what I thought. So I did. And on that day I saw Xanadu beginning to come out into the sunlight.

The packet Rolly gave me was twenty-two pages long, on simple white paper, stapled at the corner. It wasn't really a business plan. Later, we would get to know all about business plans, more than I ever imagined I would know. This document was more basic. It was part business plan, part raw vision. And it was part — a large part — simple fantasy. None of the software and systems it confidently described even existed. There was no explicit mention of the Internet. It was a set of ideas and an impulse. But it was a beginning, and we took it seriously. Why be embarrassed to be beginning?

When Rolly had gone, I sat down on the back steps of the house and took off my sneakers and socks. It was early evening. Sadie was sprawled in the backyard, snapping at the occasional bee buzzing by from our weedy flower garden. I leaned against the warm brick wall of the house and began to read.

BuildingBlocks Software
The Electronic Pattern Book Company
presents
The New Victorian Home

A. Unique Selling Proposition
1. A New Way to Design Houses

The New Victorian Home is an "electronic pattern book" on CD-ROM. It is a high-tech, high-touch version of the 19th century architectural pattern book. *(These popular, mass-market publications presented design styles and ideas, practical construction advice, and philosophical notions linking good building to healthy living. Coupled with rising affluence and cost-cutting technological innovations, they helped make possible the profusion of high-style, high-craft "Victorian" houses that homeowners today hold in such high regard.)*

Our pioneering program lets you make choices for yourself before you hire an architect or builder. It helps you to explore the design tradeoffs you think are most important. It zooms quickly from whole houses to building elements and back and highlights relationships between the parts and the whole. . . .

The New Victorian Home is as simple to use as leafing through an interactive magazine and pointing and clicking on what you like. It is a combination of a game, an educational program, and a practical home design tool.

2. Satisfy the Baby Boomers

Available in both CD-ROM and applications software versions, The New Victorian Home is designed to appeal to the rising architectural tastes, standards, and construction budgets of the baby boom generation. . . . Affluent "boomers" want houses that are the modern day equivalent of those built during the Victorian Era. . . .

The New Victorian Home helps satisfy the growing demand for customized house design by tapping into the skills, knowledge, and learning capacity of the most important — and most disenfranchised — player in the process: the home buyer or renovator. You choose the building style and details you like best. You identify the attributes (e.g.

"a ten-room house with a wraparound porch and large kitchen") and design qualities (e.g. "cute with lots of nooks and crannies") that are most important to you. . . .

3. *First to Market in Its Niche*

Rapid growth in computing power, falling hardware prices, the wide market penetration of the Microsoft Windows graphic interface, and the explosive sales trajectory for CD-ROM players have set the stage for a revolution in how people use computers. It is making possible new ways of organizing, exchanging, and using information.

Our flagship CD-ROM product is designed to create a new market. By being the first to take this approach, BBS hopes to define in our customers' minds a new class of knowledge-building software. . . .

The New Victorian Home is based on a simple premise: that homeowners need a way to sort out their home design options, preferences, priorities, budget constraints, and household conflicts, and to do so effectively. . . .

4. *A Proprietary Open Architecture*

BuildingBlocks Software will create an open graphical knowledge-building architecture for The New Victorian Home. We will create additional titles using the same interactive visual problem-solving environment. We will encourage other companies to create titles using our development platform, which will be a proprietary open architecture.

For example, building products manufacturers will be able to use customized versions of The New Victorian Home to showcase their products and services. This will create opportunities for in-context informational advertising in response to specific or open-ended customer requests. Use of BBS's object-oriented graphical environment on both user and senders' computers will allow fast downloading of complex images and information over standard phone lines. . . .

A mosquito made a pass at my ankle. I slapped it away. I was making a mental list of questions. Object oriented? No idea. Graphical environment? I guessed that meant the interface. Proprietary open architecture? I had an idea what that might mean, but it sounded like an oxymoron. Platform? I thought Microsoft and Bill Gates had a pretty good lock on software platforms, what little I understood of them.

And what was up with all this Victorian stuff? It could be right, but it sounded stuffy.

Still, something here was grabbing me. I liked a handsome house and had seen people struggle to get the home they wanted. I could relate to that. But there was more. Intuitively, this seemed to me like a big potential piece of new economy turf. It was a long way from covering the news, I thought. But this new economy, this digital stuff, might *be* the news of the next century.

I riffled through, looking for the money part. It was the slimmest section of the packet. Barely there. Bone simple. Up to fifty percent of the company would be sold, it asserted, to build a prototype, develop the product, and market it nationally. With no point of comparison, that sounded fine to me.

How big was the market? Well, the United States had 60 million owner-occupied homes, it said, and at any given time, probably half would be interested in home design software that helped them "clarify their preferences and options, have fun, and dream big dreams."

Have fun and dream big dreams. I liked that.

BuildingBlocks modestly assumed it could win a five percent share of the market for such software in its third year, or revenues of over $8 million on the sale of half a million CD-ROMs. But the real goal would be to win half of the market, or ten times that revenue — $80 million — by year three.

Eighty million dollars! Fine! Beautiful! Why not?

Sadie jerked up off the grass and snapped furiously at some bug. I moved to a lawn chair to stay in the fading light. The lawn was not looking good this year. And the house definitely needed a paint job. What would that cost me?

Never mind. Rolly's packet was getting deep into the realm of ideas.

The Decline of Modernism

For 75 years, the underlying ideology of architecture has grown out of a core set of ideas — that a "universal" design style was desirable and that ornament and attempts to achieve beauty were decadent and misguided. Buildings were supposed to be simple, boxy, and preferably white.

The modernist philosophy and aesthetic all but put architects out of the business of home design. As a result, for decades builders have been the primary arbiters of style.

Now the pendulum has begun to swing back. Consumers are again defining the market. Styles and building design details are becoming more and more elaborate, especially for high-end homes. Computer-aided design has increased flexibility. Builders are offering more choices. Architects are again designing houses.

Rising Aesthetic Sensibilities and Standards

We are living through a period of great awakening. Along with democracy and markets, artistic sensibilities are on the rise around the globe. This is not an elite phenomenon. People are getting better and better at deciding what they like — at defining for themselves what is beautiful. It is a virtuous circle, a rising tide of sensibilities and sensations. It promises to lift upward our aesthetic standards and physical surroundings for decades to come.

Something is happening to art that hasn't been seen for 120 years. Art is blossoming at every level of life — in our magazines and movies, in our greeting cards and grocery aisles, in our houses and home computers, in our hand-crafted decorative arts and our mass-produced objects from stores like Crate & Barrel. . . .

The implications of this are simple. For the next 25 years, non-artists will get better and better at discriminating, and will increasingly choose quality over kitsch. . . . The expanding market will drive down costs, permitting the emergence of an enormous consumer market for high-quality fine art, and decorative art, as well as for aesthetically-pleasing mass-market goods and services.

Okay. That was a mouthful. And there was plenty more in that vein. This was Rolly's crystal palace space/time/big bucks Xanadu analysis machine in high gear. And I loved it. I had no idea how it would sell in the real world. I had no idea if it would ever make sense as an effort for me to join. But it sounded great. Big changes. Big ideas. A bunch of exciting new technologies to support them. And big money! The Internet was still just a peep on the national screen that summer. But CD-ROMs were a phenom. And America Online was making plenty of noise. There would be lots of technology avenues opening up. Yeah, it sounded a little crazy. But weren't new things, real breakthroughs, supposed to sound a little crazy?

So I told Rolly I liked it. I liked it a lot.

And the next packet he handed me had my name in it. And a title attached. It was the second line in a hypothetical management roster: Tom Ashbrook, President and Publisher. Publisher, as in the one who would bridge the business side and the editorial side of this hypothetical operation, with its editorially presented home design information and images and ideas.

Next to my name and title was a penciled question mark. On the page it looked small. In my mind it was huge.

Who was I kidding even thinking about this? I didn't know squat about business or software or anything online. The only modems I had ever used were to file news stories as fast as I could and catch the next plane. The CDs I liked best were the ones I dropped into my stereo. This was surely not the profile of your average high-tech startup executive, not even the shadow of the profile.

And what about Rolly? Yes, he was brilliant and accomplished and knew a lot about architecture and housing and had a good mind for software. But he had never started a full-blown company before. He had never written a business plan. Rolly, the chairman and CEO of our pie-in-the-sky dream enterprise, didn't even breathe when he talked!

Yet here was the next packet, boiling again with ideas and numbers and lists and refinements. BuildingBlocks would use software and online services to help people design and furnish their homes. It would help people get the homes they really wanted, not the mass-produced junk that too many had to settle for. It would not try to turn consumers into amateur architects or draftsmen like the flood of shrink-wrapped "design your own home" software products that were beginning to hit the market. It would start with wonderful whole designs and let people easily tailor them to their own tastes and needs, right down to the individual products that would make up the house.

The company would "secure a line of venture funding totaling $5 million from the start," the new packet said. Venture funding as in venture capital, I assumed. I had a vague idea how that worked, but I didn't personally know anyone who had ever raised a penny of venture capital. I didn't know anyone who was a "venture capitalist," if that was the right expression. The phrase brought to mind pirates and adventure and sharp business school guys with boatloads of money and a pair of dice in their pocket. The $5 million, combined with cash from operations, the new packet said, would carry BuildingBlocks through its first five years. At that point "we may take the company public to raise additional capital for growth."

Simple as that! Boom! The first product would be ready in July 1995, it said. Ten months away. No problem. Big idea, big money, big future!

But it couldn't be that easy, could it? This was just a fantasy. Just a couple of twitchy guys playing catch in the backyard and bullshitting and dreaming they were major leaguers.

And yet, there was something compelling here. I couldn't let it go. Rolly certainly couldn't let it go. It was all we talked about. We would walk in the woods by his house, kicking up leaves and hopping over old deadwood and thinking it through again and again. And the more we talked, the bigger it got. And on really high days we would actually start to run through those woods, laughing like idiots and whooping and slapping trees. We would take new technology and the Internet and remake a whole industry! Hell, we would roll up our sleeves and change the way people lived, the way they slept and cooked and saw the sun and loved and breathed and the rooms they danced in. We would remake the whole freaking world, one house at a time! And we'd get rich doing it! We would not get steamrolled by the new century. No sir! We would ride this new technology like hot-damn buckaroos. We would not be bugs on the windshield. We would drive the car! I hopped up on a big rock, pissing a long arc into the woods, laughing and crowing like a goofy rooster.

We would be golden geeks!

But maybe I wouldn't say too much about this to Danielle just yet, I thought, walking back to the house. After all, I had a job — more than a job. If you believed American journalism's claims to a special, vital role in society, I had a calling.

And I absolutely did believe those claims.

And I had always loved that work.

And this was just an idea.

Just Xanadu.

But maybe it was the way.

I knew I had dreams my life wasn't touching. I knew there was a clock ticking. I knew the world was changing in ways that meant I shouldn't count on old assumptions anymore. But I didn't know if I could act on that, with kids and a mortgage and all the habits of a familiar life. Hello, boomer! Are you stuck yet?

How funny that the Internet gold rush should show up in the middle of our lives, a seductive, invisible frontier as big as our imaginations. It was the direct descendant of every wild, golden sunrise that ever set armies of dreamers in motion. We sing songs about those times and pass down their legends, of pilgrims and pirates and settlers and gold-mad '49ers.

I wasn't the only one who went chasing thrills and fortune on the Internet, but I must have been one of the least equipped. I was not a tech wizard or an entrepreneur. I had only been on the Internet half a dozen times myself. I knew almost nothing about computers beyond what it took to get through a working day. And I had never started a business before, let alone one that would require millions of dollars to get off the ground.

Here's what I did know: something huge was happening, something on a scale so large that I was lucky to see it even once in my lifetime. It was stirring economies and imaginations and possibilities like nothing I had ever known. And the more I looked at it, the more desperately I wanted to be part of it.

Here's something else I knew: I was going on forty and was desperate for fresh oxygen. I probably would have joined a mule train or a circus or any damned thing that moved if the Internet hadn't come along. I wasn't twenty-four with nothing to lose or fifty-five with a trunk full of play money. I was just a hungry soul crashing clumsily into midlife vertigo a little earlier than most. I had played out the better part of a first career and found some of its limits — and some of my own. It was time to make the leap.

It was the kind of leap that, one way or another, we were all beginning to weigh in those days. A leap from security to risk. From the known to the unknown. From well-grazed limits to open vistas. It was thrilling. It was terrifying. It changed me. It changed the people I loved most, whether they liked it or not. But I couldn't know that then. Hey, there were twenty-two-year-olds riding the rocket all around me. How hard could it be?

Danielle, who deserved better or at least easier, had always said she expected me to do something crazy in the middle of life. Just not this kind of crazy. But maybe we don't get to choose our madness. More often, it just shows up.

They called it a digital boom. I could hear it, in the distance.

Like a big train coming.

For me.

Chapter 2

Two Bedrooms

THE BOSTON GLOBE SAT like a very real brick and glass news palace on the south side of the city. For almost forty years, since the paper had moved out of its cramped downtown offices to give its fleet of green and gold delivery trucks easier access to highways and suburbs, the newspaper's complex had grown and sprawled over the old marshland by Boston Harbor.

By the mid-'90s, the *Globe* was a true showplace, one of the finest newspaper facilities in the country. The main plant stretched long and tall along Morrissey Boulevard, in handsome red brick with proud architectural curves of glass and steel that unmistakably proclaimed tradition and pride and money.

The paper's mighty printing presses were framed by a great wall of glass facing the boulevard. At night, the spit-polished, bright yellow beasts were dazzlingly lit so that passersby could see — could not miss! — the thundering production of half a million newspapers every day and more than 800,000 monstrous, fat papers for Sunday.

"Look here!" said the floodlit mountain of churning steel that sat at the heart of New England's leading newspaper. "This is power!"

It wasn't easy getting hired at the *Globe*. For years, reporters had scraped and clawed their way in from all over the country. I had shown up from Hong Kong long ago with an unusual background, a pile of exotic clips, and introductions to the paper's fabled foreign editor, David Greenway, and top economics writer, David Warsh, from an old Vietnam buddy of theirs who had wanted to hire me for the *Asian Wall Street Journal*. And even with that I had to fight my way into a dime-a-word freelancing job and wasn't hired until one poor lifer at the paper dropped out with Alzheimer's.

It was much harder still to battle your way into a senior position, with armies of competing, determined colleagues clamoring at your side.

But once you were there, once you were inside, you were golden. Golden.

Globe jobs were for life — literally guaranteed until retirement for most of the unionized staff in the newsroom. Senior editors weren't in the union, but for them — that is, for me — the embrace was even sweeter. Fine salaries, fat expense accounts, handsome bonuses that never failed to materialize, and an annual bucketful of stock options that in my first decade at the paper had showered hundreds of thousands of dollars more on top editors who had preceded me.

In the realm of inkstained wretches, this was deep gravy. It wasn't the *New York Times,* but by the mid-'90s the *New York Times* had just bought the *Boston Globe* for one billion dollars. And the gravy was still deep. You could travel the world, dine with princes and presidents and saints and sinners, have a good old-fashioned personal secretary screen your calls, and, on top of all that, have a newsroom staff of hundreds at your shoulder, ready to defend truth, justice, and the American way.

This was sweet.

This was the catbird seat.

All you had to do was put out the paper and put in your time.

And I wasn't sure I could do it.

There were so many reasons why. In the end it came down to the snowman.

After all my years at the *Globe,* I didn't know his name. I didn't want to know it. It felt like bad luck. He was a tall, awkward man, deep in his fifties, at least. His thin, gray hair was matted. His eyes were lifeless, his nose a bloodshot shade of maroon. His long, gaunt face had the jowly, hangdog, nobody-home look of a tired old beagle.

Day after day, year after year, he sat at his desk in the newsroom staring at his computer screen, softly mumbling, wrapped in all seasons in a long, knit winter scarf. Some days he would add a big, flappy winter hat. I never saw him speak to anyone. I never knew what he was endlessly tapping into that computer. Some mornings I would spot him trundling slowly toward his desk with a cup of coffee, listing slightly toward the nearest wall, muttering softly, dull eyes on an invisible horizon, swaddled in his long scarf, woolly hat perched on a walking cadaver. In my mind, he was the snowman.

I had never spoken with him. Maybe he was a wonderful, caring human being who had known tragedy or simply felt a chill. But from what I could see, this poor wounded giant, with his year-round scarf and drooping face and eyes flat as coal, was just the sad roadkill of time and surrender. He was checked out of the game. Lost in a slow inner music. Disengaged. He made me feel pity. He made me feel fear. Not that I was likely to wrap on my own scarf and go zombie. Not like that, anyway. It wasn't my style. But even a touch of the snowman was a scary thing. And I was seeing touches everywhere. Little parts of colleagues' hearts that gave up and froze and checked out. Even high-ranking colleagues, successful people. It was so easy. The cold just crept in with the private sighs of a weariness that was never admitted but began to show on faces anyway, a congealing of early retirement that hit some people long before they ever left their job.

Lately, it seemed as though the whole newsroom was wrestling with it. The *Globe* had come dazzlingly into its own in the '70s, and a great percentage of the newsroom population was still of that generation. Aging boomers, rebels, idealists. The best-educated and best-paid journalists in the history of the business. Wrestling with the snowman.

Most of us had come into journalism in the glory days of Woodward and Bernstein, of Vietnam and Watergate coverage, when reporters and editors seemed to have the power to change the world. Newspapering was romantic, even heroic. It didn't pay like some jobs, but who cared about banker's money? This was living! This was where the national heartbeat was made. This was where truth and justice were judged, where the sins of the past were laid out in the public square. This was where wrongs were lit up by bonfires of indignant news coverage until they were righted, where the whole country was called up out of bad old dreams and into the future.

Few papers had been as romantic as the *Globe*. It was a brassy writer's paper in a smart, political town. A town that had the Kennedys and Tip O'Neill and all the brains of Harvard and MIT at its back and a city-on-the-hill history of liberal aspirations and ideals that were second to none. The *Globe* was no bland, chain-owned newsrag. The Taylor family had owned most of it and run all of it for more than a century, and the Taylors were an exceptional clan. They were principled, morally upright Yankees of the old school, who sent their scions right into the newsroom to work shoulder to shoulder with the hired help until they grew up and ascended to publishing roles. They put at the helm a charismatic editor-in-chief, Tom Winship, who brought home a dozen Pulitzer Prizes for the paper and made it a rambunctious contender for top-tier status in American journalism. No crusade was too difficult. When I arrived at the paper, the newsroom was still ringed with windows of foggy, bulletproof glass, the legacy of angry gunfire a few years earlier when the *Globe* had championed school busing over the furious opposition of Boston's Irish neighborhoods.

But the romance was wearing pretty thin now. Not just at the *Globe*, but all over the newsgathering world. Social crusading was way out of style, almost forgotten. The Cold War was over, and people were tuning their lives to other, private frequencies. A feeding frenzy of reporting on tawdry scandals had left the media feeling small and dirty. Journalists' public standing had hit rock bottom. Just as newspaper circulation was headed down across the country, foreign news coverage, the mainstay of my career, was in full retreat. The very notion of newspapers as the linchpin of a vital civic dialogue was feeling distinctly quaint. The economy was driving everything. We chased behind.

Out in California, a scrappy new magazine called *Wired* had run an article in 1993 by Mr. Dinosaur himself, Michael Crichton, predicting not just that newspapers were doomed, but that the whole entire media business as we knew it was headed for the bone pile.

"To my mind, it is likely that what we now understand as the mass media will be gone within 10 years," wrote Crichton. "Vanished without a trace."

Our brick-and-mortar facade was still there, looking fine. But what did that matter? The best young college graduates were not exactly beating down the door to join us anymore.

They were going to business school.

They were talking about the Internet.

For the first time in my career, I was daydreaming on the job. It was odd, detailed daydreaming, always with the theme of something overdue. Maybe it was my own snowman alert. It felt that way. And most of all I kept thinking, as I moved through the newsroom, of Alaska and Eino Kuoppala and the best minute of every day.

My second stint working up north, years before, had begun on the second of January, which in Alaska — up between the Yukon and Porcupine rivers, where we were hunting for oil — was a fairly cold, dark day of the year.

I was twenty-one and had spent New Year's with my parents and brother and sister on the farm in Illinois and with the young and delicious Danielle, then flown straight to Fairbanks and on north by light plane to Doyon 4, a snowbound oil exploration camp in the Ogilvie Mountains, out toward the Canadian border. I had finished college a semester early and was heading north for the big money, to pay off school debts. We landed on a rough runway in the mountains. The camp foreman handed me a six-foot, twenty-pound ice pick and told me to dig a ditch in the permafrost. It was like chipping steel. For a week. Then there was word of an accident out at the blasting site, and the Indians working there said somebody had died.

They brought in a new master dynamiter, Eino Kuoppala. And they gave him a new assistant, me.

Eino was small and wiry, almost elfin, with tight, round cherry cheeks and an old pipe stuffed with cherry tobacco that he smoked whenever he wasn't on top of explosives. His family was Lapp, as in Lapland, from the north of Finland and Sweden and Norway, and he was right at home in Alaska. His mother had died young. His father died in the Homestake gold mines. Eino and his brother, orphans before welfare, had raised themselves as shepherds in Montana, hiring out to take flocks up into high pasture as soon as the snow melted and not coming down again until fall, so smelly and wild-looking, he used to say, that townsfolk pulled their children indoors in dismay.

As soon as he was old enough, Eino followed his father's path into the mines and rock faces and happily spent most of his life there. He knew earth and rock and dynamite the way a fisherman knows tides, the way a cutter knows diamonds. They called him a powder monkey, a first-class powder monkey, and he was proud of the title.

A mile outside camp, we were leveling a mountain to make stone and gravel for the construction of a huge new exploratory drilling site. All night along the blasting face, a dozen tall pneumatic drills on tank treads would punch the mountain's cusp full of deep six-inch-wide bore holes. Then, in the winter morning darkness, Eino and I would come up the mountain with truckloads of dynamite and ammonium nitrate and fill and wire those holes for blasting.

It was heavy, cold work, spreading hundreds of seventy-pound bags of ammonium nitrate above the face. It was hard, cold work slipping carefully calibrated and positioned blasting caps into hundreds of frozen sticks of dynamite and gently lowering them by wire deep into the bore holes.

When it wasn't frozen, dynamite was a reasonably stable substance to work with. It was soft and malleable and not likely to explode without a blasting cap. But when it was frozen solid — forty or fifty or sixty degrees below zero solid — dynamite became extremely volatile. At those temperatures, just the friction of a steel screwdriver trying to make a hole for the blasting cap could set it off, and had, leaving nothing but bloody parka tatters in the snow. So we used wooden sticks, carving sharp points again and again in the bitter cold, poking the eighteen-inch sticks of dynamite, slipping in the cold blasting caps, lowering our handmade bombs down the shafts, pouring tons of ammonium nitrate in behind, wiring up the whole mountainside, and waiting for the sun to get just high enough for the endless train of earth movers at the blasting face to see and stand clear. At our signal, a siren sounded. The huge front-end loaders and belly-dump earth movers far below would pull back. The whole great wilderness around would grow still. Eino would lean into the switchbox. There would be a split-second of low rumbling beneath us, and the whole wide mountainside would erupt.

It was glorious. Tons and tons of instant gravel and fat riprap rising up like stone fireworks, hissing and heaving and spuming thick clouds of rock that had been trapped for eternity, roaring up out of the mountain, then arcing and cascading, ton upon ton, down the blasting face, sprawling and tumbling with a funky hot woman scent of spent explosives and whatever dark blend of sulfur and stone powder we had unleashed that day. It was destructive. It was creative. It was beautiful. We always smoked afterward.

It was the best minute of every day.

I joked later with Danielle, when months had gone by and I had made a bunch of money and we were together again, baking out the Alaskan cold on a beach in Key West, that it was the best sex I had ever had. Until Key West.

Now I was thirty-nine and pacing and drifting back into that memory, running the explosion tape again and again, savoring the rumble and boom and the stone cascade.

And it was the best minute of every day. I was overdue to hit the plunger, to reshuffle the deck, to plow everything under. There was something in me that ached for that wild explosion. I would remember Eino sitting like a Lapp leprechaun on the riprap after the blast, smoking his pipeful of cherry tobacco on the cold mountainside. He would tell me about his own gold mine, down Kenai way. He would tell me how he loved to work it, far from punch clocks and other men's timetables. And he'd tell me this:

"You'll never be free," he would say, "working for a wage."

Maybe it wasn't my role in life to help run a century-old company. Maybe I was the wrong type for the job. I became fascinated with the founding years of the *Globe*, when Charles Taylor, a young Civil War veteran, scraped and struggled to bring the paper to life. He was the reporter and editor with five kids and a mortgage who hired on in 1873, when the paper was only a year old, and built it into a new breed of media powerhouse. Now his great-grandson William O.

Taylor II was our chairman and publisher, working to pull the paper forward in a new era.

And I was crawling out of my skin and daydreaming about blowing things up, about building brand-new things.

Something had to give here.

From the *Boston Globe*'s corporate Year in Review, 1994: "At the end of 1994, the Globe, like most newspapers, found itself operating in an intensely competitive media market and learning to cope with the dawn of a new age in media. Still, it continued to be the regional leader in news, information and advertising."

The dawn of a new age. I liked that. The rest sounded a little spooked.

Still?

From the first full BuildingBlocks business plan, December 8, 1994:

> BuildingBlocks Publishing Corporation is a start-up software company dedicated to helping consumers design their own homes. We plan to offer:
>
> - Exciting, interactive CD-ROMs that will transform the way people explore and act on home design options.
> - An object-oriented 3-D software language that permits product manufacturers to advertise more responsively in the context of specific home designs.
> - An online electronic marketplace through which consumers can review and purchase home products and services tailored to their specific needs.

There was still no office beyond Rolly's extra bedroom. There was no product of any kind, not even a tiny start. There was no investment money. But there was a seventy-seven-page business plan, almost an inch thick and spiral-bound at Kinko's. And there were projected revenues now: $20 million in year five.

Twenty million dollars! So easy to type!

Gone was any mention of Tom Ashbrook as president or publisher. This was getting to be a formal document, not a Xanadu ramble. And I already had a job.

But the margins were full of my scribbled notes. "A stronger case can be made for electronic marketplace concept," said one. "*The* realm for home trade."

That same month, December 1994, Rolly Rouse filed papers incorporating BuildingBlocks Publishing Corporation in the State of Massachusetts.

What is the sound of a tree sprouting in the forest? we joked.

Very small.

There is a famous program at Harvard for midcareer journalists called the Nieman Fellowship. It dates to a 1937 bequest to the university by Agnes Wahl Nieman, whose husband, Lucius, had been the founder and publisher of the *Milwaukee Journal*. The bequest was to be used "to promote and elevate the standards of journalism in the United States and educate persons deemed specially qualified for journalism."

Harvard's president, James Bryant Conant, was not particularly thrilled. Journalism was a suspect business, pedestrian by Harvard's standards of that day. But money talked then as it talks now, and Conant agreed that Harvard would embark on "a very dubious experiment," establishing a sabbatical program for experienced journalists to spend an academic year and be elevated at the Cambridge campus.

In early 1995 I decided I needed that sabbatical badly. It would be an academic year away from the paper, in the company of other journalists and great thinkers. I could weigh my career. I could weigh Rolly's Xanadu. I could get to know the Internet. I could play with my kids. I could listen to my heart.

The paper supported my nomination. My application essays reeked of desperation. At the interview, just back from Rwanda and cranked sky high on too much Starbucks, I practically crawled over the table to collar and beseech the reviewing committee.

"Tom, you've done so much, I'm not sure that Harvard could add to your experience," said one of the panelists early in our chat.

I almost fainted.

There were many kinds of experience, I said, struggling to keep my composure. The kind I needed now was the experience of contemplation. Yes, I'd seen the world. I'd won my prizes. But now history was making a big turn, I said, and I didn't know if our business was up to it, if we could take the curve. I needed to think about it. I *needed* to, see?

She pursed her lips and nodded. It occurred to me that I might sound really crazy.

Ron Heifitz, the renowned director of the Leadership Education Project at Harvard's Kennedy School of Government, bored in on my recent career path, wondering why such a high-ranking editor had shifted from active newsroom management to writing.

I explained, defensively, that I still had management oversight duties in the newsroom, plenty of them, but that I was looking to lead by example just now, by getting back into the field. I had high standards, and I had pushed a little too hard, a little ineptly, I said. It seemed like a good time to change tack for a while.

"Ah," the famous professor said gravely, "so you were assassinated!"

What the fuck is going on here! I thought, supercaffeinated blood rushing to my head. I was twisting in my seat and eyeing the furniture, about ready to pull down the ceiling. I've given my life to this business, I'm having a fucking midlife crisis, I'm begging for mercy, for just a minute's sanctuary to think things through, and these people are toying with me! "Assassinated" my ass! Et tu Brutus this!

Heifitz clearly sensed confusion and alarm. He smiled. "It's quite common for leaders to be assassinated, metaphorically," he said gently, with what he oddly appeared to intend as reassurance. "It happens all the time."

Okay, whatever, I thought. Just get me the time off. Get me some room to breathe.

Please.

The fellowship came through. We celebrated the news at home that night as if it were a Nobel Prize. A whole academic year, free. No deadlines. No late nights editing. No sudden rushing out the door to China or Timbuktu with a notebook and a laptop and no idea when I'd be home. Just glorious freedom.

For the first time in our family's life, we would have time — long, languid time — together. Plus all of Harvard as a playground, and a $25,000 stipend, and the *Globe* generously kicking in the balance to keep my salary whole. It was incredible.

"We'll have lunch together twice a week, three times, every day if you want," I told Danielle, as we shared a bottle of wine and made goofy toasts with the kids and their Cokes and milks at a favorite neighborhood restaurant.

"And I'll cook dinners again!"

"Cheers!"

"And we'll spend long weekends away whenever you like!"

"Cheers!"

"And Dad will fix my bike!" piped up Ben, whose bicycle had needed a kickstand forever. Why didn't bikes come with kickstands anymore?

"Cheers!"

It hadn't been easy having a journalist as a husband and father. Dylan was one when we moved to Tokyo, and for the next almost five years I had traveled constantly, sometimes six months a year, all over Asia, chasing stories. He used to curl up in my suitcase, burrowing down in the socks and underwear, and beg to be taken along. It tore me up. But I would tell Danielle, and myself, that for a serious journalist the news was like Islam. If you believed in its importance, you had to submit to it unconditionally. I did, and I had.

When we came back from Asia the work was different, but the pace only cranked up. There was no down time between assignments. Editing was every day. And most nights. I was almost never home before eight in the evening, and stumbling in much later was completely common. I would see the boys off to school. I would kiss them sleeping in their beds at night or read a last story before they nodded off. That was it.

Still, I thought, looking at the family on that happy evening, we had held together somehow. We were strong. Our bonds were deep. Dylan was twelve now, a tall, thoughtful boy who flushed easily, like me, and was beginning to see the world through his own eyes. Ben had just turned nine, still a little boy in many ways, but naturally alert and aware. He was just at the age where boys worship their fathers, and I was the lucky recipient of that attention.

Lauren wasn't even a year old yet, but she was already a force. Her newborn black hair had turned a deep tawny gold. Her big brown eyes sucked up the whole world and instantly made it her own. She was a fearless little joy. Thank God we'd had her.

Thank God Danielle had had her, I should have said. The fellowship year was still months away. In three days I'd be off again, to London and Zurich and Serbia. But Danielle would be here, packing the lunches, shuttling the boys, helping with the homework, kissing the baby, holding down her own job. She held the place together. It was a big project, like building a bridge in a hurricane. Sometimes, lately, our marriage had seemed to be only a small corner of it.

It was rare these days for a couple to have been together as long as we had. High school sweethearts turning forty together — it was almost peculiar. Some people actually arched their eyebrows with vague unease when they learned it, as if they had just realized they were talking with a Jehovah's Witness or a weekend nudist. I liked its simplicity. First there was animal attraction and gooey poetry. Then there was shared adventure. Now there was the family and providing. But keeping that covered was a stretch. And the poetry line had dipped way down, almost off the screen. I really wasn't sure what poem was running in Danielle's mind these days. And I wasn't sure she knew mine, if I still had one. We were keeping the wheels on the wagon. That was challenging enough.

I knew it had been hard for Danielle since Lauren was born. This was our last child. Definitely. And our only daughter. And I had seen how Danielle's body had actually shaken on the morning that her three months of maternity leave ended and she picked up her briefcase again and headed back to work.

There wasn't much choice, though we had spent many nights lying exhausted in bed, searching for some way out of the knot. We had moved to Newton for its good public schools. So here we were, trying to do the right thing in a suburb we could barely afford. There were plenty of grand old homes that seemed to get grander every year, with additions and greenhouses and home theaters and pools, but our house wasn't one of those. It was a simple, two-story house on an ordinary, maple-lined street with buckling sidewalks and too much traffic. The place had a tiny yard and a huge mortgage and needed work in every corner. It was cozy and comfortable and slowly collapsing.

Only our absurdly good luck in the '80s real estate boom had let us own it at all, let us pretend to be capable of the lifestyle considered ordinary here, the lifestyle we both worked like dogs to maintain. Our closets were full of ten-year-old clothes. The sheets on the bed were wedding gifts from the dawn of time. You could practically see through them. Our furniture was a joke. We did splurge on the baby-sitter, but she'd been with us forever and didn't cost much more than day care. Here we were, celebrating our virtual Nobel Prize with pizza and a half bottle of wine. Was that too much to ask? Saving for college? Forget about it. You had to be rich. But we had interesting work. Maybe even important work. And a good family. And a warm place to sleep at night.

So cheers! We should be happy!

And that night, lying there on our wedding sheets, with the kids in bed and the unbelievable gift of a free year looming, we were.

"What are you really going to do with this year?" Danielle asked sleepily across the dark gap between our pillows. I loved the way she smelled, her familiar warmth, the way her voice trailed gently off at the edge of sleep.

"You mean, other than making dinner every night and delivering the boys wherever they need to go and grabbing you at any odd moment of the day and treating you like a princess?" I asked, staring into the dark, walking my fingers down the back of her leg. I hadn't told her much about my brainstorming with Rolly. And she hadn't asked. She had a low tolerance these days for pie in the sky.

"Yeah," she breathed, fading. "Other than that."

"Oh, not much," I said. "Just figure out what the hell I'm doing with my life. Just decide whether to stick with this career I've invested half my life in. I mean, I love it, Danielle. Or I've loved it. But does that mean I should stay with it, in this way, with this paper, now? I mean, everything's changing, right?"

"Mmmm," she may have said. Or maybe she was just sighing.

"So," I said, half asleep myself, "I guess I'm thinking, just thinking, about jumping off a cliff."

She sighed again, but I don't think she heard.

The other bedroom that mattered that spring, on the second floor of Rolly's house, had no bed. It was small, maybe ten by ten, and all business. It had a modest wooden desk that sat just off center, with a brass and green glass banker's lamp on top. There were three upright cherry bookshelves, a simple wooden table — maybe Crate & Barrel — a personal computer, a nice printer, and a good fax machine that sat on a little end table. And there was a chair.

There was room for two in the office, but just. If you sat at the desk, your back was at the wall. If you stood at the end of the desk, your back was at the table that was against the wall. A narrow path ran between the front of the desk and the bookshelves. At the end of the path was the printer. We jammed a second chair between the end of the desk and the closet door. You could not polka here, but you could dream.

The two adjacent outside walls of the room each had a single window with simple pulldown blinds. No drapes. The only adornments on the white walls were a cluster of family pictures — Rolly and Carole's wedding in the green woods, Carole making kissy faces, Rolly and Kendra on the beach — and a large, striking black-on-white print of Duke Ellington, the master's arm outstretched, great fingers splayed, willing jazz out of thin air.

Before the next year was out, I felt married to Duke Ellington. I felt married to Rolly and Carole and Kendra and their two cats and that little room on the second floor, like a willing prisoner to his cell. The door was always open. There were no bars on the windows. But I was captive to an idea.

Almost every night and weekend now, Rolly and I were up in that little room, turning and turning the idea of BuildingBlocks.

I had seen productive people before, but Rolly was something beyond productive. He was possessed. He never stopped. Never. I would come by early on the way to work, and he would be at that desk, filing his morning's reading, outlining a new wing of the business plan. I'd come again after dinner, when the kids were in bed or deep in homework and Danielle had waved me out, and he would be there, kissing Kendra goodnight from his desk, writing product descriptions, running spreadsheet calculations of purely hypothetical cash flows and gross margins and pretax nets, cranking out vision statements and mission statements. We'd be there at midnight, his eyes red-rimmed and voice croaky, me staring in a groggy haze at the numbers on the computer screen, when Carole padded to the door in her fuzzy slippers and cotton nightgown to roll her eyes and point across the hall to bed.

"Goodnight, honey," I would chime, blowing kisses, playing house to send up the almost comical intimacy that our weeks of shared midnight bedtimes were creating.

"Goodnight, sweetie," she would call, yawning, heading to bed, joking wearily. And Rolly and I would churn on.

I knew plenty of other people who were fun to bullshit with, to blue sky with and speculate and rock on your feet in manly contemplation, hands in your pockets, saying "Yeah, yeah, that's a great idea, yeah."

This was different. Entirely different. Rolly had one interest. One vision. It was still gangly and wild and so big that he could hardly articulate it, so big that he could hardly find anyone who would stop and take the time to listen. But I listened. And step by little step it sunk its million little teeth into me, too.

The shelves in Rolly's third bedroom were piled with stacks and stacks of photographs he had taken of just one thing: houses. Beautiful houses. Whole houses. Old houses. Striking bits and wings and cornices and porticos of houses. Houses in full sun and in shade. Houses in all seasons.

There was a theme to the houses, I saw, pawing through them while we talked or he put out the cat or picked Kendra up at school. They were incredibly inventive, surprising houses, bursting with personality and imaginative detail. Most were from right there in Newton, a town that had exploded with wealth in the late nineteenth century, just when architectural sensibilities were busting out of the rigid old center-entry Federal style and were soaring free.

There was no cookie cutter at work in these houses. Each was richly distinctive, with gables and balconies and sweeping, shingled porches and eyebrow windows winking out of lively, flowing rooflines, with fabulous brick chimneys rising grandly above it all. Some were playful, some were rustic, some leaned toward alpine. All had a warm, open romance and exuberance. You could find hints of English cottage or Russian dacha or Italian palazzo or Swiss chalet, but these were uniquely American homes, from a time when America was first really feeling its oats, feeling affluent and confident and free to build open, embracing homes in its own image.

Like a lot of our classmates, Rolly had studied architecture at Yale with the famous art historian Vincent Scully. Scully was the first scholar to pull together and label this turn-of-the-century American effusion of exuberant and innovative home design. He called it the Shingle Style, but by the time he did, Shingle Style was almost dead. First, modernism had killed it, with its stark lines and stringent economy of design. Then the housing boom after World War II had driven a stake through its heart. There were millions of homes to be built to house the homecoming troops, to let a new middle class step up from tenement to tract house. There wasn't time or taste for all that detail. There was Levittown.

"But now," Rolly would say, eyes blazing, fingers waving over the photographs, Ellington looking over his shoulder, "now there is no good reason we can't have homes like that again. There are only bad reasons. People want homes like these, but they're too hard to get!"

BuildingBlocks would solve that, liberating the imaginations and personal living environments of generations of Americans and becoming a fabulous new media company that would help shape the next century as surely as any company had helped shape this one.

Those were the days of pure, unburdened enthusiasm in that little bedroom. We were just dreaming, so we couldn't be judged. We had incomes, so nothing had to pay. We had no product, so anything was possible. Anything at all.

Yet there was something so concrete and physical about what could be accomplished here. I had spent years in a kind of priesthood — the fourth estate, journalism — reading the oracle bones of daily events, floating through scenes of war and riot and yearning as the observer, the exempt onlooker, the scribe and interpreter. It wasn't by nature a grand priesthood, though its celebrity practitioners and their minders loved to spin it that way. But it had a magic I loved. Fires raged and I appeared. Fires died and I was gone. And what was left behind was words. Informing or dull, depending on the eye, on the day. Clarifying or confusing, depending on the mind, the delivery, the reader. But always words, from the onlooker.

A huge part of me loved that role. But something else was opening up. The chance not just to describe a world but to help build it. This new electronic arena was different. It didn't need bricks and mortar. You didn't have to be able to afford a printing press. It looked like a realm where value created in the mind could be turned directly, digitally, into real economic value. And I began to think that maybe I could dream again. I began to think that maybe I could — maybe I should! — take off the journalist's frayed collar.

On a bookshelf in that little bedroom, I saw Vincent Scully's famous book *Modern Architecture.* I took it from the shelf one night and flipped through. There was Rolly's beloved Shingle Style, and Scully quoting Frank Lloyd Wright hailing, even in his time, "the new reality that is *space* instead of matter." And suddenly, the way things do when you're enthralled with an idea, everything seemed to be fitting into that idea. Space instead of matter. Digital instead of physical. Internet instead of all that was heavy and old and owned.

"Wright's was a space compulsively expansive and flowing, like Whitman's Democratic Open Road or Twain's River," wrote Scully. And in the margin, probably in his college days, when we dreamed of open roads and rivers, Rolly had written one word, a question, in neat, ballpoint pen: "Freedom?"

And I wanted to say, across those years, now: "Yes! Freedom!"

I turned to the opening pages. Scully was quoting Camus, from *The Rebel.* I probably should have just had a cup of coffee or gone to bed. It was late. Carole and Kendra had turned in. The house was very quiet. Rolly was pecking at the keyboard, working through a spreadsheet of projections. I read:

"At this moment, when each of us must fit an arrow to his bow and enter the lists anew, to reconquer, within history and in spite of it, that which he owns already, the thin yield of his fields, the brief love of this earth, at this moment when at last a man is born, it is time to forsake our age and its adolescent furies. The bow bends; the wood complains. At the moment of supreme tension, there will leap into flight an unswerving arrow, a shaft that is inflexible and free."

Yowza! Even Camus was speaking to me. Talking about bending and changing and freedom. And I was listening hard now, moonlighting and tired and juiced up on dreams. What if this was it? The moment of supreme tension. What if there was a real chance, right at our feet, to dive into the world and change the way things worked, change the way people lived, change the way people created their very homes? There would be nothing rhetorical about that. That would be real.

The BuildingBlocks bedroom was always open, day and night. It was tiny, but somehow it felt as big as the universe, much bigger than my nice big office at work. There were no boundaries. We didn't talk too much about exactly how things might all work out in those days. We were pulling threads out of the air, weaving Xanadu into ideas that could be shared. We would run through one exhilarating thought loop after another, imagining all the ways that new media and new thinking could remake this piece of the world. We fed each other's excitement and pushed each other's thinking on and on until we could feel the epiphanies popping off like fireworks, and we would slap high fives and bang another page into the business plan.

The first plan we really loved, the one that Rolly sweated blood over and we hashed through for days and days, came together in February. A few tweaks to the spreadsheet and it now had $26 million projected for year five revenues — growing with every version of the plan! — and seventy-five pages of supporting exuberance and detail. We would blanket the nation with our CD-ROMs and online services. We would not only help people design their homes, we would help them design tree houses! And dollhouses! The brakes were off. Way off. We were cooking. "Cooking with gas!" Rolly liked to say. Maybe even burning the dishes.

Business plans are hard to write. They require a disciplined march through product strategy, market analysis, sales plans, the product launch, financial assumptions — everything. Rolly had a tremendous capacity to focus, to lay down those tracks in space. Then we'd poke and turn over and challenge and test. It took writing and rewriting and thinking and rethinking. We poured long, wired weeks into those pages. And when that first version was done, front to back and humming from the printer, we were so fevered with the vision that we decided we needed still one more page. One more quick, crowning page to say it all.

We called it the *Star Wars* page, because we imagined its text rolling majestically across the eyes of some investor someday, somewhere, like the rolling text across the heavens that opened the first *Star Wars* film. "Long ago in a galaxy far, far away . . ."

We wrote it in a bleary-eyed frenzy, shouting and banging the keyboard, short of sleep and not sure we even made sense anymore. We printed it in italics on a page all its own and sat back in that tiny bedroom admiring our handiwork like punch-drunk spacemen who had stumbled into the promised land. It was awesome! Almost too much for human eyes, we laughed, wearily spoofing our own bedroom frenzy.

Maybe this was how life sprang from the primordial soup. Some fevered germ vibrating in oblivion, in the little broodhouse bedroom of the dawn of time. And suddenly it was Xanadu dancing! It was glory! It was art!

Rolly rose from the computer keyboard like a Roman orator, like Ellington onstage, to read our effusion out loud. I threw my head back and hooted the *Star Wars* theme through an imaginary trumpet, stomping on the floor for timpani drums.

"Americans spend more than $200 billion per year on home design, construction and renovation, but the process is an awkward, frustrating tangle," the page began.

How we loved that $200 billion figure! Just to be near it! The majesty!

"Two hundred billion! Yes!" I shouted.

Rolly went on, senatorial finger wagging over the keyboard, booming with mock gravity. Laughing. Nuts.

"Consumers often can't visualize what they are buying until after it's built. Contractors fear costly midstream changes and resist new designs. Manufacturers communicate via layers of intermediaries, with a predictable loss of responsiveness and clarity."

"New paragraph!" I shouted. "Big screen! Attention, Luke Sky-walker! Let the vision roll!"

"In the digital era, these problems are unnecessary!" Rolly intoned.

"Say it, yes! Digital era! Yes!"

"No one has yet designed the electronic tools needed to transform the process of home design and renovation, but someone will!"

"Say it, brother! Go Luke! Go Obi-wan! Yes! What will we do, rebel heroes?"

"BuildingBlocks proposes to open and own that new realm!"

"Cut to Tatooine!"

We were crazed. Fried. Beyond the pale. But we liked that *Star Wars* page. We bound it into the front of the plan. And kept dreaming.

This was getting to be fun. I had no stake in the company, but what was the company? It was a vision. It was ideas pushed onto paper. New ideas about the future. And I was there from some urgent need to touch that future.

We hadn't really talked much about roles. It was too early, too ethereal. The plan had Rolly as president, and a raft of friends who had pitched in on the dreaming were plugged in as an imaginary management team. Buz and Shawn were there. And Katherine Ahern. And Rolly's pals Tom Timko and Megan Gadd.

But who knew? Maybe this was more than *Star Wars*. In the dreamers' bedroom, anything was possible.

A call came from Dad. He had a big family get-together brewing down near Philadelphia. My brother was coming in from Dallas. Mom and Dad and my sister from Illinois. There was going to be a rededication of an old family burial ground upriver from the city. Could I make it? With Danielle and the boys and the baby?

He knew I would. Genealogy was a favorite interest of Dad's, and I had heard him talk about this burial ground, in Runnymede, New Jersey, for years. It was first staked out by our original ancestor in

America, John Ashbrook, three hundred years ago. He was buried there, along with a dozen other early American settlers as well as fifty unfortunate Hessian soldiers who had died in a nearby Revolutionary War battle in 1777 and were buried at Ashbrook's Burial Ground in the middle of the night by retreating comrades. Over the centuries, the burial ground had almost been forgotten, overgrown and trashed. Now, with help from my dad and others, it had been cleaned up and was ready for a fresh coming-out.

Of course we would be there. It will be a great history lesson for the boys, I said. And the weekend came, and we drove south, and on the way the boys got the full recap of our family lore as the baby slept. Danielle, with her French and American passports, listened with a certain reserve. The boys lolled in the backseat and watched trucks roar by. But they listened.

John Ashbrook arrived on the Delaware River, near our destination, on October 1, 1682, I told them. He had sailed across the Atlantic Ocean on the brig *Antelope* from Belfast. Your grandpa, I told the boys, likes to call him Antelope John. We don't know anything about his life before the voyage. But we know he landed in America as an indentured servant, bound to work for one James Atkinson.

"What's a dentured servant?" Ben asked. We laughed, and I explained how in those days some people without much money had wanted to come to America so badly that before they sailed they agreed to work for seven years in the New World for the man who paid their passage.

"Was it like being a slave?" Dylan asked. I said no, it was better than being a slave because people chose to do it and there was an end to it. After seven years, John Ashbrook was free. He canoed up the Delaware River and Big Timber Creek and claimed his own piece of the new continent. He became an assemblyman and then sheriff of old Gloucester County, but he must also have been a bit of a rascal. He got arrested for shooting hogs in the woods, a crime in those days, when farmers' marked hogs wandered free.

When Antelope John died, I told them, he left his son a log house that had just one window, and the room behind that window he left to his wife, Mary. Grandpa had a copy of that will that they could read. One window in the whole house!

All that got their attention, and we were still only in Connecticut, so I let it roll on. Just the stuff the boys would like. About the Pigeon Roost Massacre in Indiana, and how their great-great-something-or-other had run into the brush with her two children in her arms and an Indian's arrow in her back — well, with some kind of injury — and died. And the children had been found alive two days later, so the family line had gone on.

"Native American's arrow, Dad," Dylan said.

"Well, yeah . . ."

I told them about how our German line had come from Schleswig-Holstein, near Denmark, when there was starvation in the German low country. And they had pushed west to Illinois and settled McLean County in 1822. Their cabin was just a little up the road from where Grandma and Grandpa live now, I said. And the Native Americans had camped around that cabin all winter, but our German forebears had come from starvation and they weren't going back. They carved out a farm and drove their hogs to market on horseback, a hundred miles to Chicago, through timber and tall prairie grass. And once, when they were nearly home, old William's horse had fallen through river ice. When he got home, they had to pull him down frozen to his saddle and lay him, saddle and all, in front of the fireplace like a wishbone until he thawed out enough to break loose. I told them how those settler ancestors had named their son Oliver Hazard Perry Ohrendorf, to sound American. And how the women had walked miles home at night from quilting bees at the nearest neighbors' houses, carrying blazing pine knots to keep the wolves away.

And don't think that all this was so long ago, like the Bible or something, I said. I told them how my own grandmother had been in the Oklahoma Land Rush on the Cherokee Strip, bouncing along in a wagon while her father, their great-great-grandfather, rushed to stake his claim. And how, as far as we could tell, her father had been gunned down and killed by claim jumpers, and the family had come back to Illinois without him.

I told them about their Swedish line, how three brothers had come from poverty in Uppsala, north of Stockholm, and their mother had been so bereft when they sailed west that she drowned herself in the well. But they had had no prospects and no choice. They had wanted to be Americans so much that they changed their Swedish family name to their mailman's name, because they thought the man who brought the U.S. mail must be terribly American. And then they named their own children Evar and Otto and Yarda and Hulda. Not exactly Jack and Jill. And they scraped by, over coal mines and farmland, and their sisters worked as maids for the man who built the Brooklyn Bridge. And Evar was my middle name, and Dylan's, too.

And then came your mom's family, I said, from Europe after World War II. From Paris and Niederlahnstein, robbed of parents and years by the war. They knew what trouble was, and hunger. They wanted something better.

"Were all of our ancestors poor, Dad?" Dylan asked.

"Well, most of them were, at least for a while, if you're thinking of money," I said. "That's part of why they came here."

"Are we rich now?" Ben piped up.

"That's a good question, Ben," I said. "I guess we are."

I glanced at Danielle, and we rolled our eyes and laughed.

Had we arrived yet? I wondered as we drove on. Why did we still feel vulnerable? Had we found whatever it was that they had all come looking for?

Was this it? This life we had now?

And what exactly was I looking for, dreaming in that other bedroom?

My Atlantic?

Even with the fellowship coming — praise Allah! — the present had its problems.

One was Danielle's job.

The other was money.

The job problem was a minefield. I wished I could clone my year off and give it to Danielle. She needed it.

Going back to MIT after Lauren's birth had been hard for her, the hardest return I could remember. She wanted to be with her daughter. There wouldn't be another daughter for her — there wouldn't be another child at all. Not that she wanted more. But she desperately wanted to be with this one.

She would get up in the morning and go straight to Lauren and be with her until the last minute before she had to leave for work. At night, she would drop her briefcase at the door and go straight to her daughter again. And later, when I got home and Lauren was asleep, I would find Danielle on our bed, pining. Sad.

She had always worked. Her parents had come to the United States with her when she was two. Her father had walked off the boat from France with forty dollars in his pocket and a lot of leftover hunger from the war, and that was all. They had spent their life in America carefully assembling the comforts and security they hadn't known in Europe, and their four daughters had absorbed the lesson.

I had seen Danielle, skinny and sixteen, smiling and serving burgers at the Mr. Quick in our hometown. Working her way through college without a second thought. Teaching in madhouse conditions in the refugee camps in Hong Kong. Coming home late but happy from work in Tokyo. Building a real career at the university.

She supported and advised foreign students, and MIT had many to counsel. Danielle had become an expert on immigration policy and its complex intersection with academia. The university had to decide how many engineers and physicists and mathematicians from Argentina and China and Poland it should be training. Then Danielle helped guide them in, from Buenos Aires and Beijing and Warsaw. She was tough. She was humane. She was effective. She was proud of the expertise and insight and relationships she had built. But with three children at home and time clicking by, she had begun to second-guess the whole centrality of work and career that her generation of women had fought for. It started out feeling right. Now she wondered if it really was. And that doubt was fueling her own career crisis. Our baby-sitter, Anicia, saw more of the baby than Danielle did. What exactly was the point of a woman from the Philippines taking care of Danielle's child so Danielle could drive ten miles to MIT to take care of some other mother's child from Iran or China or the Philippines?

If she had made more money, it might have made sense. Might have. But as it was, when she added up the baby-sitter and gas and taxes and all the other expenses related to working, the money left over was a pittance. So, was she working for the sheer pleasure of working? What if it wasn't all that pleasant? Was she working to make a political statement? Not Danielle. Not anymore. She was past that.

Her daughter was getting older day by day. Her sons, too. And it hurt her not to be there. What exactly, she would ask some nights, in tones that moved closer and closer to anguish, was the reason she was spending her days with biology students from Brazil and not with her own children?

I didn't know how to respond. She had always been so determined to work and be independent that this turnaround threw me. Here was my tough, beautiful, feminist wife weeping on the bed over lost moments of motherhood. I suddenly felt ashamed, as if I'd been suckered by this two-income stuff, as if I should have been stepping up to the plate all along, caveman style, to bring the whole side of bacon home to my woman. What kind of wimp was I?

"So quit," I told her. "Just quit."

"Oh, Tom," she said, almost angry, "you know it's not that easy."

"But you could."

"But I can't!"

And the pain of it was, she was right. And just because of money. Stupid, mundane, necessary money.

Her take-home pay, even with all the bites chomped out of it, still mattered to us. I hated to admit it. But it was true. She kept the budget. She knew where the money went. She had every incentive to make it add up without her income. And it wouldn't.

I was usually the one in disbelief. How, I would ask, can we make $150,000 and be broke? This is ridiculous! We don't live in a fancy house. We don't drive fancy cars or wear fancy clothes. Our kids don't go to private schools or fancy camps.

"So how can we be broke?"

It made her furious when I asked that. It just showed how little I knew, she would say.

"But $150,000!" I would say, as if repeating the number would make it stretch and grow. "How can $150,000 not be enough to run a house?"

My rant would build. I was starting to think more about income distribution. Like everyone else, I had seen the charts. Our household income put us high on the heap. How could it be this hard to make ends meet? How was everybody else around us making it work?

"We're in the top five percent of incomes in the whole country!" I would pompously point out. "We make more than ninety-five percent of families make! That ought to be enough!"

The boys would scatter when this conversation came on. Danielle's eyes would narrow. I had always avoided dealing with the checkbook. I just wanted to make the money. And now I was insisting on some miracle cure for budget imbalance, for some beanstalk to grow out of the checkbook. And she knew it wasn't in there.

I'd put the knife in deeper.

"What about the Visa balance?" I asked. "How are we doing on that?"

She cringed, but her eyes stayed right on mine. The credit card balance was well over $5,000 and had been ever since we bought the house. There was always something that needed fixing. Always something. And I damn well knew it.

We didn't talk about it often. Neither of us was naturally inclined to dwell on money. It was just something you needed to live. But when it did come up, it was lousy.

I kept going. I was willfully ignorant, casually merciless. I did not want to believe that $150,000 couldn't cover us.

"You know, Dylan is going to college in five years," I said, stooping lower, twisting the knife. "Five . . . years."

I really was an asshole. We had almost nothing saved, and we both knew it perfectly well. Did I have some great suggestion here? Something constructive to add? Or was I just the jerk I appeared to be? Just determined to punish the messenger, to work off a little fiduciary angst by torturing the bookkeeper, my hardworking wife?

Danielle isn't big. Maybe five foot four. A foot shorter than I am. But she's a pistol when she's mad.

"Look, Tom!" she said suddenly through clenched teeth. "You just sit down here and look!"

She grabbed a pencil off the dresser, her bathrobe flying, and a book and sheet of paper from the nightstand. She slammed them on the bed and began scribbling off monthly numbers that, to my amazement, she knew by heart. Gas, groceries, child care, mortgage . . .

"Some are exact," she said slowly and angrily as she wrote, as though talking to a difficult idiot.

"Some are approximate."

"Now you just watch, Tom, and think about what you see. And then you tell me — you tell me! — your brilliant solution."

And the numbers slashed down the page.

She was fighting back tears of frustration and trying to hide it. I kept my eyes on the numbers. It was dangerous to look away just now. She was on a tear. And I realized I really was ignorant and she was the one who held all this together, who juggled and plugged the dike every month. We were top five percent, and living hand to mouth.

"We don't live in Kalamazoo, Tom. We live in Boston. It's expensive, remember? And you want to know why the Visa bill doesn't come down? You want to know why we don't have a hundred thousand dollars saved for Dylan's college? Well, you figure it out!"

And she slammed the pencil down on the scrawled column of figures and pulled her hair back sharply over her shoulder and walked out. Looking good, I thought, slapped alert but admiring her spunk. I always liked her spunk, the way she glowed when she was mad. God, she'd kill me if she knew I was thinking that.

She'd be back and we'd talk in bed. Maybe we should sell one of the cars. That would save a couple hundred bucks a month. I could take the train to work. Or maybe we should move to Kalamazoo. But what would we do there?

Maybe Danielle was right.

Maybe I should get off my ass and figure this out.

Johnny's Diner was the hot new place in Newton Centre, the little commercial cluster between Rolly's house and mine. It was just about a year old, but it was decked out like a 1950s soda fountain and storefront diner, only nicer. John Furst, the owner, had designed it like the diner everyone wished they had had in some storybook youth, but lighter and hipper and better equipped than the real thing had been. Like the house we wished our grandparents had lived in. Like memory, only better.

It was breakfasttime and the place was hopping. People paid handsomely for their nifty nostalgia trip at Johnny's. But the atmosphere was so evocative and pleasing that they paid happily, the same way they paid happily through the nose at Starbucks.

Rolly was already there, reading *Investor's Business Daily*. I had never heard of it before we started hanging out. I wouldn't have dreamed of picking it up at a newsstand. Are you kidding me? But he read it religiously, and I was starting to grab his old copies.

I was just back from a reporting trip through Paris and Zurich and down to Belgrade. It had been grim. We sat in the diner, and I told him a little of what I had seen and heard — of bombed-out Vukovar, of ghoulish skinhead militiamen along the Danube, of neighbors ax-murdering neighbors and stakes driven through familiar foreheads in revenge. Horrible stuff.

"Thank you for sharing that," said Rolly, his eggs and home fries arriving. The place was packed. Who were all these people, lounging over eggs and lox and coffee on a bright workday morning? And who was I to drag that other reality in here? Rolly's mind was somewhere else.

"Tom, I'd like you to have a five percent stake in BuildingBlocks," he said, changing the subject.

"For what?" I asked.

"For what you've contributed already and for what I hope you contribute in the future," said Rolly, putting on his mildly facetious businessman's voice. But this, of course, was serious.

"In what relationship? In what role?" I asked.

"I don't know," he said. "We'll have to work that out."

And in our next version of the business plan — before I had really decided anything, before Danielle had more than half a mumbled warning in the night — there I was, in the magic realm beyond the *Star Wars* page, a founding partner in the business.

This was getting to be a lot of realities to handle at once.

Chapter 3

Kryptonite

T HERE WAS ONE MEMORY I had never known what to do
with. It was a simple, difficult memory, one image really, from
when I was eight or nine. It was the kind of memory a person is
aware of but doesn't call up casually. The kind we approach carefully,
respectfully. The kind we suspect may be wired into our character in
ways that are beyond our control or understanding. The memory
was mainly about my father.

When Dad got out of the army, he and Mom lived in a succession
of small central Illinois towns. Good towns, but towns so small you'd
never hear of them unless you lived in the next town down the train
tracks. Taylorville. Fairbury. Wenona. Just specks in the cornfields
with water towers.

Wenona was the one they loved best, and so did I. The sign at the
edge of town, where the last, little, crumbly street met the fields,
said POPULATION 1,000. Looking back, I suspect that was an exag-
geration.

Wenona was tiny, but it had all its functioning parts the way little
American towns did in those days. It had its own school, K–12, with a
big orange banner in the gym for the school team, the Wenona Mus-
tangs. It had a grain elevator and a five-and-dime and a library and
two little groceries, Kurrle's clothing store, and a bank and barber
shop and soda fountain and bar and the Shortstop Grill, all on Main
Street. It had a hundred-year-old post office where everybody in
town fetched their mail from rows of little bronze P.O. boxes. It had a
sweet town park with a fine Little League diamond and a bandstand

and a refreshment shed that the young married couples opened on summer evenings when the town band came out to play and we ran in the grass and chased girls and leaned exhausted against our parents' backs while they drank coffee and talked in happy, laughing groups at picnic tables.

The town didn't have a movie theater. You had to drive to Toluca for that. But Wenona did have a landmark you could see for miles in that flat country, a great red hump of a slag heap left over from a coal mining operation, maybe three hundred feet tall, that we all called Wenona Mountain.

As small as it was, the town had at least five churches. The cherry-wood cross in the sacristy of ours was a gift from my parents in memory of my youngest brother, Timmy, who died when he was ten weeks old. He was born with Down syndrome and a weak heart. A hole in his heart, I told my younger brother, Todd. That was a sad time, and my mother sobbed in the gravel driveway of our small house while our minister held her, and my father stood with his head down. Todd and I watched from the screen door. My sister, Cynthia, hadn't been born yet. A few days later, Todd and I stood in the funeral home next to Timmy's casket in the receiving line. The casket was white and looked so small. Like a fancy shoebox with handles, I thought. I couldn't believe he was in there.

Even with Timmy's death, we all loved Wenona. Especially my mother. She was a sociable, emotional young woman and a sharer, and in Wenona everything was socializing and sharing. She and Dad were the first generation in both their families to go to college. Dad had taken his agriculture degree to jobs selling farm equipment and hog feeders, the jobs that had kept them hopping from town to town. But in Wenona he had stumbled onto something different.

In this little town, of all places, my father connected with a very smart engineer, maybe a genius, named Ken. Ken knew about plastic, something new and exciting in Wenona in 1964. My dad knew something about selling. And before long they had a plastic molding machine set up in the old stables across from the big grain silo on Main Street. They made plastic cups.

When we promised to behave, Todd and I were allowed to visit the old stables, with their sweet smell of strange chemicals and hot oil. We were instructed to keep a distance from the big, hissing molding machine, but we didn't mind. All we wanted to do was climb in the tall pallets of flattened cardboard boxes stacked just inside the big wooden doors of the stables. The boxes were new and smelled crisp and fine and had a nifty blue logo that had FLAIR CUPS stamped on their sides.

And this is my simple memory, the one I can never call up casually, the one I keep at a respectful distance, like something alluring and dangerous:

It's evening. I'm up on top of those tall stacks of crisp, new flattened boxes, all the way up in the dark rafters of the stables. The boxes are packed tight and smooth under me, steady and waiting to be filled and shipped. Down on the stable floor, next to the big molding machine, my dad and Ken are standing in a pool of yellow light, sleeves rolled up, hands on their hips, looking at the big machine, looking proud. And I'm curled up in the rafters, invisible, watching them, sharing that pride. A pride I don't really understand but that feels good. That feels very good.

And that's it. That's the whole memory.

But it's got a tail.

The business failed. My dad wasn't paid for six months, maybe a year. The town shared and shared, but we could only go on so long. In the muffled, snowy middle of my fourth-grade school year, we packed up our tiny house and ripped our happy lives out of Wenona and drove back down Highway 51 to Bloomington, back to the farm where my mother had grown up.

We moved into her grandmother's house, down the road from my grandparents, up the road from my cousins. The house sat on a low, wooded bluff not far from where my family had settled in 1822. It still had stiff purple horsehair furniture in the living room, portraits of severe ancestors in oval frames high on the walls, and the big indoor ferns that were popular at the turn of the century. It had an abandoned outhouse out back with a moon in the door. Under the stairs in the cellar there were dusty old Civil War belts and bags and a sheathed bayonet, thrown downstairs when old Uncle Marcus came home from Vicksburg, still there when Walter Cronkite read the news from Vietnam.

The place was wild and overgrown. The day we moved back, it was covered in fabulous winter ice. Within a week I loved it, in the way a boy couldn't help loving that wild paradise of cricks and haymows and steam-snorting livestock.

But falling back on the farm was humbling for my father in a way that knocked him back hard. He was a stoic, not a complainer, but I didn't see his hands on his hips in that same happy way for many years.

And it hurt my mother, my emotional soulmate, who had dreamed of a new life and had never imagined that she would be turned back to live among the ghosts of the farm. She had been a top scholar at the University of Illinois and had dreamed of everything. And now she'd been whacked hard and was broke and was back in her grandmother's house, suddenly wondering, too early, if it might have to be the next generation that stepped beyond. Sometimes it was so bad that there really wasn't a penny and we were eating eggs from my grandfather's henhouse three meals a day. That fall hurt my parents deeply and for a long time, to my child's mind.

And somehow, I felt responsible. I felt that in my one instant of looking down in pride from the rafters on my dad and his partner in their dusty stable by the train tracks, I had blown it. I had dared to hope too much. I had hoped, without words or really knowing, for triumph for my father, so happy in that pool of light. I had cheated in imagining in that moment that it was already his. And in my boy's mind that warm, satisfied moment, that peeking too soon, had cost him everything.

Rolly and I were alike in some interesting ways and absolutely unlike in others. The differences were a strength, part of what drew us together. They could also be a minefield.

First there was the breathing thing. We both loved to talk, especially about abstractions and possibilities and cool ideas. But I breathed when I talked, rambling happily on, and Rolly didn't. It didn't seem quite fair, but it was a fact of life, like the matter of living in one's skin.

"I don't know if you can imagine what it's like to live in my skin," Rolly said one day over lunch at O'Hara's Bar.

We had been working together long enough in his upstairs bedroom that I guessed he was right. His sense of urgency and compulsion and will to hyper-exacting analysis were clearly set notches above mine. I admired enormously what that high setting produced. When he was focused, which was most of the time, he was miraculously productive. But I couldn't say I knew what that level of minute-to-minute urgency felt like from the inside.

"No, I'm sure I don't know what it's like," I said.

"Well, it's not easy," Rolly said. "Think of it this way. I feel all the time like I'm falling out a window. It's that kind of nonstop adrenaline surge. Like I'm being chased by a bear."

"Jesus, you're kidding!" I said, but of course he wasn't. He was almost never kidding. He was telling me something important, something that took me a long time to really understand.

We went on talking about the radical advantages and disadvantages of such a way of living, about how difficult it was and how often he was misunderstood. How that constant flood of urgency put his mind in overdrive and sent it looking out over horizons that most people didn't even perceive. How it gave him the power of vision but could also rob him of the ease with which to simplify and communicate that vision in a way that people wanted to hear it, in a way that they *could* hear it.

"Now you," he said, nodding across the table. "You've got this ease as big as an Illinois cornfield."

I decided to take that as a compliment. I could see he meant it that way. And I could see it pained him a little, too. I already knew how devoted he was to his own relentless, kinetic mind. But a kinder God would have somehow schemed to wrap that mind in a more comfortable skin. For Rolly, life was a charging bear aiming for the adrenaline glands. For me, it was a big cornfield, coming up sweet. Except when it was not like either of those for either of us. Nothing was ever totally consistent. But there were patterns, always patterns.

Maybe his urgency and my ease made a good yin and yang, I said. He nodded. He had thought the same thing. Maybe the two of us working together made a whole that was greater than the sum of its parts. Maybe we were each magnified in this relationship, he said. Maybe together our personalities could accomplish something greater than all our individual efforts might ever amount to.

I nodded. I had been thinking the same thing. We were an odd pair in some ways but maybe a good fit. We clearly relished working together.

There were systems at work here, Rolly said. Everything fit into a system — except things that didn't.

Rolly's bible for systematizing types of temperaments in people was *Please Understand Me*, by David Keirsey and Marilyn Bates. Keirsey and Bates had seized on the Myers-Briggs Type Indicator test, published by Isabel Myers in 1962, and used it as the basis for a highly detailed delineation of temperament types. Rolly was a true believer in the test and the book's interpretation of its results.

The test was a carefully constructed series of multiple-choice questions that classified people along four temperament poles. Extroverted or introverted. Sensory or intuitive. Thinking or feeling. Judging or perceiving. Everyone who took the test fell into one of sixteen types, and Keirsey and Bates analyzed each in depth.

Big categories of personality emerged — impulsive, useful, power-seeking, self-seeking. And specific types were pulled from specific combinations of traits. An Introverted, Sensory, Feeling, Perceiving result (an ISFP in Myers-Briggs shorthand) was described as the Artist type. An Extroverted, Intuitive, Thinking, Perceiving profile (an ENTP) was described as the Inventor type.

Rolly had been introduced to the test and the book some years before and had felt an epiphany when he saw his result. He tested Introverted, Intuitive, Thinking, Judging — INTJ, the mastermind builder type, a Scientist in the book's lexicon. It was illuminating, he said, because the analysis of his type pulled together and made sense of so many characteristics he had seen and wrestled with in himself but never managed to perceive with such clarity. It was a relief because in Keirsey and Bates he found, as the book's title suggested, people, or at least a system, that understood him. At last!

These mastermind builders, as described, made up no more than one percent of the population, so it was hardly surprising if they were often misunderstood. Like all Intuitive Thinking (NT) types, they were rational. They were supreme contingency planners, capable of anticipating and coordinating many steps in a complex process. Like all NTs, they were abstract in communication and utilitarian in implementation. Their self-image was based on being ingenious, autonomous, and resolute. They trusted reason, hungered for achievement, sought knowledge, and prized deference. They were prone to strategy over diplomacy. To a mastermind type, life was a chessboard for playing out strategy.

I had to admit, the quick thumbnail fit Rolly well. My friend, the mastermind builder. Excellent! What could be better? I had taken the Myers-Briggs test as part of a training program at the *Globe* years before and remembered marveling briefly at the same flash of recognition of self in my type analysis.

"What was your type?" Rolly asked, his eyes gleaming with anticipation.

I was wracking my brain to remember, but the name of the category escaped me. I remembered I had been delighted by it but had been skeptical about taking it too seriously. I didn't think I would mention it to Rolly just now, but the whole thing had smelled a little like horoscopes for eggheads to me, with its big gumbo of letters and pat descriptions.

I remembered in one category, my results had been almost evenly balanced. And then I had it.

"ENTJ!" I said, pleased to have dredged it up.

Rolly blanched, shrinking back with a look of horror. "No!" he said.

"No?" I asked, confused.

"ENTJ is the Fieldmarshal type," he said. "You can't be a Fieldmarshal!"

Ten seconds earlier I had been musing that the whole thing was maybe a crock of horoscope. Now my title was being challenged and I instantly clung to it.

"What do you mean I can't be a Fieldmarshal?" I asked.

The Fieldmarshal type was an NT, like the builder, said Rolly. And an NT was a scientific temperament. I, he said flatly, with the single-minded certainty of a Scientist, was not a scientific temperament.

"And why do you say that?" I asked.

"Because it's obvious," he said. "You're an NF. Intuitive Feeling."

"And what about the test?" I demanded, reluctant to relinquish such a grandly named type. Fieldmarshal! NT! Cool!

But then, Intuitive Feeling wasn't bad either.

"People test wrong all the time," said my scientific friend. "It might have been close, but I guarantee you're an NF."

The next morning, in my mailbox, I found *Please Understand Me*, with pages carefully marked by Rolly.

"Portrait of an ENTJ," I saw on a page one over from Rolly's type, INTJ.

"The basic driving force and need of an ENTJ is to lead," wrote Keirsey and Bates, outlining the Fieldmarshal type. I flexed my shoulders and sat a little taller as I read over breakfast, nudging Lauren's gooey oatmeal bowl away from the book, slowly peeling my banana, feeling the natural urge to greatness coursing through my veins.

"Although ENTJs are tolerant of established procedures, they can abandon any procedure when it can be shown to be indifferent to the goal it seemingly serves." Damn straight, I thought. No musty old harness for me!

"They are natural organization builders, and they cannot *not* lead. They find themselves in command and sometimes are mystified as to how this happened."

I could live with that. Of course I was an ENTJ! Born to lead!

I turned the page to Rolly's type. The Scientist.

"INTJs are the most self-confident of all the types, having 'self power' awareness. Found in about 1 percent of the population, the INTJs live in an introspective reality, focusing on possibilities, using thinking in the form of empirical logic. . . ."

I could see why Rolly loved this. Keirsey and Bates had him nailed so far.

"To INTJs, authority based on position, rank, title, or publication has absolutely no force. The type is not likely to succumb to the magic of slogans, watchwords or shibboleths. If an idea makes sense to an INTJ, it will be adopted; if it doesn't, it won't. . . ."

Geez, we were a rowdy couple of wave-makers. Bullheaded. "Promethean" in the book's puffed-up description of our types, bringing fire to the world.

"INTJs are natural brainstormers, always open to new concepts and, in fact, aggressively seeking them. INTJs manipulate the world of theory as if on a gigantic chessboard, always seeking strategies and tactics that will have high payoffs."

Yes, I could already see all that in my fellow traveler. Not a bad profile for a business partner, I thought, as long as he was on the right course. In fact, very encouraging.

I turned to the other bookmark, the one for intuitive-feeling types, the big camp where my friend would place me. The Apollonian Temperament, in the words of Keirsey and Bates. The seeker, the one who quests for self-actualization.

Apollo! I remembered why I loved this test. All these beautiful, ego-stroking choices!

"To act (to achieve, to become) is to destroy one's being, while 'to be' without acting is sham and therefore nonbeing," wrote Keirsey and Bates, defining this type's challenge and dilemma.

Whoa! Heavy. Mysterious. I loved it.

I turned to the specific subsection within the group where Rolly pegged me, the type my test result had put me a hairsbreadth from, ENFJ. The book's descriptor: Pedagogue.

Pedagogue? Me? A teacher? Right out of college, I had taught for a short time in Hong Kong. It was a fiasco. I was utterly bored. I had run off to Borneo, made a fool of myself in Balikpapan . . . Well, never mind.

I quickly searched the text for something to grab on to in its characterization of my near-miss temperament: "Unusual charisma . . . at home in complex situations . . . longing for the perfect . . . always trustworthy . . . influential . . . excellent executives . . . can read other people with outstanding accuracy . . . highly developed ability to empathize by introjection . . . restlessness whatever their jobs . . . genius that other types find hard to emulate."

Well, hey, I could live with that, too. So there was the buffet. The mastermind and the seeker. The mastermind and the marshal. The bear and the cornfield. Whatever. We could make this work.

But "empathize by introjection"? What the hell did that mean? More egghead horoscope.

Rolly had quickly moved that spring and summer from a part-time commitment to BuildingBlocks to a full-time effort. He had taken a deep breath and simply dropped his lucrative consulting business.

This was cutting the cord. The big step. He still had some contractual payments coming through the pipeline, but there would be no fresh consulting work, no new income beyond Carole's modest state salary to support his family.

It was brave, but he did it as if there was no alternative. Carole, who knew him best, shuddered and accepted the decision. Rolly's working life had been full of accomplishments, but he never sounded satisfied when he described them. They had never quite lined up with his own vision of the way things might be. He lashed himself to BuildingBlocks as if he'd been born to do it. I had begun to think that he was.

I wished I had that certainty, but I did not. Rolly had pondered it longer, since 1991, and had made his peace with the move. I was still the moonlighter, pitching in hard to see and learn and for the pure satisfaction of helping shape something new. But I was still enmeshed in a career. I had only begun to consider the risk that came with a move like his. And Danielle had not considered it.

Our BuildingBlocks planning was firming up that summer. Rolly had begun using a pile of multimedia software — Director, Photoshop, Studio Pro — to start roughing out a product "demo," a staged multimedia presentation that would demonstrate the basics of what the finished product would look like. His old architecture instructor from Yale, Jim Righter, and Jim's associate Jacob Albert were working in Boston. They had given us photographs of some of their work to use as raw material.

And we were reworking the business plan. Rolly's old friend Peter Thorne had taken one look at our seventy-five-page opus and informed us it was far too long and too heavy on romance and vision. Peter's father had been a founding partner of a company in Boston called Greylock, one of the oldest and most successful venture capital firms on the East Coast, so we listened.

Peter showed us a copy of a business plan from another startup company that he knew was getting a good reception in the investment community. He had blacked out all the key names and numbers and strategic sections but had left enough for us to see this successful young firm's approach to writing a business plan.

We were stunned. The plan was less than twenty pages long and absolutely dry in its presentation. Where we were florid, it was factual. Where we were visionary, it was intensely practical. No hand-waving exuberance, just the clear, cold presentation of a plan.

There were other differences, too. We were novices with no credentials. The principals of this firm had had relevant experience and major technology skills — technology "chops," we had learned to say.

And while we were proposing a consumer product company that would be supported by CD-ROM and the Internet, they had been outlining a technology company that would create infrastructure for supporting Internet use itself.

And they were getting investment money. Lots of it.

"It's a great time to go out for money," Peter told us. But don't just say you're building a better mousetrap, he said. Offer breakthrough solutions. Offer solutions to chores that are laborious. Take an onerous task and make it easy.

Focus on what is essential when you talk to investors, said Peter. Get the hooks in, get them intrigued. "Sell the sizzle, not the steak," he said, because there wasn't much meat there yet. And be prepared to sell it fast. Most investors would decide in about two minutes whether they were interested or not.

Two minutes? How would they ever grasp our magnificent vision in two minutes? After all the nights and weekends we had poured into the first plan, we were going to have to go back to the drawing board. We couldn't change our backgrounds. We couldn't change the fact that we were not proposing to build Internet infrastructure. But we could simplify and tighten our presentation. We could squeeze out some of the cosmic stuff. It wasn't our nature, but we would try.

We sat back to rethink. What was the essential story here? What was the big frame? Rolly took the keyboard and we pushed forward, phrase by phrase, completing each other's sentences across the screen.

"We are in the midst of a revolution," he typed. And right away we were going cosmic. But how could we not? If you didn't buy that there was a revolution going on, then nothing else made sense.

There had been a lot of hype about multimedia software and on-line connections, we wrote, but beneath all the hype were emerging opportunities, some of which would be enormous and profound. The real opportunities would be in changing the fundamentals of specific industries, not just in dragging old ways of doing things onto the Internet. The best opportunities, we wrote, were in frustratingly inconvenient industries in the brick-and-mortar world, the only world most people had access to then.

We talked about Intuit, the Mountain View, California, company that was a favorite reference point of Rolly's. A guy named Scott Cook had figured out how people could use their personal computers to make balancing their checkbook easy. From that simple base, taking the hassle out of keeping a checkbook in order, Cook had changed an industry. Intuit had created a huge market for personal finance software. Its main product, Quicken, had won seven million customers within a decade — a seventy percent market share. It had a market valuation of more than a billion dollars.

Intuit, we said, was our model.

What Intuit had done for personal finance, BuildingBlocks would do for home design. Our target customers would be affluent and quality-conscious consumers with home computers, CD-ROM drives, and — as quickly as they emerged — online connections. We would take a frustrating, time-consuming process and turn it into one that was exciting, empowering, and convenient.

The product we described had not changed: a CD-ROM that would make it easy for nontechnical consumers to design beautiful homes. But its title had changed. We had decided that "The New Victorian Home" sounded too narrow. We would call it "The New American DreamHome." In addition to selling the CD-ROM, we would sell advertising space on the disk to home design product manufacturers. And we would follow up the CD's release with the creation of an online marketplace that moved home design, construction, and finance into the digital realm.

Consumers were hungry for the information and functionality we would offer, we said. The home design and construction industry was notoriously fragmented. The process of building or renovating a home was too difficult, too likely to produce a result that was not what consumers wanted. Even the process of dreaming effectively about a new home or renovation was difficult.

Broderbund was already selling ten thousand copies a month of a sixty-dollar product called 3D Home Architect which let enthusiasts build simple electronic home designs on their home computers. We would have a much cheaper product with a much more consumer-friendly approach paired with a powerful online strategy.

We wouldn't just give people a pile of electronic Tinkertoys and expect them to build their own house. We would give our users wonderful, whole electronic houses, lots of them, photorealistic and beautiful, and let them modify those homes to their own tastes and needs. Drop in whole dormers, add whole wings. Try out different windows and doors, different mantelpieces. Try out different furnishings, different paint colors. Really make them their own.

And when they were satisfied, when they had what they wanted, we would enable them to go online to make the project happen, to get the products and the financing and the professional design and construction help to wrap it up right.

At a minimum, we said, we would have a lucrative business selling our CD-ROM — the CD we still had not even designed. And if we did better than the minimum, if we approached the online service of our dreams, we had a shot at establishing a software standard for the entire home design industry. We could own the heart of a huge, transformed sector of the economy.

Rolly took our thinking to Len Schlesinger, his old neighbor and friend who was a hotshot professor at the Harvard Business School. I wasn't at the meeting, but Rolly took copious notes.

His first note was not encouraging:

"Not a bad idea, but not fundable."

That hurt.

We had no experience, said Len. We had never run a software company.

Did Scott Cook have experience when he started Intuit? asked Rolly, knowing the answer.

No, said Len. But he also didn't jump right in trying to raise five million dollars, which is what we were suggesting. He had bootstrapped his first work out of his garage. He had launched Intuit with sweat equity and with his own money.

And it would help, said Len, to get affiliated with some hot name in the software business. Maybe Mitch Kapor, the founder of Lotus. Or Esther Dyson, the digital guru and media darling. Somebody who could give us credibility.

We didn't have any big-name guru in our circle.

Then fan your own flame, said Len. Work out the product's look and feel, at least, so that you can show it off. Bring some more experience into your effort. And work on your industry connections.

And don't try to raise all the money right away, he said. Raise some. Become a going concern. Get cracking.

We were trying. It would happen. Our first phone calls to potential investors had gone nowhere, but we would get better. And we would only raise $700,000 to begin with. A mere $700,000. That would get us started.

We would make the right calls with the right message, and the money would come, right?

After all, it was a great time for raising money.

We crunched our thick business plan down into a dry nine-page executive summary. Then we couldn't resist celebrating with a new *Star Wars* page. The whole page was in italics, all effusion.

But we didn't holler when we wrote this one. We just wrote it:

Dreaming about homes is the true American pastime. Each of us carries an evolving vision of our perfect living space. We spend countless hours imagining, shaping and sharing our visions of how to make our homes ideal.

Some of us are able to act on our dreams, spending $200 billion each year on new homes and home renovations. More of us pursue our dreams vicariously. We buy 20 million home-oriented magazines every month. We spend weekends driving by attractive houses and browsing through stores, searching for inspiration and options. Home improvement planning is a perpetual dream machine.

And yet, for most of us, the avenues for exploring and acting on our home design fantasies are outdated and clumsy. Our society is rich with ways for children to play with their dreams: toys, computer games, Disney World. But for the consuming adult dream of a more perfect home, the options for engaging play and satisfying action are limited.

In the digital era, it will become far easier for consumers to imagine, shape, plan, and — when they are ready — build their ideal home. No one has yet designed the electronic tools needed to transform home design and renovation, but someone will. BuildingBlocks proposes to open and own the avenue to a vast new marketplace for dreaming, designing and doing.

Summer moved toward fall. Danielle and I took the boys and Lauren home to the farm in Illinois for Lauren's first birthday. My sister, Cynthia, made her a marvelous cake in the shape of a tiger. This girl was a tiger.

Cynthia had her own place in the country now, a gracious spread ten miles east of town, five acres, with a pool and barn and shed, sweet, towering sycamore trees, and a thousand-mile view of the cornfields beyond.

My parents were still on the old home place. It was simple and in need of repair, but to me it was beautiful. And my parents had become beautiful in it over the years. They were profoundly kind, engaged, and sharing people. They had spent their lives as community pillars, on school boards and 4-H committees and church councils and international friendship groups — all the things I never had the time, and maybe not the goodness, to do. They were bright, shining spirits that I wanted our children to know.

My grandparents' place up the road had been sold. All the outbuildings down at my cousin's place, where we had put up hay and sheared sheep and raised hogs, were gone. But the green bluff and pasture behind my folks' house, where Danielle and I had been married under tall oaks, looked great. The ghosts were easy.

"What are you really going to do with this year?" Dad asked, when Mom was making dinner and the kids were running in the hayfield. He and I sat out back watching them, watching the sun go down over Kickapoo Creek. The cicadas were whirring. My parents had been incredibly supportive over the years. With moral support. The best kind. And their happy, driven boy had spent his life trying to play redeemer.

The fireflies would be out soon.

"Well, Dad," I said, "I'm going to study income distribution at Harvard. You know, the rich getting richer and the poor getting poorer. That really bothers me. That's not the kind of country I want to live in. I want to understand why it's happening."

He nodded.

"And I'm going to pay a lot of attention to new media. You know, online stuff, the Internet, all that."

He nodded.

"And, uh, I've kind of got a business idea on the side, too. Something I want to really check out this year. You remember Rolly Rouse from Yale?"

"Yep."

I felt the déjà vu whisper down from the tall old backyard trees before I even began to recognize it.

"Well, we've been spending some time thinking about a new media company. You know, our own. I don't know where it will go. But it's pretty exciting."

My father nodded, looking at me deep for a second and then way off.

"He's a brilliant guy, Dad. Maybe a genius."

"Good," my father said. "Good."

We had flown back to Boston, and I was back at Rolly's house, catching up.

He showed me new numbers he had run, and we shared our thousand thoughts, like always. We talked about going to New York to see an old friend of his who was close to a lot of the manufacturers that BuildingBlocks would want to work with. We talked about getting together with his attorney, Gene Barton, at Rubin and Rudman, down on Boston Harbor, to take care of share distribution. He wanted me to meet Gene.

"You're really doing this, aren't you?" I said.

"We," he said, pointing with his chin at a reminder note on the desk for us to see Gene about my shares. "We are doing this."

"And what about the money?" I asked.

The plan still called for us to raise $5 million — not all at once, but eventually. Neither of us had ever raised a penny before, and our first groping inquiries over the summer had not exactly been promising. At Len Schlesinger's suggestion, we had cut back to looking for just $700,000 right now.

But when we really got down to the work of doing it, even raising just $700,000 was no easy trick. Try it sometime. It's not like borrowing lunch money. It's not borrowing at all. It's getting real people to put real dollars into a dream. It's money they may never see again, and they know that very well.

On a complete whim, I even put in a call to Ted Leonsis at Redgate. He had launched this damned itch, I thought, with his "digitize or die" challenge. Maybe he could point us to some money.

His secretary said he was on an island somewhere. And who was I again? He never returned the call.

"Oh, the money," Rolly said quietly, as if he was thinking of something else. "The money will work out. You'll see."

"Yeah," I said, distracted. I thought about Danielle's impossible budget on the bed, those damned credit card balances that never got smaller, and the money we had just spent flying to Illinois. Money was such a pain.

Rolly was staring at me with a weird smile. It was long and thin and slightly crazed, like the grinning movie madman threatening to shoot himself.

"And if it doesn't work out . . . ," he said, trailing off. He kept his eyes on mine and reached his hand out slowly to the top corner drawer of the desk, just the way the detective reaches for his pistol in the movies. Real cool and slow. I followed his fingers as they climbed into the drawer and came out with what I, for a long second, took to be a hunk of wood or an extremely fat little book.

He slowly pulled his hand under the green shade of the banker's light.

It wasn't a hunk of wood. It was a stack of credit cards as thick as a fist. More credit cards than I had ever, ever seen in one place. Neatly bound with two fat rubber bands stretched thin by its size.

"Oh, fuck!" I gasped.

"Fuck me! Oh, fuck a duck! Oh, nightmare on Elm Street!"

I danced toward the door, hands in the air, fleeing. "Get that away from me!"

Rolly just held the stack out in midair, like a prize snake on a pole.

I don't know how many cards were in that stack. Fifty? A hundred? He could barely hold them between his fingers and thumb. I couldn't remember when I had felt such a sudden recoil. This was Grade A 1990s American horror. This was fucking kryptonite.

"Just a little insurance policy," Rolly said, holding his crazed grin, cocking an eyebrow.

Those were the days when banks were flooding mailboxes with free credit cards. Sometimes five or six a day — a day! — would flood in. No muss, no fuss, no service charge. Just wicked, alluring, hideous credit in dandy royal colors, laid out like chunks of crack cocaine.

I hated those slick, easy cards raining down on my house, so blithely tempting and deadly. I threw them away as soon as I touched them. We had enough of those in this house, thank you very much. Now get the hell out!

But Rolly hadn't thrown them out. Rolly had kept them all. Every single glittering one.

Jesus.

From the doorway I pointed, arm stretched full length, at the hideous stack.

"We . . . will never . . . use . . . those," I said. "Never!"

"I hope you're right," Rolly said, dropping them back in the drawer.

"But just in case . . . ," he said.

And I remembered: He had already committed here. He had locked in. I supposed he could still crank his consulting business back up if he had to, but who could know? This was getting serious.

The next day I started saving my own stack. Quietly. In a dresser drawer where Danielle never traveled.

It made me sick to look at it, even when it just had its first few cards. I must be crazy, I thought.

Kryptonite!

Chapter 4

In the River

I T WAS A PERFECT September evening, sweet and clear, and the Harvard boathouse looked like an American palace, all rich Victorian wood and turn-of-the-century ornament perched above the Charles River. Its cool interior was stacked high with racks of long rowing sculls, ready for a new year of students to slip in and dip their oars. And the students were there, among the boats, chatting in clusters of two and three, tanned and rested from the summer, looking for all the world like J. Crew models in a setting J. Crew would love.

On the slatted wooden ramp that led to the river's edge, a different crowd was gathered. A couple of decades older. A lot more care around the eyes. Some with children. Definitely not J. Crew models. But this crowd was glowing in its own way, frankly giddy with astonishment at its good fortune, at being here, in this place, with a wide-open academic year ahead and no job — no job! no deadlines! — to report to.

There were twenty-five of us in that lucky class of Nieman Fellows. Thirteen Americans. Twelve more from all over the world. All journalists. All midcareer. I was the only local, with a house five miles up the river. The others had just arrived in Cambridge and were piling onto a tubby riverboat that evening for a sunset cruise down the Charles, a time to get to know one another and celebrate the amazing jackpot we had all just won in the rarest sweepstakes of life. For nine months we would have in abundance the very thing that nobody had anymore. We would have time.

The fellowship was deliberately designed to take some of the world's most deadline-driven people and set them free from the clock. It required a bare minimum of coursework at Harvard. The point was to unwind, to explore, to learn about the things you didn't know, and, it was hoped, to come out a better journalist.

This was already a pretty impressive crew on that score, cruising down the Charles that sweet September evening. Mary Schmich, the no-nonsense *Chicago Tribune* columnist, was there. Gwen Lister, the courageous founder and editor of the *Namibian,* in southwest Africa, was there. There was Tim Golden of the *New York Times* and David Marcus of the *Dallas Morning News,* both highly respected Latin America correspondents. Jenny Lo from the BBC and David Bank, a brilliant telecommunications reporter from the *San Jose Mercury News.* Ying Chan, the tough-as-nails reporter from the *New York Daily News,* was all smiles and amazement as we watched the proud turrets and ivy-covered walls of Harvard drift by.

This really was unbelievable.

Bill Kovach, the growly director of the Nieman program, said a few words in his feisty southern drawl as we headed downriver. Gray-haired and dark-eyed, Kovach was a stern Tennessean who had made his mark at the *New York Times* as a standout reporter and editor. He had been wooed back south to edit the *Atlanta Journal and Constitution,* had clashed spectacularly with the paper's owners, and left the paper for Harvard, first as a Nieman Fellow himself, then as curator of the whole program. Now Kovach had emerged as a national torchbearer for journalistic standards and ethics. From his dour expression, you would gather that was a little like being a famed physician in a time of plague.

It wasn't a great time for journalism, particularly in America, Bill told us that evening on the river. But it was a great time to be figuring out how to make things better. It was high time, he said.

We lifted glasses to that. But then, we would have toasted almost anything that night, with all the riches of Harvard and open time spread before us like a waiting feast. Riches! Was this how the rich felt every day?

That evening we were all free. We were hard-bitten, skeptical journalists turned into immortals. We were free to put down our note-pads and game faces, free to check at least a couple of our bags of cynicism, free just to be.

Yet even then, on that very first night, we all knew the year would be fleeting. The clock would strike midnight. The fairy tale would end. And we each had issues to resolve before it did.

I made my way to the front of the old boat. The moon was up. We had taken a quick turn through Boston Harbor and were now headed upstream again, plowing past the great domes of MIT where Danielle's desk waited for her every day, past the Back Bay, where an explosion of railroad and mining wealth a century earlier had turned marshland into a glittering paradise of handsome town-houses and charming red brick architecture.

The river was smooth and calm that night as I leaned over the prow. The water was still warm in early September. The Charles wasn't exactly a mountain spring in its purity, but it looked inviting in the rippling moonlight.

How did people make changes in their lives? We faced so many layers of obligation and responsibility, of habit and expectation. How did anybody cut through all that?

The conventional wisdom now was that we would all have half a dozen careers in a lifetime. I could see how that worked if you were truly a free agent. But what if you weren't? What if you had a con-suming job, a role, even a calling? How did you know when it was time to change? If it was the right change? Or whether you should change at all?

I was coming to the fellowship torn in a way that couldn't be sus-tained. I suspected I wasn't the only one. Whatever their public story, most people who sought the year came at a turning point in their lives, in their careers. The way I saw it, in this particular year we were also coming at a turning point in history. Everything was changing right now, and each change would bring more changes in its wake. And that made the question of how to proceed all the larger, all the more pressing.

The water really was beautiful and not too deep as we wound our way upstream. I was never baptized in a river but always wished I had been. It had some primitive appeal. I'm sure a lot of people waded in, went under, and only got wet. But the symbolism of that moving water, that surrender and rebirth, was so strong. It spoke to me.

It was time to wade in, I thought. I needed to wade in all the way over my head and come out fresh, come out new.

If I was reborn in the old religion, so be it. I would stay at the *Globe*. And if I went under and came up changed, I would embrace that change. I would take a new path.

I would not be passive. I would push on with Rolly. How could I decide whether to jump full onboard with BuildingBlocks if I didn't keep my teeth in it? And I would push with this excellent crew of journalists to study and reflect and grow. And I would come out with a decision.

Either way, Harvard would be my river. This would be my time in the water. I was lucky to have it.

In the car on the way home, Danielle wanted the bottom line. No walk-in-the-water stuff, please. Just tell me what you're thinking, Tom.

So I told her. I would dig into Harvard. And I would dig into BuildingBlocks. I would go full bore on both fronts, which might not leave time to cook some of those dinners I had promised. And at the end of the year I would decide.

"Decide what?" she asked.

"Decide whether to stay at the *Globe* or jump into this new company."

"But didn't you promise to go back to the *Globe*?" she asked. She was right. It was part of the fellowship agreement. But she was also, suddenly, reaching for any brake to pull. This third-bedroom pipe dream, this Tom and Rolly fantasy, was somehow becoming a contender for our future.

"Yes, I did, and I will go back," I said. "But I can't say for how long. I mean, I've given them almost fifteen years already. I feel like I've paid my dues, like I've paid up front."

Paid. That got her attention. She knew I was searching for a new way. She also knew the grocery bill and the mortgage.

"And what about money?" she asked.

We were almost home. The kids had come with us on the boat trip and had loved it. Now Lauren was asleep in her car seat and the boys were sprawled in the back of the van. It was cavernous back there, with captain's chairs and yards of legroom. Not like the crowded backseat that Todd and Cynthia and I had squirmed in as kids while our parents drove us all over the country. We had loved those trips. Were my kids happier because we had this marvelous van? Not in any way that mattered, I thought. On the other hand, this big rig did let us carpool to the max. It let us load up an army of soccer boys on the weekends to try to pay back all the parents — God bless them! — who had carted our kids around during the week while we worked.

These calculations were impossible. You just had to do your best, to deal with what was. We passed joggers out late, padding along in pairs. It was still warm. Maybe I'd take Sadie out and over the train tracks later for a run around the lake. I could use it.

"We'll have money," I said, turning onto our street. Danielle began to gather up baseball caps and Lauren's bottle and the diaper bag. "I won't jump unless BuildingBlocks has money."

My first official act at Harvard, by my own reckoning, was to give up coffee. Cold turkey. No cheating. Fini.

I bought my last tall cup of Starbucks, drank it with enormous pleasure, turned the cup upside down on the sidewalk, and stomped on it. It made a nice pop, and that was it. The next two weeks were complete misery. The third wasn't much better. But I wanted to live this next stretch as a "human bean," as my Ben once said, not a coffee bean. I wanted to see if life itself might be more than enough stimulation again, like when I was a kid. I wanted that natural high or no high at all.

What a spiritual guy I was becoming! Practically a monk.

My second official act was to ditch books on tape. They had become a fixture in the glove compartment, a constant companion when I was dreaming of another life. But this was get-naked time. This was time to get real about my own story.

Oh, and one more thing. No more lottery tickets. I had never bought them often, but maybe even once in a while was too much. Just more food for illusion. Empty dreaming. I decided I'd be done with that.

Then I went to class.

It was paradise. Ron Heifitz, my old "assassination" interviewer, on leadership. Lawrence Katz, the hot young economist, on social problems of the U.S. economy. E. O. Wilson, the famed naturalist, on evolutionary biology. Robert Coles, pediatrician turned social philosopher, on the literature of social reflection. Robert Levin, extraordinary interpreter of the arts, on chamber music. Alan Dershowitz, whenever I could cram him in, on something at the law school. And Amar Bhide, at the Harvard Business School, on entrepreneurial management.

Just writing out the list was thrilling. It was brain sex. I had to pull myself together after I wrote it.

This was good.

And so a new rhythm emerged. Crack of dawn at Rolly's house, while Carole got Kendra ready for school and herself off to work. Days at Harvard until the last class and seminar had ended. Dinner with the family. Back to Rolly's extra bedroom until crashing for a few hours' sleep. He had given up coffee, too, but not late nights or early mornings. Then I was back on campus.

"The median income in the United States hasn't changed in twenty years," Lawrence Katz was saying in a packed classroom overlooking Harvard Yard. I was surrounded by J. Crew models again. Some taking notes, some nodding off, all looking smart. I wondered how much older I looked to them. A lot, I figured.

"The difference is," Katz was saying, "that there are now more people clustered at the low end and more clustered at the high end."

Okay. The middle class is dead. So what's new?

"When you look at wealth distribution as opposed to income distribution, the skew is even greater," he said, turning to the blackboard.

The top five percent of American earners, he said — and I exhaled comfortably, anticipating a little ego stroke — have eighteen percent of the nation's income. That didn't seem so bad, I thought. After all, it left eighty-two percent of the pie to go around. And I was on the happy side of the equation.

But when you look at wealth, Katz continued, the top two percent of the population have four fifths of the nation's wealth. Four fifths!

For two percent of the people! Wasn't that ridiculous? Extreme? The word *revolt* came to mind.

I looked around the room to share my dismay. I couldn't see any response in my classmates' faces. Not even a furrowed brow.

"How much money would you like to come out of this with?" Rolly asked one late afternoon as we winged down the highway. We had been in New York, working on our industry connections, following Len Schlesinger's advice.

Rolly's question assumed I was hooking into BuildingBlocks. He knew that wasn't a foregone conclusion, but it suited him to assume it. We were going at this for real and, in any case, I was a shareholder in our expanding empire of the mind.

"That's hard to say," I responded. We weren't even out of New York State yet. Soon we would head north through Connecticut's low hills. There was plenty of time to consider his question. It was so nice and open-ended. Pick a sum! Any sum!

My old friend Tony Barbieri, from the *Baltimore Sun,* had a useful measure of enough money, I said. He would roll it out at the end of a crazed day of dodging tear gas canisters and chasing soldiers or politicians in Manila or Seoul. We would be back at some hotel, with our stories on the day's mayhem already filed. Around midnight, after a few beers and our second or third pack of cigarettes of the day, Tony would loll his head back and start extolling the supreme importance of "fuck-you money."

"Fuck-you money?" asked Rolly, and I could tell right away he hated the phrase. To Rolly, money was the logical outcome of value creation, and value creation made people's lives better, made the world better, so money — well-made money — was a good and noble thing. I was from a more rumpled school.

"Yeah, fuck-you money," I said. "You know, enough money that you could say 'Fuck you' to anybody, or any situation I guess, that you didn't want to deal with."

He made a face. That wasn't his approach. But if the middle was falling out, I thought, then you had to think about which side you would be left on, right?

"Okay," I said. "I admit, it's not melodious. And it doesn't exactly conjure up the brotherhood of man. But isn't that what it boils down to? Enough money that you can call your own shots? Isn't that why people do these things?"

These things. Like trying to start a company out of nothing.

"Well, let's say so," he said, not committing. "How much money would that be? For you?"

I thought for a minute. We were in the hills now. I liked the big views to the west. There were dairy farms in the valleys. I wondered if my folks would have to sell the farm to cover their retirement. It had already been carved down over the years. My cousin Steve farmed it along with his acreage now. But still, after 180 years on that land, it seemed a crime to let it go, for our extended family to become another bobbing dinghy on that shrinking Middle American sea. At least with a farm, even a little old farm, you had something at your back, some anchor in the world. You could plant potatoes there. Sweet corn. Beans.

"I'll say . . . three million dollars," I said with a note of hesitation. I didn't know why I settled on that number. It seemed big. Big enough. I didn't need a bazillion.

"Is that it?" he asked.

"Yeah, three million," I said. "That would do it for me."

He was quiet. I had the distinct impression he found the number absurdly low. Quaint, even. Maybe this wealth gap was even bigger than I thought.

E. O. Wilson looked like a big bird and talked like a matter-of-fact genius. Evolution meant change, he told us. Nothing else was constant. Generation by generation, meiosis and recombination would tear up our individual genetic legacies, reducing even our genetic echo to fractional insignificance.

So this really is it for my gene pack, I thought. Right here, right now. A one-time only appearance. Let's go, boy!

Robert Levin, leaping from piano to podium, took us through the great cathedral of eighteenth- and nineteenth-century chamber music, and all I heard again was change. Changes in tempo and pattern and key that left the music rolling on but always changed, and in that change somehow irresistible.

I was too jacked up to handle Robert Coles, with his lovely, mournful lectures on literature and morality. He walked us through soulful renderings of common men and women struggling to understand their place in a tortured universe. And I could not listen. In ordinary times, this orbit was my natural home, but now I was somehow too cranked up, too revved. And I hadn't known it until I hit Coles. Peter Lynch, the great, white-shocked mutual fund investor of Fidelity fame, was there one morning, hands clasped between his knees, soaking up the hard knocks epiphanies of the lost and poor and literary. But I could not. Not now. I was the jumpy monkey, keyed up and restless. Change was all I heard and all I cared for. Mere authorities are pawns of the systems they inhabit, Heifitz told us in his leadership seminar. But leaders recognize the need for change and lead in change, however difficult that may be.

Change. Again.

"If you don't perceive how much in the thrall of a system you are," I scribbled in my notebook, "then you are a slave."

Packet from Rolly:

We expect that over the next 50 years, as in the period from 1870 to 1930, much of the housing stock that currently exists will effectively be rebuilt from the ground; either incrementally or, as is increasingly the case, in one fell swoop. The bland, ungainly ranch and split level homes built during the 1950s and 1960s may be the first to go.

The trends are already clear:

- A shift toward traditional design (albeit too often expressed through awkward builder models with feaure-itis).
- Demand for higher and higher product quality (including more and more traditional, inventive, customized, unique-feeling features).
- A shift toward larger houses with more and more specific design amenities.
- A gradual shift away from the do-it-yourself movement, which may have already peaked, toward use of skilled designers and builders. (This shift is especially pronounced within our target

market: the top 25 percent in terms of affluence plus the top 25 percent in terms of quality consciousness.)

As new houses and new home design innovations get better and better, existing homes will become less and less attractive by comparison. This will be true even for many of the beautiful homes created in the period from 1870 through 1930.

We believe that the shift we are living through is tectonic. The digital revolution is already changing dramatically the logic of business and organizational models that work best. Changes in the logical order — and hence organization — of the home may not be far behind.

Change. Always change.

A whole country full of houses slowly crumbling. Mine certainly qualified. And a lot of the younger ones, the cheap, flashy, fast ones thrown up since midcentury, were crumbling even faster than the old ones. And people would rebuild, but differently, better than last time. And we would help them.

Cool.

The real shock to my system was across the river, at the Graduate School of Business Administration. The B-school.

All of Harvard, with its eight-billion-dollar endowment and its brick and spire architectural splendor, had the smell of fortunes on it. But the main campus at least had a grimy feel around the edges. Paths worn in the grass. A little peeling paint. Attitude kids hanging out in Harvard Square with dirty hair and lots of body piercing and boomboxes pumping reggae and ska and music edgy and obscure.

Not the business school. The B-school was perfect order, perfect everything. It was a gleaming, vitamin-enriched, brick and marble and white-trimmed monument to economic steroids. It was a hypermaintained, superpolished, glittering empire of its own. The buttery new buildings instantly evoked the old, in their rich wood trims and gracious cornices and pilasters and priceless Greek mosaics. And the old buildings always looked next-to-new, like rich, pampered matrons on full-dose nip-and-tuck regimens of estrogen and plastic surgery. They reminded me of the beautiful Japanese temple behind Mount Fuji that was torn down and rebuilt every twenty years, whether it needed it or not, just to keep the smell of fresh wood in the air.

Armies of groundskeepers and brass rubbers swarmed over the place. Not a blade of grass was out of place, not a branch untended or untrimmed. Unworldly perfection.

What a torrent of money it must cost to keep a place like this, I thought on my first day across the bridge. Typhoons of money. Gales.

But that was nothing compared to what I saw in the classrooms. If Coles was the moon, reflecting and emoting and parsing shadows, then this was the sun. Blazing. Hot. In your face.

The students had none of the comfortable slouch and intellectual wayfarer look that reigned on the other side of the river. They were pumped. High wattage. Hungry. Attuned. Bionic. They sat on the edges of their chairs and sucked up real-life lessons from the school's vaunted case studies like wolves on meat, like jazzed athletes about to go into the big game.

These were players.

I talked my way into Amar Bhide's course on entrepreneurial management. Entrepreneurial. The word of the hour. The B-school course book was crammed with it. Entrepreneurial Marketing. Entrepreneurial Finance. Entrepreneurship, Creativity and Organization. Field Studies in Entrepreneurial Management, and on and on.

The class was packed. I sat in the aisle.

This was foreign territory for me. I had reported on business, on biotechnology and simple economics. But always as an outsider. Now I was inside the palace — or on its ramparts anyway. I felt like a spy, like an impostor. How did they all make their eyes glitter like that? Where did they all get that ready-pounce-kill posture?

Amar Bhide was a slim, high-energy provocateur in the pit of the lecture hall. There was a giant screen behind him and a deep half-circle, tiering three rows up, of these young firebrands in front.

If I had any shred of hope that the old order would somehow be exempt from change, I began to drop it in my first five minutes of this class. There would be no safe haven from change, from the new economy and whatever came with it. I was sitting in the very boot camp of creative destruction. There was no loyalty here to bricks and mortar, or the way things were, or my retirement plan, or anything else. There were just brains and hunger, and those glittering eyes.

"Simple laws don't work for complex tasks," Bhide began. He was quick, eyes flashing, high metabolism, from somewhere in India. Somewhere with good schools and an ambitious family. And he set out from the very start to instruct these hellhounds how to tear up the world and remake it, no matter how complex that process might be.

He did have one simple law. "It is dangerous to take entrepreneurs too literally when they describe their work," he said. Because entrepreneurs were too far into their dreams even to know, very often, exactly what they were doing, why things were working, or why they weren't.

I wondered if I qualified as an entrepreneur or was still just a dreamer. Dreamer.

But there are broad rules that work, Bhide said, and anyone who wants to set out into the entrepreneurial realm was well advised to develop a personal vocabulary to describe what works. A vocabulary that would speak to you intimately, that you could remember when things got wild. Because they would get wild. They had to — or you weren't doing anything new.

The first rule, he said, holding up one slender finger like Siddhartha under the Bodhi tree, was, find good models.

Intuit, I thought. We liked Intuit.

The next rule, he said, was, learn the right lessons.

Oh, shit. It was already getting slippery. The "right lessons"? Which lessons were the right lessons? How were you supposed to know?

Good observation was key, said Bhide, answering the unposed question. And good observation required work.

That I knew. That I could relate to.

The last rule, he said, was to be prepared for lifelong learning and modification. And not to expect that those would be easy.

I was feeling a little sweaty in the aisle. The wolf pack was restless. It was rippling, leaning on its leash, heating up the room. Bhide leapt on, but I was lost in my own thoughts.

Lifelong modification. There was that change thing again. It was everywhere. Rising. Overwhelming. Relentless change. You might try and cling to the shore, but there was no guarantee the shore would stick around. And there were wolves, young wolves, fired up and hungry and doing what came naturally.

Notebooks slapped closed. The class was breaking up. The reggae from Harvard Square floated up in my mind and with it, an old lyric from somewhere. Nothing heavy. Just sweet Jimmy Cliff, putting it to me:

> *You're gonna run to the rock for rescue, and there will be no rock.*
> *You're gonna run to the rock for rescue, and there will be no rock.*

That left the river. And I guessed I was in it.

Chapter 5

Geek Gods

ONE EVENING when I was twenty-seven, not long after Dylan was born, I got a call from a college classmate. I hadn't spoken to him in years. His name was Steve Gottlieb. He was at Harvard Law School. I hadn't known.

Could we get together? he asked.

Sure. When?

What about right now?

There was an odd urgency in his voice. He was politely evasive about why he wanted to meet. I only lived a couple miles away. He named a bar. I said I would be there in an hour.

But for what?

Danielle and I had just scraped together the money to buy our first house, in Somerville, then a tightly packed working-class city next door to Cambridge. The house was a creaky old triple-decker, a Somerville specialty. Triple-deckers were three-story frame houses with an apartment on each floor. They filled blocks and blocks of Somerville, separated only by narrow driveways. Triple-decker, driveway, triple-decker, driveway. For miles. When we threw open our windows in the summer, we could hear the conversations of at least six different families floating through. But real estate was going up and up. We put our little savings together, borrowed $5,000 from our parents, made the down payment, and bought the place for $73,500. We lived on the second floor, and with the rent from the two other floors, we could just make the payments.

It was tight. A bad moment for Steve's agenda.

We sat over a little table in a dark corner of the bar and caught up. I had always liked Steve, and it was good to see him. He was a straightforward guy, good-looking, with long black curls. There was a touch of pirate to him, but likable pirate.

He was raising money for a new venture, he said, and was asking anyone he could think of who might be able and willing to invest. Maybe $20,000. Maybe $10,000.

Nobody had ever asked me such a thing before, and I was impressed. It took nerve. But I didn't have any money. I had just closed on a house and my sugar bowl was empty. What was his venture?

He was evasive. Something to do with recording.

Music? I asked.

Yeah, music. A chance to get a big return fast. But he couldn't really say much more about it.

I was apologetic. It just wasn't a good moment for me, I said.

What about $5,000? he asked. Maybe just $5,000.

I apologized again. I didn't have it.

We finished our beers, made small talk, and said goodnight.

The next time I saw Steve was in a photograph, maybe a year and a half later. I was on a long flight over the Pacific, chewing through every magazine the airline offered. I was down to the in-flight magazine, *Golf Digest*, and *People*. I flipped open *People*, and there he was. Lying full length on his side, a huge grin on his face, big head of curls cocked up on one elbow, spinning a globe on his fingertip. He had formed his own recording company, cut a novelty album of old TV theme songs, hit the boomer nostalgia market at just the right moment, and made a mint.

What a goofy idea, I thought. But he was grinning now. Right there in my lap, at 36,000 feet. He had made a fortune.

And with none of my money in the deal.

Damn!

The next time I read about Steve, he had come across a bone-crunching band called Nine Inch Nails and had turned its success into another bonanza for his recording company.

Still none of my money in the deal. But I remembered he had asked. He had felt he could ask me.

Now I needed money for a new venture. From his perch at the

B-school, Len Schlesinger was encouraging Rolly not to go straight to venture capital. The venture capital guys were too greedy, he said. They would chew you up and spit you out with nothing but their own quick profit in mind. Try to get started with private money, Len said. "Angel money," he called it. Money from private individuals. Angels. Much better to start with angel money.

But angel money was tricky. Unless an angel had a net worth of at least a million dollars, it wasn't a great idea to take his investment. If you did, and later on he got unhappy, he could sue, saying he had been taken for a ride. The mere possibility of that kind of suit could make more sophisticated investors reluctant to get involved at later stages, when you needed bigger money.

But if an angel had a net worth of more than a million dollars, he was considered, by the courts, savvy enough to know what he was getting into. He was considered, by the measure of his wealth, a "qualified" investor. And it was much tougher for a qualified investor to sue, so that's what later investors wanted to see.

There was one category of investor, our attorney Gene Barton explained, that would probably be okay without the million-dollar net worth qualification: close family members. Close relatives could usually invest, regardless of their net worth, without drawing unwelcome attention from regulators or subsequent investors. But our families, Rolly's and mine, were not exactly gold mines. Far from it. And very soon we were going to need money if BuildingBlocks was really going to come to life.

So we began to poke around. This was new terrain for both of us, and when we culled our list of acquaintances down to those with million-dollar net worths, the number got awfully small.

We made a few calls, scratched our heads, made a few more calls, got nowhere. Our inquiries were through third parties. Here's what we're doing, we'd say. We thought you might know some interested private investors. Not really, they'd say. End of story.

We talked to my neighbor's accountant. He had a network of doctors and lawyers, clients mainly, whom he occasionally encouraged to look at an investment. He had been involved with the early funding of Boston Chicken, the restaurant chain that had turned into Boston Market and made its early investors a pile of money before it stumbled. But he asked around for us and got no takers. His circle of clients understood takeout chicken. CD-ROMs and the Internet were another story. Too new to judge.

It was time to expand the hunt a little. Time to ask directly. No more third-party shield to hide behind. If we were serious, we would have to put our own chins out.

I called Steve. We had not talked since that night in the bar when he asked me for money. I hadn't had any money to give, but he had felt free to ask. So that made him fair game, right? We were looking for individuals to invest a minimum of $100,000. Steve could do that easily, I thought. He must have made a ton of money by now.

I tracked down his company, TVT Records, on East Fourth Street in New York. Directory assistance gave me the phone number. I sat down at the telephone at home, in the jammed little study off our living room. The room was a mess, as usual, strewn with the boys' lurid computer game boxes, *Sports Illustrated for Kids,* and wrinkled stacks of old homework piled around the Apple computer. Danielle was at work. The boys were at school. Lauren was napping. The house was very quiet. The phone was right there, waiting.

My palms started sweating. I felt flushed. That damned easy flush. I was cursed with it. But, hey, this was scary. I was about to call someone I hadn't seen in more than ten years, and ask him for $100,000. Not a gift. Please! An investment. A great investment. He could read the plan. He could read the *Star Wars* page. He would see how great it all was, how incredibly promising.

But $100,000! How could I call a guy completely out of the blue and ask him for that much money?

My hand went to the telephone receiver but made no move to pick it up. I stared at the phone number but did not dial it. Who was I kidding? I couldn't do this! I jumped up from the desk, hot and short of breath.

"Come on!" I was talking out loud now. Sadie looked around the corner from the kitchen, staring. I stepped back, turned away from the phone, wiped my hands on my trousers.

"Okay!" I shouted, suddenly pumping my fists. "This is a test!"

If I could not bring myself to ask Steve Gottlieb for $100,000 — right here, right now, on this phone, before the baby got up — then I didn't deserve to go down this road. If I couldn't pick up that phone right now, then I did not have the right stuff. If I couldn't dial that number, then I wasn't cut out for this entrepreneurial thing. I was old economy, I was dinosaur, and I always would be. I was just another good schmo on the assembly line, waiting for his plant to close. If I couldn't do it I was blind, stupid, pathetic.

But how could I?

I was roadkill!

But $100,000? From a guy I hadn't talked to in ten years?

I was history!

I saw a tall gaunt man in a thick scarf and winter hat. His eyes were dead. He was lying down in the road. I heard a Mack truck coming.

Snowman! Frozen, doomed snowman. Me.

I dialed.

The phone rang in Manhattan. My mouth was parched. There was a click. No human. Just a rush of seething music. Very loud, angry, blaring music, like an electric shock to the brain.

Nine Inch Nails.

It sounded like a train wreck, like guitars and machine guns and hell. I had the phone clamped in a death grip on my ear. My gums ached. Nine Inch Nails. Nine Inch Nails.

And then a beep.

And then complete silence.

This was my welcome mat to the world of big money? Nine Inch Nails and an answering machine beep?

I was breathing hard. I tried to hide it.

"Uh, this is Tom Ashbrook, ah, calling for Steve Gottlieb," I managed to squeeze out. "Steve!" False bonhomie. Obviously false! "It's been a long time."

I sounded like a dork! He was a recording mogul. He had the world spinning on his finger. And I was a dork, sitting with "Reader Rabbit" and an Indiana Jones game and crumpled fourth-grade homework under my elbows.

"Give me a call. Let's catch up."

I left my number and I dropped the phone back in its cradle.

I had done it. Or at least started it.

I might be a dork. But I wasn't going snowman.

Not yet.

On October 10, 1995, the MIT Media Lab turned ten years old. To celebrate, the storied fountainhead of new media hype and magic threw a gala all-day symposium and party. Everybody who was anybody in new media would be there, I was told. It would be a great gathering of the digerati, the elite of the emerging digital world. My old friend David Levitt was coming in from California. I decided to go.

It was the triumph of the geeks. The campus was swarming with an even higher than usual density of computer heads and techno-visionaries. I knew it had been a long time since geeks were nerds. I hadn't truly realized that geeks were now gods.

The Media Lab made sure we all understood.

It wasn't difficult. The very air around this celebration was crackling with opportunity, with optimism, with pride and great expectations. It was in the way geeks walked. It was in the way geeks talked. It was in the program notes and the huge festival tent set up on a broad MIT green for a free, fancy lunch and way-cool party favors. It was in the rich laughter rippling over every cluster of conversation. It was in the "anything is possible" aura that shone from every geek eye.

The future was theirs. And they knew it.

I had never been to a newspaper industry gathering that cast this kind of cocksure eye on the future. Never. And in the last half-dozen years, those gatherings had always had an in-the-bunker atmosphere that was chilling. Maybe the print world had partied like this in the Gutenberg Bible days, I thought, when the geeks of that day carved movable type and got high on three copies a week of Leviticus. But here, in the Media Lab's twinkling spell, today's tomorrow was wide open and marvelous, and every new geek thing was hip, hip, hip.

David was hip, as always. He was just in from Palo Alto. His big banana curls were flailing like a sea anemone, his wide-set eyes were sucking up the scene by the gigabyte. He looked like Jimi Hendrix with a slide rule. He gave me his crushing hug and introduced me to a friend from New York he had just run into. Wave.

That was his name. His whole name. It said so right on his calling card. Wave. I didn't know any journalists named Wave.

For Wave and David, this was old-home week. David had taken his doctorate in artificial intelligence, studying under Marvin Minsky at MIT. I remembered dancing in Minsky's living room at a party years earlier, a geek party, where everyone was miming improbable machines to improbable music. It was a wild little scene. Kinky and cool, I had thought. Now here it was, ten years later, and that little geek scene was huge and taking over the world, spawning a new global zeitgeist, rewriting every game book that mattered. Geeks ruled!

Now David worked in a Palo Alto research lab, Interval Research, that was funded by Paul Allen, the billionaire who had founded Microsoft with Bill Gates before moving on to his own ventures. David was by nature a fabulous dreamer and thinker, and he had been giving us good feedback on our BuildingBlocks plans all summer.

"You're coming to my wedding, right?" he was asking.

His wedding. Right. Up in Sonoma Valley in just a couple of weeks. "You've got to be there, buddy," he said. "Leary's going to do the ceremony. He's sick, but he says he wants to do it."

Leary. Timothy Leary, officiating at God only knew what kind of wedding ceremony for my old friend at a big old farmhouse in Sonoma County. David and Leary had become pals in recent years, and even now, when the '60s guru of psychedelic adventure was in failing health, they stayed close. David's father, a hugely outsize character and spiritual mentor to me, had died in the mid-'80s. He had been a hard act to follow. Leary came close.

But Timothy Leary, officiating at David's wedding? Was that hip, or what?

"Count on it," I said. "Danielle, too. We're there."

The morning program was The Future of Media. The afternoon's was Things That Think. (Cool!) The host and emcee of the day was Douglas Adams, the author of *Hitchhiker's Guide to the Galaxy.* (More hipness!) Nicholas Negroponte, the Media Lab's uberguru, kicked off. Negroponte had just come out with his big book, *Being Digital,* and today was his glory day. The lab's tenth anniversary! Ten years of moonbeams and modems. In those ten years Negroponte had emerged as a leading proponent of — some said huckster for — new media and the wired world.

By the year 2000, Negroponte was saying now, one billion people would be connected to the Internet. And in this crowd, no one had an interest in disagreeing. Never mind that in the fall of 1995 the Internet was barely a reality. Even "early adopters," the forward-leaning few who are always the first to try out a new technology, a new way, were just dabbling with it. Only a week before I had sat in a darkened Harvard computer lab with most of the two dozen Nieman Fellows, and only two or three had ever even seen the Internet before. It was terra incognita for almost everyone, including me. I had tracked its approach for years. I was thrilled by its theoretical possibilities. I had turned on the TV late one night and heard ponytailed old Grateful Dead songwriter John Perry Barlow call it the first nervous system connecting the whole world. I had seen the endless references to the Information Superhighway. But the Internet had only barely begun to be part of my life — or of anyone else's beyond the digerati and a fringe of online enthusiasts.

That was changing, though. And here, at the East Coast pole of the digerati universe, the future was now. Negroponte said a billion people would come in the flash of an eye. Why doubt it?

One after another, the Media Lab's homegrown heroes took the stage and spun out their visions. Minsky was there, by now the grand old man, but lively and challenging as ever. Patti Maes, the Web world's first bonafide sex symbol and an MIT professor, was there, with her latest line on electronic agents that would be our personal butlers on the Internet. Damn, she looked good, went the nods down my aisle. When geeks looked as good as Patti, the geekdom had arrived.

The crowd was mostly unruly, of course, loaded with geeks who ambled in and out and chatted on their own wavelengths. But there were suits there, too. The Media Lab floated on a sea of money from big corporations who expected that one day all this geek firepower would produce a truly huge payoff. The world would be changed in fundamental ways, there would be a paradigm shift, a whole new way of seeing and organizing and doing things, in every nook and cranny of the economy. And when it came, the suits would be there, arm-in-arm with their new best buddies, the geeks. And they would be rich beyond imagining.

Paradigm shift! Yes! They said it with such casual, cosmic authority, like Billy Graham noting the Second Coming. A paradigm shift here, a paradigm shift there, and damn! We'd have a brand-new world.

Michael Bove was up front now, talking about a shift from photographic images to models, a future when cameras would not just capture flat images but produce 3D models with "intelligent interoperability." I made a note. That sounded good for BuildingBlocks.

Then Walter Bender, all fired up about how the pipes were growing, about how we would soon have "signals with a sense of themselves."

Pipes! I loved this lingo. Pipes meant the wires or cable or optical fiber or whatever it was that brought a media signal, let's say the World Wide Web, into your home.

Narrow pipes made everybody bummed. Narrow pipes meant "low bandwidth." They meant only a skinny little trickle of an electronic media signal could squeeze into your house, onto your computer screen, or, someday, onto your TV. Narrow pipes were what almost everybody had, and narrow pipes sucked. They meant slow Web connections. They meant too small a connection to push this crowd's big dreams through.

But big pipes — big pipes were cool! Big pipes meant big bandwidth, enough delivery capacity to flow the wonders of the geek's ever-expanding computing power not just around the Media Lab and Palo Alto but around the world. And the bandwidth would come. Oh, yes. Big pipes would indeed arrive. The cable companies or the phone companies or the electricity companies would lay those big pipes down, mile by precious mile, and one day big pipes would become . . . *ubiquitous!*

Ubiquitous! Another favorite word of the geeks and, especially, of the guys in suits. The guys with money. Because when you finally laid down your big pipes and those big pipes were ubiquitous, then the whole freaking Barnum and Bailey Circus could be piped into anybody's living room, anywhere, anytime, upside down, in 3D with surround sound, and live video, and maybe even the smell of the elephant's doowops. And that would be new media nirvana. That would bring a mother lode of paradigm shifts. And then every wild-assed, bandwidth-hogging new media fantasy ever concocted in the Media Lab or anywhere else could come roaring right into Negroponte's billion homes. Then the geeks' dreams would truly rule. And the guys in suits would need their own big pipes and big dump trucks to load up the money.

"Rolly, you've got to get over here," I said on the phone when the symposium broke up and flooded into the big tent for a very hip catered lunch of delicious, unnamable concoctions. "You've got to see this stuff!"

He came over. And we toured the Media Lab when it threw its open house that evening. Danielle came over, too, after work. And I ran home and got the kids and brought them, too. Because if all this was the future, then I wanted them to get a noseful of it, too. I wanted them to know what a groundswell felt like, what bursting optimism felt like when hundreds and thousands of people under a big tent were feeling it, were riding a moonbeam. There wasn't much of that in the papers lately. Not much of that on TV. Not in 1995. No, sir. But here it was. Big as life, in all its geeky glory.

We wound our way through the open house, through the Media Lab's mounting floors and tangles of computer cables and pileups of huge computer screens. There was a lot going on here. A lot of it was tremendously subtle or so very simple that you had to cock your head to see how this very simple thing would someday change the world. But who could doubt it?

And then we spotted a screen with an electronic image of a house on it. The house was a photographic 3D model, maybe the kind Michael Bove was talking about. Yeah, we had heard about this. We picked our way over.

A Media Lab Ph.D. student was playing with the model, turning around in 3D rooms that magically responded to his mouse. Rolly and I asked him how it all worked. And he showed us, politely and patiently, exactly what he had designed. He told us he could turn two-dimensional photographic images into 3D images using elaborate math. He could do it whether or not he knew anything about the focals of the camera that had taken the picture.

We were blown away.

His name was Shawn Becker. We introduced ourselves, shook hands, and said we'd like to learn more sometime.

Anytime, he said. Anytime. And the surging crowd of geeks and gawkers pushed us on.

Timothy Leary didn't make the wedding. He was dying, and the trip to Sebastopol would have been too much for him. But his spirit was all over the ceremony.

David and Gail stood in a great circle of flowers behind Gail's wonderful big farmhouse looking over her rolling apple orchard and the Sonoma Valley and the Macayamas Mountains. David wore a blazing dashiki, Gail an angel's gown. They were blessed with the smoke of burning herbs, serenaded by a trio of half-naked muscle-man musicians called Thoth, and embraced by a seer who specialized in spiritual tours of the Egyptian pyramids. There was feasting and dancing and a general floating through sublime consciousness that would have made Leary proud.

And almost everyone there was a geek. They worked for Microsoft or Viacom or Apple or Netscape or themselves, for some little company you had never heard of but wished you owned stock in. And they didn't seem burdened by the same things my colleagues and neighbors seemed burdened by. They took all these wonderments and resources and great expectations absolutely for granted. They were dancing to some different music. More assured. More promising. More pixie dust.

"Have you noticed how these computer people are so . . . confident?" I asked Danielle as we flew back East, dazzled by our California weekend. We had rented a convertible and looped up along the ocean on the way to the wedding. It was spectacular, and we walked on the beach and marveled at the redwoods along the Russian River and savored the time together. It was a miracle when life slowed down enough, even briefly, for us to really see and touch each other. She still had that beautiful fire, that gentle, captivating energy that had knocked me out as a kid. But when was there time to invite it out, to revel in it? I resented the way time had been squeezed out of our lives for years, the way days were carpeted wall-to-wall with work and errands and more work. When we were kids and dreaming, I had dreamed of something richer, of a life with more time for passion and for counting stars. What happened to that?

This was supposed to be a year of suspended animation, but it felt more like the slightest calm before a storm. I had turned forty that fall with at least the comfort that I was testing a new path. My stake in this thing called BuildingBlocks had been bumped up to ten percent, which maybe — and what an over-the-moon maybe! — might possibly, if I committed to it, be worth something someday. But between Harvard and nights in the other bedroom, my time was, if anything, more packed than ever. I was not cooking dinners after all. And Danielle could feel tremors in the ground of our lives, tremors of unknowable consequence. We were walking some fault line, holding hands and hoping we would keep our grip.

"You won't throw everything over," her eyes said, searching for reassurance. We have three children and a life to support. However harried and rushed it might be, it was ours.

"I don't know anymore," my eyes said back, pulling away from guarantees, from the even keel, in a way that could only be unnerving. It may be now or never, I signaled but didn't yet say. It may be time for something radical.

But it was all too vague even to really talk about that weekend as we drove along the Pacific. I hadn't thought we could afford to make the trip. But David had come to our wedding on the farm in Illinois all those years ago. How could we not be there for him? Then Danielle's parents had chipped in on the air tickets with an old voucher, and Danielle had somehow wangled the balance of $150. As for the rest — the car, the motel — Uncle Visa would have to cover us one more time.

Was I wrong, or did this shimmering high-tech crowd never seem to worry about money? Money just appeared.

"It's like everything's going their way," I said. "They've got all this amazing technology, they've got the Internet, they've got skills people are dying to throw money at. They can call their own shots."

The Rockies were sliding under us. The snow was starting to creep down from their peaks. I had been reading about the migration of well-heeled techies and new media buffs to Telluride and other alpine sweet spots. They built their lodges in the mountains, shared their work over the Web, and then went out to ski. What a life. I had never skied the Rockies. I wondered if I ever would.

"This geek thing looks pretty sweet," I said. "It's like they own the future."

"You're not a geek, Tom," Danielle said softly, pointing out a potential problem with the direction of the wheels she could sense turning in my head.

"I know, I know. But maybe you don't actually have to be a geek to be part of it. I mean, it's exciting. And there's got to be a place for people who imagine how to apply all this new stuff, whether they're geeks or not."

"Yes," she said, squeezing my hand as if I were a starstruck boy who wanted to run up front, jump into the cockpit, and fly the plane. "It's exciting."

"I've met an amazing guy," Rolly told me. I was running between classes, leaning into a pay phone by Harvard Yard. He was up in the extra bedroom, stitching together more pieces of our product demo, churning out fresh plans and sketches for packaging.

"His name is Art Bardige," he said. "You've got to meet him."

We had been expanding our circle that fall, sharing the Building-Blocks idea with every potential good critic and guide we could persuade to sit down and listen.

In New York, Peter Rush, an old acquaintance of Rolly's with great connections in the world of building product manufacturers, heard our pitch and saw the crude beginnings of a product demo. Photographs of beautiful homes. An electronic scrapbook for saving favorite home design ideas. Some elementary interactive 3D scenes. Tim Johnson, an MIT architecture instructor and a whiz at creating photorealistic 3D models of buildings, was beginning to build some interactive home settings for us. He was a master of computer-aided design (CAD) software, a wildly complicated art unto itself.

Yes, Peter said, he could see manufacturers buying advertising space on our CD-ROM if we made it dead easy to use and could guarantee some minimum distribution, maybe thirty thousand units.

Yes, we said to ourselves, we can do that.

In Worcester, an hour from Boston, my neighbor's accountant, Bob Charron, was still putting out feelers for potential angels. There was one question, he said, that he was consistently hearing: How could we be sure that Microsoft wasn't going to come in, overpower this market, and squash us like a bug?

It will never happen, Rolly responded with the conviction of a true believer. We are focused with laserlike intensity on this one market and a key core of services we will bring to it. Microsoft, he said, will never be as perfectly focused as us on this market. Think of it like this, he said; in our niche, we'll be the Nature Company and they'll be Sears. We'll have atmosphere, a sense of style, beauty. They'll simply be huge. And huge alone doesn't win.

Look at Intuit's case, he said, citing his favorite touchstone. Intuit built a powerful franchise in personal finance software centered on Quicken, its dead simple software for balancing your checkbook. It made personal finance its sole focus. Microsoft tried to beat Intuit at that game and failed. Microsoft tried to buy Intuit out, and failed again.

And if potential investors don't swallow that, we told Bob, tell them the worst that's likely to happen is that Microsoft buys us. Then we swore to each other on the way home that we would never sell to Microsoft unless our lives depended on it. We had no product, no sales, no revenues, and no staff. But we had a firm position on selling out to Microsoft.

No way.

We talked with Amar Bhide at the business school. He read our plan and pronounced it "very intriguing." Someone, he said, would do the thing we were proposing. Someone would bring the complicated, fragmented home design industry into the electronic realm. But then, what business would not be addressed electronically? Banking was already there. More, maybe all, would follow.

BuildingBlocks faced one grave danger, said Bhide. Our plan was too ambitious all at once. It had, he said, "too many moving parts." The biggest danger startup companies face, he said, is trying to do too much right out of the gate, when they don't have the resources to do more than one thing well.

All right, we said. That makes sense. And we carved the plan down for a tighter focus. We would aim to come out with one CD-ROM title, to be updated annually, not the absurd eleven titles that were still knocking around in our business plan. And we would not attempt to produce proprietary 3D technology (a vain hope, anyway, since we still had no tech staff) but would buy what we needed "off the shelf," from someone who already made the software.

Then we went to see Art Bardige.

I don't know what happens to big dreamers who don't find someone like Art. I suspect that most entrepreneurs do, in one form or another, find someone who plays his role. Art was the one who stood with one foot in our world of dreams and another foot in the real world and pointed the way between the two. Art was the bridge.

Peter Thorne, Rolly's old friend, had introduced us. Art was Peter's neighbor and had been a pioneer in educational software, building a successful company called Learningways in Cambridge. Art was a former teacher who had taken his passion into new technologies. Learningways did many things, but its bread-and-butter was taking paper-and-ink textbooks and turning them into interactive, multimedia formats on CD-ROM.

At their first meeting, Rolly and Art weren't sure why they were sitting down together, except that Peter had suggested they meet. They talked, shared ideas, and parted. But they both saw a spark. At the next meeting, it was the three of us. Art's company spread over the fourth floor of a large, modern office building overlooking Fresh Pond, the Cambridge reservoir. Employees hummed through a large central field of cubicles surrounded by glass-walled exterior offices with a view of treetops and more office buildings. It was bright, well appointed, down to business. So this is a software company, I thought, walking in for the first time. Yeah, this looks right.

And then there was Art. He was maybe fifty, built like a bear, with big, slow eyes that seemed to drink in everything instantly. He wore blue jeans and sneakers and a denim shirt and greeted us with open arms, as if we were old best friends.

He made us tea. Rolly and I were both off coffee now and took tea only when he insisted with such good-humored hospitality that we couldn't refuse. After two clean months, the caffeine stoked us up instantly. Between the tea and Art's warm glow, we were feeling pretty good. We were sitting in a real software company, with its real chairman, and he was making us tea and taking us seriously. This was good.

As usual, Rolly had come prepared. He had a neatly typed, three-page agenda tucked into his pocket. We didn't get to half the items, but it drove the opening movement of the conversation.

Thinking back on their first meeting, Rolly was concerned that Art saw our product like a TV program on a network channel, in this case a program focused on home design. That was not our model, Rolly said. Our goal was to be the channel itself, even a network of channels.

Our immediate problem was that we needed to turn our rough prototype into a working product, and we did not have the technical capacity to do this. Art did. His staff had plenty of multimedia production horsepower for our CD-ROM. Plus, Art was nursing a new notion of how to package daily doses of electronic content for online delivery. He called it "software broadcasting." We could use that, too. There was room to do business here.

And, by the way, we could use his help in raising money.

Art nodded, grunted good-naturedly, fidgeted. We walked him through the budding prototype on Rolly's Apple laptop, with a long accompanying narration of our vision and goals. Art fidgeted extravagantly.

The instant we finished, he leapt to the white board on the far wall, grabbed a marker, and began to scribble furiously.

First of all, he said, we had to learn how to organize a presentation. Our tour through the prototype was far too long and complicated. If we were going to go down this road, he said, we were going to be making lots and lots of presentations. So learn the basics now.

The iron rule of presenting, he said, was to create eight slides, or screens, with three points per slide. No more than that, no matter how much you love the other points. And it didn't matter if the screen showed text or images — the organizing principle was the same. Make it simple. Make it tell a story. When you're raising something up out of nothing, you've got to have a simple story that describes it, that helps people understand it before it exists. Find your story. Make sure it works. Good story, bright future. Bad story, no future.

We nodded gravely, taking notes. If he was willing to groom us for the big world, to teach us how to walk and talk and get our little boat to the other side, we were ready to listen.

He turned to the board again and began sketching his vision of how our home design content would feed into his software broadcasting service. A big circle in the middle for his technology and our content, with lots of spokes radiating out — to the Web, to e-mail, to bulletin boards. And the heaviest line to the BuildingBlocks database. It may not exist yet, he said, but it would. The online world was made for tapping great databases and distributing their data far and wide. And home design images and information were a database waiting to happen.

We were essentially proposing an online home design magazine, he said. We both winced. We did not think of our product as a magazine. We thought of it as a unique new animal designed for a new medium. But never mind. We'd work that out. For the time being, it was just pure oxygen having someone so smart get so engaged with our dream.

And he was really getting into it now. He was stoked. This barrel-chested guy with his blue jeans and gray halo of Roman curls and years in software and aura of complete confidence was deep in his white board sketch and chasing the vision farther and farther. His diagram grew bigger, with more pods and connections and slashing lines around the perimeter. And the more he drew, the more enthusiastic he got.

"This is great!" he muttered under his breath, diagramming, lost in thought. It was as though we had brought in a missing piece for some puzzle he was working on. As though we fit into a picture he had already been drawing in his mind. "Yeah, this is great!"

Rolly and I looked at each other like stranded islanders who had just seen a sail on the horizon.

This was new.

This was good.

This was a powerful kindred spirit.

And you understand, said Rolly, that even if we use your shop to

help build this, we still intend to eventually develop our own proprietary open architecture for presenting home design information?

There was a pause.

Rolly was wedded to the idea that the software structure (or "architecture") we developed for supporting this industry belong to
us ("proprietary") but be available for anyone to use (therefore
"open"). This was one key to our goal of having everything Building-
Blocks did be enormously "scalable" — that is, capable of being endlessly scaled to greater and greater volume and market reach. An
open architecture meant that if we built something great, others
could pile in and use it, pushing our architecture toward ubiquity,
the godhead.

Art squinted with a look of bemused fascination at these two guys
with their big dreams and empty pockets and no product. He understood, he said kindly. He had the empathetic tone of a man who
knew what it was like to get the conceptual cart before the practical
horse. But we had some basics to get to before we worried too much
about all that high-flown stuff, he said.

He was right. We cherished the big dreams because in the realm of
dreams we were powerful. It was the realm of practicality and getting
it done that made us feel ill equipped, puny. But it was time to move
to that realm. And somehow it was easier to acknowledge that fact
sitting here with a guy who was extending us such a big embrace.

And what about money? I asked. Any ideas?

We'll think about that, said Art, his big arms crossed on his chest
at the white board, rocking on his sneakers. We'll think about it.

Two phone messages. One from Steve Gottlieb, one from *Newsweek*.
Newsweek came to visit. Steve I just called back.

Nine Inch Nails again. Brutal. Then a secretary. Then Steve. I had
talked to his office and sent down our business plan. He had read it,
skimmed it anyway. He sounded in a hurry. A busy mogul.

"Hey, Tom! How ya been?"

We ran through the bare minimum of catchup. I lamely referred
to the time he had come to me about chipping in for his first record.
He didn't remember. Why should he? I hadn't chipped in, and now
he was a mogul. He cut to the chase.

"It's interesting, it's interesting," he said. "But great software development is a very tough nut. And I don't see a big enough opportunity in this. Not a grand slam. It's a CD and something else . . . I don't know. I'm into some projects now with the promise of really big payoffs. Really big. I don't think this is going to make my screen."

Ooooph. Our dream was too small! Puny! It couldn't even pluck a string in the world of his deals. Ouch! Steve was polite, in a hurried sort of way. He was honest. And he was my first straight-in-the-face rejection.

But, okay. No problem. I understood. Different strokes. Hey, good talkin' to ya. Yeah, yeah. Catch you later. I had the feeling I could still hear Nine Inch Nails going full blast in the distance behind him.

Rejection.

Nine Inch Nails.

I would never pull them apart.

Newsweek had a better song, but what the hell to do with it?

I met with one of the magazine's top editors at the Harvard Faculty Club. She was an alum, on familiar turf. And she brought a juicy proposition. The magazine needed a foreign affairs columnist. They had their other big bases covered, with George Will and Sally Quinn and Robert Samuelson and Jonathan Alter. But they needed a cleanup hitter on world news. Would I do it?

There would be lots of perks.

A global readership.

Plenty of free rein.

How 'bout it?

Oh, God. Rejection and seduction. Nine Inch Nails and *Newsweek*. Why was I even thinking about CD-ROMs and the World Wide Web?

Why does the tide change?

We needed money now. Seed money. Five hundred grand to get started. Art was sharing ideas. Len Schlesinger had joined Rolly and me on our tiny board of directors. But cash was the missing ingredient. Rolly's leftover bits of consulting income were running out, and he had begun to put his own money in. We needed to start spending on talent and on product development and on really figuring out the market. We needed half a million to begin building a team. I needed to see the money to convince Danielle, and maybe myself, that this was a viable path. Our latest business plan described a $100,000 investment in BuildingBlocks now turning into a potential $2.2 million payout when the company went public in an initial public offering, the sacred IPO. Now we needed the simple affirmation of investors — even one investor! — willing to believe, willing to step up and commit cash.

They say look close to home for your first money, and we did. Rolly's mother agreed to invest $30,000. She was retired and divorced. It was not small money to her, but she was there. She was a sweet, soft-spoken woman who saw that her son was lashing himself to a dream. And she supported him.

Who next? It was late afternoon, and I was pacing the three-step length of the extra bedroom. Rolly was scanning photographs of beautiful homes into his computer, endlessly pushing our tiny wave forward. We needed to feed the wave — and soon. Who did we know who had money? Someone we could ask.

Stone!

"Should we?" I asked.

"We should," said Rolly. "It's time."

Stone Phillips had been a brilliant student at Yale, a philosophy major who could argue Kant and Kierkegaard with the best of them. He was the quarterback of the football team. The girls absolutely fainted for him, and so did the professors. He was disciplined and focused beyond belief. He was also a Missouri good ol' boy who could raise hell and get crazy, though you wouldn't guess it now. We had shared a bunk through sophomore year, until I went off to India. He had spent his freshman year rooming with Rolly as well. Stone was always cut from stiffer cloth than I, but not as stiff as most people thought. We drank and danced and bullshitted a hundred nights away, howling and debating free will and pure reason and the nature of truth. When I finally decided to lose my long hair, he was the one who cut off the ponytail in the dorm bathroom. We put it in a Valentine's Day candy box and mailed it to Danielle in Illinois.

Now he was a genuine media star, up on TV every time you turned around, with Jane Pauley and the *Dateline* gang. Danielle and

I had just been down to New York for his fortieth birthday party. He had a sprawling home that overlooked a majestic piece of the Hudson River valley. On the occasional weekend, he would cross the river to play basketball in Bill Murray's private gym. He was shopping for a mountain getaway in the Rockies. He was making megabucks.

I dialed his office in New York. It was almost Christmas. In my mind's eye I could see the ice skaters whirling in Rockefeller Plaza, far below Stone's gleaming office windows. Why hadn't I called him earlier?

He was there. Same voice as on TV, but more ease, less rigid cadence.

"You know, I've always wanted to have a chance to share some of my good fortune with you guys," he said, all warmth and good feeling when I described what we were up to. "It sounds really fascinating," he said. "Yeah. Pretty cool. Can you send me something to read, maybe to share with my accountant?"

Sure we could. Right away. And a merry Christmas to you, too!

Excellent. It was so obvious. Why hadn't we thought of it earlier?

The semester was wrapping up. Heifitz led us in a meditation on the assassination of Yitzhak Rabin. You see? he said. Leaders do get assassinated when they lead, and it happens even in arenas far more mundane than Rabin's. Change is necessary and good, and leaders create conditions for change. But remember, he said, that change also involves loss. Remember to take into account the learning capacity of the opponents of change. They will feel the loss, and if they cannot be brought along, they will be dangerous.

Before the term was over, he brought a tape of wolves howling to the class and sat silently while it played. He had implored us to practice stepping back from the rush of events, even as they consumed us, to observe the human dynamics of every situation, to watch the dance "from the balcony" even as we danced. And then to know that seeing would be lonely. Like the loneliness of the wolf.

At the Nieman Foundation, Bill Kovach kept us focused on the challenges facing the news media. As I listened for his own formative path and reference points, I was struck by the lucky arc of history his generation of journalists had ridden.

It hadn't been easy history. Far from it. But Bill's generation had covered profound, galvanizing events that unfolded in an era when the press was taken seriously, when it mattered, when it even led. The major stories of his career were the news royalty of the American century. Selma and the civil rights movement. Vietnam. *The Pentagon Papers.* Watergate. All the big ones, I thought. And as chaotic and difficult as those stories surely were in the unfolding, there was also a tremendous majesty about the lineup, a nobility in its heft and consequence.

My generation caught the scruffy tail end of glory. The stirrings of democratization in Asia I had seen at first hand, in the Philippines and Korea and the glimmer in China. And we reported the fall of the Berlin Wall, of the Soviet Union and the end of the Cold War.

Then it got ugly. Petty. Tawdry. Marginal. Vaudeville. We got the Clarence Thomas brawl. The Menendez brothers. OJ. Whitewater. Paula Jones. News became news entertainment, and the news industry barely knew how to resist. And the energy, I thought to myself, was flowing elsewhere. The world was being shaped by forces that had damn little to do with the news business and its old assumptions and too-apparent weaknesses.

How do we compose Christmas letters that tell all and tell nothing? That sketch outlines of a family idyll and flat-out ignore career crisis, meltdown at home, and a clearly looming storm of family risk? That hint at a seven-year itch and a wife on the verge but camouflage everything in a goo of honeyed words and honest pleasures?

We do it like this:

Friends hither and yon,

Greetings, fa-la-la, rum punch and snowballs. Have you noticed how cruelly time collapses around this letter ritual? It seems about 42 hours ago that we shipped the last one. At this clip, we'll be in the year 2525 by next Tuesday. Lord, slow us down and make it last.

It's been a fine, gentle year at our house, a year of blessings. Despite the rush of time, 1995 has somehow had a warmly familiar feeling to it. The seventh summer of dinners in the same backyard. Christmas lights pulled from the same box in the same amazingly cluttered attic. Happy, familiar terrain, but hardly uneventful.

Our littlest one is the year's hot pistol. Lauren is proving the most self-possessed, precocious starter of the brood. She's 16 months now. Height is off the charts. (I'm predicting 6 feet-plus. Danielle insists not.) Talking a blue streak. Yards of tawny hair. Deep, probing eyes. Running through the house, hands full of everything. The girl is a force of nature. And we are all helplessly smitten. What a gift!

Then, the excellent brothers. Dylan, shockingly man-sized now, 13, verging on his first shave, master of academe, Uechi Ryu, swimming lanes, rehearsals for Meet Me in St. Louis and, of course, the Net (home page: http://www1/usa1.com/pickle22). Benjamin, lithe-cubed, 9, he of the supple intuition, the tendriled imagination, the jazzy clarinet and magical prowess in all games with balls. These guys are brawny, sassy, boisterous fun.

Personally, I've had a year of ambrosia. The appetizers were pungent: reporting trips to Rwanda, Somalia and the Balkans. Since September, pure honey. I'm halfway through a Nieman fellowship at Harvard. Full pay, no work, just study whatever you like for an academic year in the company of wonderful, midcareer journalists. Until June, I'm a renaissance lout, and loving it.

Which brings us to the keystone, our tender goddess of mercy, compassion and savory curries, Dean Danielle. She's the one who deserves the sabbatical but carries on juggling sixteen bundles instead. She holds MIT together, keeps us all on an even keel and lights every day with her gentle smile. Except for envy of my current lark, she's in fine form. Lucky for us.

So that's it, folks. We count our many blessings and pray for those in the world's hard corners. To friends near and far we send our warmest good wishes and undimming affection. May your year ahead be full of joy.

Peace!

Danielle, Lauren, Dylan, Ben & Tom

Not a whisper of the earthquake coming.

Chapter 6

Astrodome

I T WAS TIME to be "in the market." History was at a turning point. So was I. No more dreaming. It was time for doing.

We hadn't built the product yet, but we were close to having a demo we liked. It would be short and sweet. It would show the major features of our planned CD-ROM, "The New American Dream-Home."

We needed to get the demo in front of manufacturers, our first market, and get their feedback. If the manufacturers liked it, and if they believed consumers would like it and use it, then we had a shot at their advertising dollars.

And if they didn't like it . . . well, we'd scramble.

At the end of January, most of the country's major manufacturers of home design products would be gathering for the annual convention of the National Association of Home Builders. It was a huge convention, Peter Rush told us, with fifty or sixty thousand attendees from all over the country. All the big manufacturers, and many smaller ones, would be there, showing off their latest products, said Peter. They'd be showing windows and doors and tile and wood flooring and whirlpools and kitchen appliances and a thousand other products that would be going into American homes for the next year and more.

The Builders' Show, as it was called, moved around the country every few years. This year it was in Houston, at the Astrodome.

"The Astrodome?" I had said when Peter called from New York to encourage us to go. Astrodome, as in the football stadium?

Peter handled public relations for a bunch of trade associations in the industry. He had met Rolly years earlier, in another life, at a solar energy conference. (Talk about history!) He was low-key, but this show brought a superlative.

"Yep, the Astrodome," he said. "It's a big show. The biggest."

This is your shot, Peter told us. You can't afford to fly around the country and visit all these companies one by one. And they probably wouldn't see you if you tried. They've never heard of you. But here they'll be all in one place. Fish in a barrel. With all their top brass on hand to make nice with the builders, their biggest customers.

So go get 'em, boys, he said.

And we decided we would.

It would have been nice to have had a crack team of multimedia designers at our disposal to help pull the demo together.

It might have been nice to have had a pile of market research confirming what consumers wanted in a new home design product.

It might have been nice to have tested a demo on focus groups and polished it and reworked it until we knew it was drop-dead wonderful.

It would have been nice to have had a killer marketing department to whip up some great printed materials to distribute.

But we had none of that. Whatever we took to Houston, we would have to imagine and produce ourselves, with Tim Johnson kicking in the 3D scenes.

Our very first test audience would be the biggest manufacturers in the industry, our most important target customers. If there was time, we would get some feedback in Boston before we flew south. But the calendar was looking tight. We had two weeks to get ready.

Harvard was on its winter break. I buckled in. And Rolly was always buckled in. He would just stretch those long days a little longer. He was good at that.

We lived in his third bedroom. We worked there, ate there, and sometimes, late at night, nodded off to sleep in our chairs there. I saw twenty times more of the big Duke Ellington print on the wall than of Danielle and the kids.

Think of me as on a news assignment overseas, I told her. Think of me as out of the country. I may as well have been.

Piece by piece, the demo inched together, consecutive scenes of electronic craftsmanship that showed what our full-blown product would be like. I wished we had a real working prototype of the actual product. But wishing wouldn't make that happen. If the demo was compelling enough to fire up a strong manufacturer reception, that would help us raise investment money. Then we could develop the product.

Rolly made a virtue out of that necessity, a habit I was beginning to notice pulled him out of a lot of tight spots. The old way of doing business, he liked to say, was to design a product, then build it, then sell it.

When products were physical things, he said, there was practically no way to proceed other than to build first and sell later. If you didn't build a physical product, it was awfully hard to show how it worked.

With new media products, he said, that approach was outdated. An electronic product could be shown in design form, in demo, and endlessly tweaked and improved before it went into production. And so it should be rolled out that way!

So, out with the old mantra of design, build, sell. In with the new mantra, our mantra: design, sell, build.

Perfect!

And perfect for our circumstances. We felt better already about having no production capacity. We hadn't done a deal yet with Art Bardige, and who knew if we would. But what did it matter? As any new-thinking person could see, it wasn't time for production! It was time for a demo. Houston would be our first test. The industry heavyweights would either connect with our dream or they wouldn't. And the demo was the key. A demo could portray almost any effect, whether or not you had the underlying technology required to actually pull that effect off and scale up its application. The demo could represent almost any dream. Beyond that, you only had to believe that the dream could be made into a product. And we absolutely believed that.

In fact, we believed something more. We believed it was better to be coming to the party naked. It was better not to be already loaded with technology and piles of money and a lifetime of industry experience. All those things came with their own limits and entanglements and blinding assumptions.

We came with something stronger, Rolly loved to say. We came with beginners' eyes. The eyes of children. With no sense of limits, no burden of history, no conflicting interests about embracing change, no presumptions about what could and could not be done in the world.

Beginners' eyes saw the world as a clean slate and imagined its ideal configuration. Beginners' eyes were honest and unencumbered. Beginners' eyes saw what could be and asked, Why not? No wonder we loved this idea. It was practically the anthem of our youth, the soundtrack of Bobby Kennedy and answers blowing in the wind. We never spoke of it that way. Never. But what a miracle to find a new realm, now, when we needed it, that would reward beginners' eyes.

And the demo would bring to life the first glimpse of what those eyes saw. The demo would be the keyhole on a new universe, on the castle in our minds. Or the mess in our minds if we didn't hurry up, I thought. The days were flipping by. The Astrodome was looming.

Rolly was a self-taught putterer at Adobe Photoshop and Macromedia's Director, the basic software tools behind the explosion of multimedia CD-ROM titles that were flooding onto the shelves of computer stores. They let designers capture and manipulate images, then stitch them together into interactive sequences of scenes, scenes that could simulate almost any software application.

It was slow, tedious work. Using Director meant flipping between the unfolding scenes on the computer screen and the thousands of tiny checkboxes of the background software that made the scenes play out. It was like assembling an electronic player piano cylinder. But little by little, our beautiful homes and interactive models began to flow into a package that looked pretty spiffy for third-bedroom stuff. Pretty spiffy, we hoped, by any standard.

Our core electronic image — maybe our logo, we thought — was a house-shaped scrapbook. What did people do when they dreamed of building or improving a home? They started a scrapbook or folder of design ideas and products they liked. They tore ads and photos out of magazines. They collected brochures and pages from catalogues. And the scrapbook became the record of their home design thinking and wishing. It became their tool for communicating to others what they wanted.

BuildingBlocks would make that simple tool its core metaphor and graphic symbol. A house-shaped scrapbook. A dark green leather cover — electronic, of course — to suggest luxury and good taste. A substantial 3D brass spiral to hold the cover and give definition and depth to the image. A picture of a lovely Shingle Style home embedded in the green leather cover to convey that this was all about homes.

Then there were the homes. Rolly's old architecture instructor from Yale, Jim Righter, was good enough to let us use photographs of two houses he had designed to populate the demo.

One dramatic home, on Fisher Island, off the Rhode Island coast, we used behind an introductory message telling manufacturers that home computers and the Internet were a new force that needed to be reckoned with.

"Your best customers are plugging in," said the text overlay. "Talk to them!"

Photographs of the other Righter home had been used by Tim Johnson as the raw material for two interactive 3D home design scenes. The scenes had a unique design that was central to a core BuildingBlocks tenet. Instead of offering a pile of "electronic Tinkertoys" and expecting users to create their own home design from many tiny pieces, these models offered whole homes and design scenes and let users integrate or remove whole parts. Adding a wing? The receiving wall would reconfigure to accept it. Removing a dormer? The roof shingles over the hole left behind. That's "object-oriented" design. Programming the real software to do it remained far beyond our resources. But a demo, the holy demo — that we could do. Maybe.

With Rolly's scripting of Tim's interactive 3D models, we began to approximate how whole houses would be manipulated electronically. Wings on, wings off. Living room fireplace with stone mantelpiece, same fireplace with a very different wooden mantelpiece. Furniture in the living room, no furniture in the living room. It was fun.

Just point and click on the electronic homes and, as long as you followed the careful script and sequence of the demo, they appeared to
pop brilliantly to life, endlessly changing form at the click of the
mouse.

This was cool. This we had not seen before.

To Tim's models, Rolly added his own touch. Even the best 3D
models — and Tim's were excellent — still had a cartoonish feel
about them. It was almost unavoidable. But people designing a
home didn't want to deal with cartoons. They wanted photographic quality in the images they saw and dreamed over. They
would want the same, we thought, in images they could manipulate electronically.

We had already used all our photos from Jim Righter. The clock
was ticking. We needed an image now. We dived into a stack of
Carole's home design magazines and came out with a jaw-dropping
shot of a beautiful Connecticut home, Shingle Style again, with an
elaborate door and window facing the camera straight on from the
end of one gracious wing. Perfect.

The magazine was slapped onto the scanner, the photo came up
on our computer screen, and we breathed a silent thanks to the paper-and-ink publisher. We would never sell or distribute this lovely
piece of work, but we sure were glad to have it for the demo. A great
spreading oak stood nobly over the house. Dewy, early morning light
flooded the green strip of lawn in the foreground. The house was
warm and inventive and inviting, with young shingled walls the
color of rich leather and crisp white trim at its windows and eaves
and doors. It was gracious and gently imposing and casual, all at
once. You wanted to live there.

Into Photoshop it went, and the magic began. The soaring door
and window set that opened onto a wide patio went into electronic
surgery. In one layer, the set stayed complete. In the next layer, the
arched window above the door was removed and shingles from the
surrounding wall were copied into the void left behind. In the next
layer, the door's side windows were removed and the voids were
filled again, leaving only the simple, attractive door.

Then the layers were reversed and sequenced in Director for a
startling effect. The house appeared first with the simple door. Click

on it once and *voilà*, side windows. Click again and the top window was added. And an attractive wing was turned into a splendid wing before your eyes. One more click and it was just a simple door again. No complicated CAD. Just clicking.

Next came the demo scrapbook. Any scene or product in the program could be saved into a personal electronic scrapbook, to review or share later. Click on a saved product and all its key information would be displayed — manufacturer, model name, model number, and a brief product description. If the manufacturer was a BuildingBlocks advertiser, the user could go deeper, could find out where the product was available for sale locally and see a marketing message from the manufacturer. At that last step, "The New American DreamHome" became a tool for selling. And BuildingBlocks, we hoped, made money.

The show came closer. We worked later. Designing our first business cards. Drafting our first marketing material. Getting a contact list from Peter of companies likely to be attending. On and on.

I dashed to Harvard one morning for a Nieman seminar. Joe Bower, a professor from the B-school, was taking our group through a short course in U.S. economics. By early 1996, the long-running story of the American economy was still one of recession and layoffs and insecurity and fear. Bower didn't promise any quick respite.

The basic U.S. strategy has two goals, said Bower. Creating rich individuals and creating strong allies. In the pursuit of those goals and the conditions that create them, he said, the United States tended to use harsh tools, the equivalents of fire and flood.

"The United States uses the flood and forest fire method of forestry," said Bower, drawing an analogy to the fires that had recently been allowed to devastate large sections of Yellowstone National Park.

"It looks pretty bad when it's happening," he said, "but over a century it works. The question is, how much fire and flood can the system bear?"

And, I thought, where any individual falls in the cycle of destruction and creation. I didn't want to leave my place to fate. Not these days.

Back to the third bedroom. No response from Stone. I wished he would hurry up. We were spreading the investor net wider now, but it would help if Stone would break the ice. We needed money.

On the positive side, the list was in from Peter Rush of fax numbers for the Builders' Show exhibitors. We knew none of the names, but we would try to set up appointments before we got to Houston.

We faxed out our first marketing document. It was fresh from the printer, another expense we could hardly afford. But it was ready, with no time to spare. It called the company BuildingBlocks Software. We had decided on the way to the printer's shop that "Software" sounded more current than "Publishing," even though we were a publishing company.

Perhaps we had a few jitters?

Never mind. The faxes went out, inviting manufacturers to meet with us in Houston. For the first time we were in the market.

"BuildingBlocks Software presents," it said in bold at the top of the page, "The New American DreamHome™." We loved that little trademark sign. It made us feel in business. And just dropping it on was all we needed to do for now to protect our empire of the mind.

Then came the pitch. It was unabashedly earnest. It was hardly sophisticated. It was choppy and corny. But what the hell. It was ours. Beginners' eyes, beginners' marketing.

"Your customers are changing," we wrote.

Affluent Americans are plugging in. They're hooking up multimedia computers in droves. They're catching the online bug. They're getting wired . . . Wired consumers want sharper, deeper home product information. They want exciting, interactive images. Customized options. Personal relationships with brands they can trust.

Are you ready to catch the wave?

We've created a powerful new way for you to sell your products and services. Right into people's homes. To motivated consumers . . . It's a new breed of software. For women. And for men. It's simple. Powerful. Gorgeous. Useful. Fun.

Let it work for you.

Catch the Wave!

We're BuildingBlocks Software. We're dedicated to helping your best customers make their dreams real and to serving you.

Ad space available now for September '96.

Call us.

We sent out scores of the piece by fax. Never mind that the software didn't exist yet. We thought our sell was pretty catchy.

We got one response, asking for a meeting. One!

But that one was from Ham Shirmer, the vice president of marketing for Masco, a $4 billion conglomerate and the largest manufacturer of home design products in the United States.

That would do for starters.

The day before our flight to Houston was mayhem. At the last minute, when Rolly ported the demo from the desktop computer to the laptop, he realized we needed a more powerful laptop to run the program. We needed the brand-new Apple machine. It was expensive. It was hard to find in stock. And we needed a thirty-day return policy in case even the new model couldn't handle our program. We finally got the machine. (Charge it! Just charge it!) We brought it home and struggled to load the demo. The new machine didn't have enough memory either. The stores were closed. Rolly worked with it for half the night, but it wouldn't play the demo. Our flight was at 10 A.M. We couldn't lug a desktop computer around the floor of the Astrodome. We were screwed! Totally screwed!

At eight o'clock the next morning, we were at the doors of the computer store again. It was bitter cold. My fingers stuck to the steel handles when I shook the doors, hoping that someone was in there somewhere. But there was no one. It was dark. There was no other store we knew on the way to the airport. We sat with the nose of the car almost in the door, our bags in the trunk, heat on High trying to beat the cold, waiting. At last, one light came on. We jumped to the windows like maniacs, like bank robbers. When the frightened manager realized it wasn't a heist, he let us in and sold us the memory we needed. And we were tearing down the highway to the airport, to Houston.

We landed at the wrong airport. We rented a tiny car and bounced

down Houston's torn-up central freeway to our motel, a grim cinder-block bunkhouse at the bottom of the convention's accommo-
dations list, miles from the city center in a worn-out zone of strip
malls and sagebrush. No problem. We were a startup. We liked the
rough road.

We plugged the new memory into the laptop, ate a bag of burgers,
and dropped off to sleep before midnight for the first time in weeks.

At nine o'clock the next morning we were at the Astrodome. It
was vast and flanked by its even larger convention hall sisters, the
Astrohall and Astroarena. There were miles of parking lots, all full.

We registered and crept into the bleachers, two tiny specks in the
Astro megacomplex. We had our suits on. I hated wearing a suit, but
Peter had given us the dress code for everyone here looking to do
business. And there were thousands of them. Waves of builders and
exhibitors were flooding in everywhere. We could see the manufacturers' exhibits, rising like palaces, two and three and four stories
above the show floor. We could not see the end of the exhibits. They
stretched beyond eyeshot.

Rolly had the new laptop on his knees in the bleachers, making
last-minute fixes in the demo. He had wrestled with it all the way
down on the plane — wrestling with the software, wrestling with the
framing of the screen. He was stressed. A thin, blue vein pulsed hard
in his temple.

What are we doing here? I was thinking, squeezed into a bleacher
seat next to him.

He was making the houses come up on cue.

Who are we fooling?

He was making sure the wings and dormers would come and go.

Why will anyone pay attention? We're just two little guys with a
laptop and a shoulder bag. In this vast arena, packed with tons of industry muscle and mountains of marketing firepower. We are dust!
Less than dust. We are mice in the land of giants!

He was making sure the doors and windows would appear and
disappear. That paint colors would magically change and fireplaces
would morph on command.

Get a grip, I thought, looking out over the sea of manufacturers' proud exhibits. Remember, they may be big, but they need us. Say it again: they . . . need . . . us.

"Okay. Okay. It's working," Rolly said. And I turned to look.

And I glanced over my shoulder as I turned.

There behind us, on a narrow landing between tiers of bleachers, was a line of men I took to be builders or maybe architects. They didn't appear to know one another but were standing tightly bunched, right behind us, peering intently over one another's shoulders.

The great hall stretched before them, full of million-dollar booths and miles of famous corporate logos. But they weren't looking at that.

They were staring at our demo.

They had stopped dead in their tracks to gawk.

They were fixated.

"Do some more," said one, pointing to the laptop, and the others nodded.

So we ran through it again, with the houses dancing and rooms morphing on the screen. Hey, this was fun.

And the little crowd grew.

"How can I get that?" asked another man, a builder. And I gave him a BuildingBlocks business card, the first one I had ever handed out, and got his in return. We would send him a copy when it came out, I said.

"Thanks!" he said. "Thanks very much!"

Other hands reached out.

Maybe this wouldn't be so bad after all.

We snapped the laptop closed and hit the exhibition floor. We must have walked a hundred miles that day. We were nomads, with a laptop and a fast patter. Peter Rush was right. The top brass was there. And to our delight, nearly everyone we approached was eager to see what we were showing. They were there to sell, not to be sold. It wasn't easy to get their attention. We had to start with the lowly show help and talk our hearts out. But almost every time we did, the staff bumped us up and up until we were talking with the top executives of these enormous companies. It was as if there were no gravity in the Astrodome that day. We just kept going up, right up even to the skyboxes where the muckety-mucks sipped their drinks and looked down through the million-watt blaze of Astrodome lights. The moment was on our side. There was talk of an information revolution in the air. These guys wanted to keep up. Suddenly, maybe they *needed* to keep up, to have somebody fill in the picture.

And there we were.

We might be nomads on the show floor with nothing but freshly printed business cards and a newborn demo. But when the laptop whirred to life and the screen lit up, they paid attention. They felt the hinge point, too. They wanted to know what was coming. CD-ROMs they knew, but most had barely grasped the Internet. They wanted to know more.

And they liked what they saw. Ham Shirmer at Masco watched the demo go through its paces, nodding yes, yes, as he watched. We were on to something here, he said. Something good. Would we be willing to come out to Masco's headquarters, outside Detroit, and talk business?

Absolutely.

At Du Pont Corian's booth, Carol Gee, the global brand manager for Corian, heard our story and took us straight into her temporary office, away from the surging crowds. She was smart and focused and running her own quick calculations on how a new marketing vehicle like ours might unfold. This was the best new media presentation she had seen in her industry, she said. Would we be willing to visit her advertising agency, BBDO, in New York? She wanted them to see this. This was different, she said. This was really good.

Yes, we would be happy to follow up in New York.

Delighted.

We talked to Viking, and Jacuzzi, and Andersen Windows, and American Standard, and the keen-eyed marketers at Grohe. We talked to Jenn-Air, and Marvin Windows, and Kentucky Wood Floors, and DCS, and Moen, and Baldwin Hardware, and U-Line, and Dal-Tile, and Amana, and Caoba Doors, and Broan, and Velux, and Finlandia Saunas, and Sub-Zero, and a hundred more.

We talked to the undisputed king of the Builders' Show, the biggest of the big exhibitors, Kohler. Kohler's towering exhibit was a huge, cocky celebration of water: water gushing through deep, luxurious showering pavilions, high-pressure water shooting in alarming midair arcs over visitors' heads, a wide, four-story waterfall that spelled out Kohler as it thundered down behind a booming country and western band.

Would we be good enough to come to Kohler, Wisconsin, to tell them more? they asked.

Count on it.

By the time the first day of the show was done, we were dog-tired and giddy with triumph, hooting and high-fiving our way out of the Astrodome, ready to kiss the Apple laptop as we bounced back to our cinder-block bunkhouse.

They liked it. They really liked it.

No, they loved it!

Yeeeeehaa!

We had come to the Astrodome like waifs to the palace door and left affirmed and grinning wide. We weren't just dreaming. We were on to something here.

We tore off our suits and headed up the highway, whooping with the windows rolled down, to a noisy Texas roadhouse for dinner. I was singing all the way at the top of my lungs, goof-drawling every cornball Texas song I could dredge up. Rolly played bongos on the dashboard. He looked like a crazed Civil War rebel in the dashboard light, with his hair blowing back and the tips of his big mustache streaming. I wished he had his guitar.

"This thing is real, buddy," he shouted over the roadhouse din as we tucked into ribs and beer.

"Yessir, I do believe it is," I shouted back.

"We're going to build a great company," he shouted. "It's going to be fun."

It was fun right now — that much I knew. I was getting invested in this adventure. It was fun being on the leading edge for a change, cracking open the future. Walking out on that Astrodome floor today had felt like some kind of ancient rite of passage. You had to be crazy enough to dive in and smart enough to succeed when you did. But what a feeling!

The roadhouse crowd began to thin a little. The din was easing. And we talked. We had dived in so hard on BuildingBlocks that there was still much we didn't know about each other. We knew our college personas. We knew the outline of each other's adult life and family relationships. But we were getting in deep here, the way this thing was going. Maybe we should know more.

So I told him about my mom and dad, and memories of the farmstead covered in ice when we moved back, and how that all stuck with me and prodded me in ways I couldn't fully understand. I told him it hadn't been all glory at the *Globe*, that I had stepped on toes and sometimes been an asshole in my urgency and arrogance. I told him what a miracle it seemed to me that we had reconnected around such a project at just this time. I told him how empowering it had felt to pair our energies, the mastermind and the seeker, or field marshal, or whatever. I told him I was getting wedded to the little sprouts of this company and that I was worried about how Danielle would respond if I really gave up everything else and made this move.

And I told him I was feeling some guilt about pursuing this wild vision on the quiet. The *Globe* certainly didn't know. The Nieman Foundation certainly didn't know. How could I tell them? If I did, even in confidence, they'd be forced to either betray a confidence or betray the *Globe*, which had long supported the foundation. I couldn't put them in that position. Only a couple of the other fellows had the barest inkling of what I was up to. I didn't like the double life. It was something new to me, and distinctly uncomfortable.

Yet what other way was there? The pontificators were saying that as the economy changed, we would all need to be ready to pursue half a dozen different careers in the course of a lifetime. How were we supposed to make those transitions? Employers were obviously no longer expected to be loyal. So how could employees? How could anyone pull off the run up to a leap except with stolen time, or at least with stolen thought. Maybe this was part of a new structure of work and commitments. More fluid. Overlapping. Interwoven in time.

"It's just nature," Rolly said. "You can't stop it."

Then he opened up. About a childhood filled with the awkwardness of being too bright and too shy. In grade school, he had tested as a two-year-old on IQ tests that were too easy to bear. A problem child, they had said, with a mind wired too densely for ordinary routines. It had always been his blessing and his curse. He could see what others could not. He could think things through in such depth and detail that he could look ahead, over the horizon. But that vision had often not been paired with a knack for conveying what he saw in a way that brought people along. The world had sometimes been uncomprehending and cruel.

But this time it was working, he said. The vision was there. And the vision was communicating. Maybe not perfectly yet, but it was working. And in ways that I might not be able to fully relate to, he said, this felt like his main shot. Like his one big chance to build something that put his power of vision fully to work. And to build an environment, a company, that was fully hospitable to his restless, unique mind, because that mind was at the heart of the company.

He felt empowered by our work together too, he said. We had complementary strengths. We were greater than the sum of our parts. And it was working.

You're damn straight, I said, full of ribs and beer and feeling big as Texas. Turn on your love light, mama! Make a path straight and clear. Catch a train to glory.

Hell, we were heroes of the Astrodome!

Chapter 7

Leap Year

STONE WASN'T calling back. I left messages. They didn't get returned. Glad to help, he had said. Then radio silence.

Never mind. I was beginning to understand that this path wasn't going to be easy. And it wasn't for everyone. We would live with that. If it were easy, everybody would be doing it. If it were easy, somebody else would already be doing what we were aiming to do.

So be glad that it isn't easy, I told myself. And I made twenty other calls, to twenty other people.

And still it gnawed at me that Stone didn't call. I hadn't felt so exposed in a long, long time. There was no institutional armor around me now. No ranks of staff. No buffer of bureaucracy or corporate grandeur. Nobody else to blame anything on. There was just pixie dust and pure will and a plan and a demo (at last!). And everything was so personal.

Let it go, I would say to myself. You've got bigger fish to fry.

And that was true.

This romp, this toe dip, was getting serious. We came back from Houston on fire, showing everybody we could corral the demo and recounting our taste of triumph at the Astrodome. The money from Rolly's mother had come in. Rolly had put $10,000 in. It was time for me to do the same.

The ante was going up. My year of freedom was ticking by. The noise and distractions were receding. I could see the issues standing tall and stark in front of me.

There were two questions:

First, could I personally make this leap?

And, second, if I made the leap, out over the canyon of risk and uncertainty that was surely ahead, could this little company land on the other side?

The first challenge, the leap, was all about tearing out old roots and attachments, letting go of salary and of certainties, and committing to something entirely new. Not just a new job. The leap I was staring at was a leap to a whole new economy. From the known to the unknown. From the trappings of security to the opportunity of risk. It was thrilling. It was frightening.

And if I was honest with myself I could see that it was a leap I was already sprinting toward.

I hadn't cut the cord. All the old comforts and perks were still there waiting. Come back, they beckoned, and watch the retirement plan grow!

But in truth, I was already running. Somewhere along the line, my center of gravity had shifted. There was no explicit commitment yet, no blood oath. I could still jump off this train. But my heart was in transit. It was headed for the canyon rim, ready to fly.

Everything seemed to be urging me on. A page 1 *Wall Street Journal* article on the New York Times Company said the New York paper had paid far too much for the *Globe,* that big-city newspapers were a declining business, that the Times company was not making an adequate profit, that its stock price was stuck in the cellar, and that spending on "editorial product" — the content of the *New York Times* and the other papers it owned — was the place that analysts were expecting cuts. *Editor & Publisher* magazine reported that the Times company management projected staff reductions for the *New York Times* and the *Boston Globe* in 1996. There was talk of the *Globe's* being sold yet again. Who knew where it all might end up?

But it wasn't the gory details that pushed me most. It was the overwhelming sense that everything was changing and it was time to go. I figured that any boomer in the country with six ounces of awareness was asking him- or herself how the hell he or she was going to make it in this new economy, where nothing was certain, where there were no guarantees, where bricks and mortar could be closed down overnight, and where the rewards were all in moving fast and free. Every time an AT&T announced forty thousand layoffs, a hundred million people shivered. They felt the tremor and wondered whether it was time to break camp, whether it was time to run for new ground.

I was running, I realized. I wasn't a tech-head. I wasn't twenty-one anymore. But, dammit, I was in the game. I was running for the new frontier. I was racing toward the leap.

Which left the second question.

Could this little company make it to the other side? Could we cross the canyon? Or was this just the overture to an elaborate midlife crash-and-burn?

Don't think too much.

Just go.

And we were really going now. Showing that demo nonstop. And as we showed it, we fired up the circle of friends and acquaintances around us who had been casually paying attention. We showed it to Bernice Cramer, an old friend from my days in Tokyo who was now a marketing consultant in Boston. We showed it to Louise Citron, my friend and neighbor two doors down the street, who had been watching me wade deeper and deeper into this venture. We showed it to Len Schlesinger, our board member from Harvard Business School. We showed it to Art Bardige.

Everybody loved it. Friends looked at it almost with relief. We had been talking so long and loudly about this vision. Now they could finally see something. And in seeing it, I suspected, they were able to put away quiet fears that we were simply nuts.

Bernice offered to get more involved in helping us think through marketing issues. Louise's eyes opened wide and her mind bubbled with the possibilities beaming out through the laptop screen, and she smiled big and pronounced it a sure thing. A winner. Len began making introductions.

We took the demo to Len at the B-school on a snowy February day. We were so excited nearly all the time now. I sped over a hill with my bald tires, slipped sideways, slid fifty long, downhill yards, and crunched into a tall cement lane divider. Never mind. It was just a crumpled bumper, an alignment job. Nothing at all in the scheme of things we had brewing now. We had to get to Len.

Len Schlesinger was a B-school powerhouse. He was a brash and brilliant dynamo, a success in business and a big man in academe. He had been chief operating officer at Au Bon Pain in its hot growth years. He had helped to completely restructure the B-school's curriculum at Harvard. He was only in his early forties but had the accomplishments and air of a lifetime of high-voltage success. He was on the board of directors of Borders Books and The Limited. He was an adviser to the high and mighty, including Jack Welch at General Electric. And on this snowy day, the first time I met Len, the first thing I heard him yelling from his office was "Pigs!"

"They are such pigs!" he was bellowing as we walked in, my crumpled car stowed in the perfectly maintained B-school parking lot, beyond perfectly shoveled, swept, and salted B-school walkways.

"Soooooweeee!" Rolly chimed in, popping his head in Len's door. "Who are the pigs?"

"You don't want to know," said Len, throwing both hands high over his big head in disgusted good humor. His office was jammed with trophies of companies helped, courses led, projects completed: fancy silver groundbreaking shovel, inscribed hard hat, big framed back-slapping notes from CEOs and government honchos, thanking him for prodigious labors, joking that he should take it easy sometime. I had known him for three minutes and already I doubted he ever took it easy.

"Believe me when I tell you that people sometimes do not know when to stop!" Len was almost yelling. "They make piles and piles of money, and they want more piles and piles. Piles! And there's a point at which they hurt themselves. And they can't see it. Because they're pigs!"

He laughed at the splendor of human folly and spun around in his big chair. His eyes didn't just have the glitter I had seen in the B-school students' eyes. These eyes were furnaces in the tough-guy face of a well-read prizefighter, blazing with intelligence. He planted his big hands wide and flat on his desktop.

"So, how are you guys doing?"

A huge smile cracked across his face. The B-school was all about case studies, and case studies were all about human scheming and yearning and folly. Some follies turned into great companies. Some turned into laughingstocks. Len looked at us as if he was ready to be helpful and ready to be amused at the same time. Businesses were built on ideas and passion and analysis and folly. He was ready to hear ours.

So we poured it out. Our latest plans, our struggles, our reception in Houston.

"Show me," he said, pointing with his broad chin toward the laptop. And we did. And the high humor danced again in his eyes. The demo laid out the audacity of our ambition. Our unique folly. He was grinning wide, with approval. This was ambitious enough to be interesting.

We told him about the desperate race to prepare for Houston, about the last-minute tweaks in the Astrodome bleachers and the magic crowd of onlookers before we even hit the floor. We recounted our meetings with manufacturing executives, and Rolly read off the glowing comments he had carefully recorded as we worked the floor. Find your story, Art Bardige had said. Tend your story. And we were. And those flattering quotes were part of our story.

Len's grin got wider and wider. "So, they loved it, huh? They really loved it."

His eyes were dancing, shining. We basked in the glow, a little too pleased with ourselves. He kept grinning. "How many sales did you get?"

"Pardon?" said Rolly.

"How many sales did you get?" Len asked again, grinning harder. Human folly was so terrible and so wonderful.

"Well, it won't happen that fast," said Rolly, smiling right back. "We got meetings. Great meetings."

Never let even the most modest success be discounted. Another Rolly trait I was noticing.

"Uh-huh," said Len, beaming, lapping up the marvel of eternal, irrepressible high hopes and good storytelling.

"Fifty touches," Rolly said in his mysterious authority style. "I read it takes fifty touches to make a sale like this. Phone calls, meetings, postcards. Each one a touch. Fifty touches."

Fifty touches! I was horrified. We would be ninety years old before we could touch all these companies fifty times. Surely he was joking. Fifty touches, my ass!

But Len wasn't laughing now. He was nodding yes. Yes, it takes time. How was our money situation?

We told him about Rolly's mom's money and Rolly's ten thousand. And I heard myself saying, to my dismay, that I would also be putting in ten thousand. When was that decided? Danielle would kill me.

And we told him about Art Bardige, and the string of meetings we had had with him since November. Art was quickly becoming a mentor, we said. He was a mensch. He knew so much. He was a great thinker with practical experience, too. And Art just might be a connection to money. He had been making cryptic comments about possibilities, about his brother-in-law and others. A real long shot, Art had said. But worth talking to, if only for the benefit of insight.

"Is the brother-in-law a VC?" asked Len. VC. Venture capitalist, not Viet Cong. Len said it with an extra twist on his grin. He didn't like to see young companies take venture capital. The venture capital companies, he said, promised the world in terms of what they could do for you. The contacts, the leverage, the wise guidance. Then far too often they took a huge hunk of your company for the money they put in and didn't deliver value. If you succeeded, they took the credit and the lion's share of the reward. And if you struggled, he said, they too often dropped you cold.

"They don't call it vulture capital for nothing," said Len.

Vulture capital! Great.

No, Art's people were not VC, we said. We weren't sure what they were. We hoped we would find out. We agreed that private money was better for now. We were working on it.

"Work hard," said Len, grinning and scribbling down names for us to call. The president of Crate & Barrel. A top ad agency guy in New York. More. His phone was ringing. His secretary was at the door with a fistful of messages. His next appointment was waiting outside. Len was spinning in his big chair, eyes ablaze, eyeing the stack of e-mail that had poured in while we talked. All this folly! Folly and human endeavor and threads of genius, all wound so tightly together that most people could not tell them apart. But Len could. Oh, yes. Without question. And he was nodding us encouragement and taking the phone and handing us his scribbled names with a thumbs-up and that big, fully amused smile. Hey, the world is full of folly, and the world goes on splendidly anyway. And some people make millions. And some become pigs!

He covered the mouthpiece, grinning, waving us out.

"Are we having fun yet?" he asked in a gleeful stage whisper, eyebrows shooting high. Then he spun in his chair, and we were gone.

"Come down to White Plains," Art Bardige had urged us. "You've got to meet Rick."

Today we would. We were on the road again, driving south from Boston toward New York and White Plains. The great Rick had agreed to see us.

Rick Segal was Art's brother-in-law, an investor of some kind, we deduced, though Art was always a bit vague when he spoke of him. Rick was very smart, he said. Rick knew people, he said, in a tone that was so respectful that I wondered if I heard fear. Rick didn't invest in things as small as BuildingBlocks, but . . . Come on down. Talk to him. He'll have good advice. Show him what you're up to.

We were hurrying across Connecticut now, through forests, toward Hartford. Rehearsing for Rick.

In the three months we had known him, Art had already come to seem like a co-conspirator. He had taken a fast and deep interest in BuildingBlocks. He believed that people would go online to learn things that were difficult to learn otherwise. He loved beautiful homes and beautiful things. He knew it was often difficult for people to learn exactly what they needed to know about home design and home products exactly when they needed to know it. We were going to solve that.

But it wasn't just business that connected us to Art. He had a soul-

THE LEAP / 134

ful spark that we loved, and somehow we had sparked an attraction in response. We were on fire with this idea, and that passion was attracting lots of people now. Not big money yet, but people and their minds.

Art's mind was the biggest catch of all. He was a software builder, but he was also much more. He was a big thinker. He worshiped Charles Darwin. He loved to explore the texture of knowledge itself, how it was created.

Over Chinese noodles at lunch one day in Cambridge, when we had talked for hours about BuildingBlocks, Art had begun to share his bigger project. Knowledge didn't just magically pop into being, he said. Knowledge was invented. Constructed, even. And the tools, or elements, of its invention evolved over time. Symbols, for the earliest tribes. Universals, like math and logic, for the ancient Greeks and Romans. Then interacting objects — the planets, Bach's interplay of melodies and instrumentation, Henry Fielding's lovers and enemies — during the Renaissance and the Enlightenment.

I'm not in Kansas anymore, I was thinking, sipping the last of my dark tea. This may be the tornado. Or it may be Oz. But it's definitely not my old stomping grounds. Software revolutions and a wide-open online future. Big money and the mysterious Rick. Aristotle's thought patterns and Bach's guitar and Henry Fielding's lovers, all over Shanghai noodles! If this was bricks and mortar, these were yellow bricks.

The twentieth century, Art said, on a roll now, came to knowledge through environments. Think of Einstein's "frames of reference," he said. Or Freud or Joseph Conrad or Heisenberg. Think of quantum mechanics. I was beginning to lose my footing here. I tried to think of quantum mechanics. Bach's guitar was easier.

And now, said Art, his lunchtime short course nearing its end, we were reaching the end of one great period of knowledge invention and entering another. We had lots of thinking and activity, but few breakthrough ideas. Which meant, he said, that we were likely on the cusp of a great new explosion of profound knowledge development. And the central knowledge-building tool of this new era, he said, the successor to symbols and universals and all the rest was . . . the unique artifact.

The unique artifact. Artifact, as in anything constructed by humans, whether physical or conceptual. Unique, as in special, singular.

I surrendered. This was more than I could digest in one lunchtime. But I was hooked on his mind. I now had two minds in my immediate circle that thought in terms of big patterns in time. Between Rolly and Art, I got the message in stereo: the world was changing. We were on the verge of something new and great.

I got it.

"What do you think this meeting is really all about?" I asked Rolly as we drove into White Plains. All the way down we had rehearsed our message for Rick — the size of the market, the frustration of consumers, the needs of manufacturers, the opportunities in bringing new media to bear.

"Maybe it's advice, and maybe it's money," said Rolly. "Art says Rick doesn't invest at our level. We're too small. If that's right, we'll just take his advice and be happy for it. The reality of the situation is, we don't have any choice but to step ahead and see what happens."

We were pulling into Rick's office park, on a commanding hillside above the tree-lined highway. His offices were in a central building on the fourth floor, behind a wide, solid wood door, no window. We rang the bell and the door buzzed open. A wide hall, with a dozen or more private offices opening onto big windows with a good view of pine and hardwood hillsides. Nothing ostentatious, but someone was an art collector, of large, hyperrealistic oil paintings. Rick's secretary beckoned us to the end of the hall. Rolly set down the shoulder bag with the laptop and we waited, two guys in frayed khakis with a demo and an introduction. We were mice in the temple again.

Rick was around the corner, on the phone. No one had explained to us exactly what went on here, except that there was family money being managed. Maybe several families' money. And Rick was the helmsman.

He was trading shares right now, from the sound of it. We couldn't help overhearing snatches. Let's sell three hundred thousand shares of that, I thought I heard him say. Let's buy a hundred thousand there. It was a soft voice, but firm. Not one to argue with. And unless we were hallucinating, it was moving millions of dollars' worth of stock, just around the corner from us, on an ordinary trading day in February.

Rolly and I stared at each other across his shoulder bag, eyes wide. "Wow!" I mouthed soundlessly.

And Rick was there.

It was hard to pin down his age. Maybe late forties. Casual, button-down shirt, no tie. Expensive blue jeans. Italian loafers. No socks, in February. And very well tanned ankles. He was tall. Handsome, with a high, smooth forehead and keen glance. Friendly, but reserved. Welcoming, but with an aura of permanent skepticism around his eyes. He sat us down on a deep leather couch with two wide side chairs and called in a partner or colleague from across the hall, Ray Lamontagne. Ray gave us a hearty handshake, but had an even cooler demeanor. I was thinking Frank Sinatra and the Rat Pack. Cool power.

The view from Rick's corner office was sweeping, over snow-streaked hills and a wide ribbon of highway. The art on his walls was the best. He must be the collector. On his desk I saw a copy of *Gunfighter Nation,* a book I admired. We asked tentatively about the office, the business they were in. "Capital maintenance," Rick said cryptically, and that clearly was the end of that line of inquiry.

Well! Okay. . . . Where the hell was Art!

"Art says you guys have an interesting project going," Rick offered, noncommittal but open, and we dove in. This was what we came for. To tell the story. The market. The opportunity. New media. The demo. We opened the laptop on Rick's coffee table. My mouth was parched. Rolly was barely breathing, I knew. Rick and Ray watched the images flicker on the screen, lolling comfortably in deep leather. Polite questions. Probing. No rejection, but no Astrodome applause either.

I was beginning to quietly despair. Here was our first big money interview, and the voltage was just polite. Smart questions. Attentive. But cool. And we were almost finished with our pitch!

Then Art arrived, thank God. And just behind him, Rick's wife, Monica. Art's energy warmed the room immediately, but it was Monica who flipped the tone. She glimpsed the demo. She sat down. She was immediately engaged.

We ran the morphing houses through their paces. Her eyes widened. We told our story again. How we intended to help people get the homes they really wanted. She was into it.

"Rick, this is great!" she said, and the meeting wasn't over after all. We would all go to lunch. There was a lot to talk about. We took Rick's car. It was a brand-new BMW 750, delivered to his office by the dealer that very morning. I slipped into the backseat, onto the virgin, caramel-colored leather, and dropped my feet onto the pristine carpeting. They were muddy! I was the first person ever to sit in this rich man's backseat, the backseat of a guy so cool he seemed to float, so exempt from ordinary struggles that he didn't wear socks in February, and I was fouling his beautiful new car with my muddy, worn-out shoes.

But it didn't matter. Lunch was good. Art was in high spirits, Monica was full of warmth, and Rick and Ray warmed, too. It became clear that it wasn't just advice we were talking about here. It was investment. Yes, we were small potatoes. But new media and the Internet were becoming hot. Very hot. And Art was vouching for us. And Monica liked our stuff.

Our blood started to flow again. Rolly was breathing. We bubbled about our reception in Houston. Ray was skeptical. People will always see you at trade shows, he said. They're bored out of their minds, you come along, they see you. Okay, I thought. There was nothing guaranteed here, but this encounter was warming. Rick had a friend, he said, who was a former software analyst with Donaldson, Lufkin and Jenrette. His name was Scott Smith. We should see him. If Scott liked what we were up to, that would be a good sign.

A good sign? Did that mean a green light? Did that mean money? Could we ask?

Rolly did.

Rick was positive, but completely noncommittal. He would wait to see what Scott thought.

But that definitely meant maybe. And maybe meant maybe yes. A long way from no, certainly. We drove back to the office, with Rolly talking nonstop now about the possibilities here, the scale of our opportunity. He was still talking when Rick walked us to the elevator, polite and cool, but listening. The picture must have seemed outrageous by any traditional standard of what two guys with a demo could represent. But who knew? Technology had made a lot of fortunes, and the Internet was starting to look like a potential new gusher.

Rolly was pulling out the stops.

"On our projections, you'd make twenty times your money in five years," he was saying as Rick showed us into the elevator. "If we hit it big, it could be a hundred times your money," he said, pitching everything we had as the elevator doors began to close.

"Yeah," said Rick, cool but listening. "Yeah, that's right."

The doors slid together. Our first major investor meeting was over. We had survived.

"Did you hear that?" said Rolly. We were both staring at the closed doors. Almost afraid to move.

"He didn't say we're nuts!"

Back in Boston, Len Schlesinger had called to say he had a potential team member for us. A guy named Steven Robbins. He had worked for the godhead, Intuit. Don't rush into anything, said Len, but he might be worth talking to. The answering machine clicked ahead through the circle of friends who were leaning in to help now. Bernice Cramer had called to check in. Kathy Ahern, too. And Peter Thorne, and half a dozen others. We had a buzz going.

And there was a message from Danielle on the answering machine in Rolly's third bedroom. Just wanted to know where you were, Tom, and when you might be home. Shit! I had been running so fast lately, I hadn't even told her I was going out of town.

So much for cooking dinners. This year, which was supposed to be a time of long, quiet evenings and slow weekends with the family, was turning out just the opposite. I wasn't kicking back. I was pushing forward. Hard. On every front except home. How could I explain it?

There was a calculation growing in my mind that went like this:

There was a window of opportunity here. It wouldn't last forever. But it was cracking open huge right now. Right in front of me. I was forty. I would probably never have a greater sum total of energy and insight than I had at this moment. My insight might grow. My energy probably wouldn't. But it was there, right now, at the very moment that this incredible vista was opening up.

So I had a choice. I could stay where I was, hoping the old world would see me through. Or I could jump. I could make the leap to a new world, a new economy. And if I made that leap, I would not only be on the side of the future, I would *own* a piece of that future. I was never going to own a printing press, but I might own a real piece of electronic turf.

And then, who knew? I wouldn't be marking off years on the calendar. I would be riding a rocket. I wouldn't be hiding out from the future. I would be embracing it. I would be reveling in it. I would be part of it! The wheel of history would not grind over me but would lift me up. And my family, too. And my children would see a father stepping up with courage to grasp a new day, showing them the courage and flexibility they would need in their lifetimes, lifetimes without economic guarantees, lifetimes that would reward courage and risk-taking.

And if it took me five years to make the leap, and land, and prosper on the other side, it was worth it, I figured. I would be on the right side of history. I wouldn't be cowering. I wouldn't be making excuses for why I had let one of history's most amazing turning points pass me by. I would be out in the teeth of this new life, not peering from behind the trembling walls of an old industry but right out there in the new battle. I would feel the steel. I'd be alive!

I knew that for Danielle, this kind of wild calculus was nauseatingly metaphysical. She could feel me straining on the leash but couldn't understand where I was going or how I could believe with adequate confidence that there was a real possibility of our landing on our feet. And what price would be paid along the way? I was already missing soccer games and school concerts and our rare meals together chasing the merest wisps, I knew she thought, of anything firm at all.

She would try to humor me, she would try to be supportive, but she refused to drink the whiskey. These dreams were toying with her world. She would not get drunk with me.

I told her about Houston. She asked if we had any contracts signed. I told her about White Plains. She asked if we had any money invested. I showed her the demo (the fabulous demo!), with Rolly sitting right there with us in the living room, and she could hardly find a good word to say. There were people effusing about this demo all the way to the Rio Grande, I protested and cajoled, trying to hide my disappointment. But the woman whose family might depend on this demo and what it represented would not effuse lightly.

For the first time in many years, I felt myself falling into a true rage. I was gathering all my strength to make a leap for her, for our children, for our future, I told myself. And it all depended on believing. On every old "clap your hands and you can fly" fairy tale cliché ever whispered. Because we were pulling something out of thin air here. We had endlessly thought and analyzed and worked through the numbers. But there would never be enough proof that it would all actually work unless we threw ourselves completely into it when it was far too young and nebulous to be a sure thing. If you didn't believe, you couldn't leap. And if you couldn't leap, you couldn't get there.

And she would not believe.

"You think I'm crazy for thinking these things? For having doubts?" she asked. "Everyone we know has the very same questions about what you're doing! I'm the only one who will ask them to your face. But I'm not the only one wondering, Tom."

I wanted to put my hands over my ears and shout and kick the walls down. Her doubt made me crazy.

She loved me, I knew, but she could not believe in fairy tales. And I could not force her to believe in fairy tales. And I could not show her what she needed to see. And on the afternoon, a week earlier, that she turned her eyes away from our little demo with more fear than delight, something tore between us that had not torn before. I was already pulling hard for a shore she could not see and I could only dimly describe. And she knew it. And she had not agreed to go along. She could not agree because it was not a rational choice in her mind, and she was a rational person, and she was afraid. And my rage was great because I was afraid, too. But I could not tolerate acknowledging that fear. If I did, even a little, I was not sure I could go on. And I desperately wanted to find a way to go on.

If I had learned all I should have from Heifitz about leadership and change, I would have seen and understood all this. I would have stepped back to see that moment from the observer's balcony of life. I would have stepped above my emotions to see what was going on in detached, objective, empathetic terms. But I was not detached. I was going into a kind of battle I had never been in before. I was working myself into some kind of deliberate frenzy of psychological momentum to tear loose from a life. And anything that put a drag on that momentum, I repelled. Brutally.

Already time was racing by. It was almost the middle of February. My time for tearing loose was growing shorter. And little Building-Blocks was not close to having a team or a product. Investment money was a mere possibility, no more. And Danielle knew that. She was trying to be supportive, but she knew what she knew. And I was still running for the brink. And we could hardly talk about it.

The calendar behind the basement door off our kitchen kept the record of family events — ball games and karate exhibitions and teacher conferences and doctor's appointments. I was home staring at that calendar, realizing everything I had missed in the last month alone without even a thought. Almost unannounced, I realized, I had begun a journey and just assumed that they would come along. That she would come along.

Valentine's Day was coming up. We were always corny about Valentine's Day. I would try to make up. Maybe there was a way to explain.

And something else about February I noticed, with gratitude. There was an extra day.

It was a leap year.

That figured.

I put the roses in the garage. It was cold there, but not freezing, and the red buds would stay fresh until the next morning, Valentine's Day.

Danielle would be home in half an hour. I had dinner going, at last. We would sit down, all together, and things would be better. I had been brooding for days. I had to get over it. She had been brooding, too. We hadn't spoken of it. We didn't know how.

The table was set. The kitchen was warm and bright. So what if the metal cabinets were fifty years old and scarred like battle tanks? They were friendly. The boys were helping out and giving me a rare update on school and their lives. Lauren was conducting the proceedings from my shoulders. Sadie paced the kitchen, ferociously wagging her tail, happy to have everyone home for a change.

I thumbed through the mail. Lots of junk. Another new credit card to stash away. And the new *Time* magazine. Its cover caught me right away. It was Marc Andreessen, the twenty-four-year-old tech brains behind Netscape. He had been posed by *Time* sitting barefoot in blue jeans on a gold and velvet throne, with a wide, sassy smile across his baby face. The banner headline at his elbow: THE GOLDEN GEEKS.

"They invent," read the subhead beneath the banner. "They start companies. And the stock market has made them INSTANTAIRES."

Instantaires? That would never make the dictionary. But I got the idea. I flipped inside.

HIGH STAKES WINNERS went the cover story's inside headline. "Meet the get-incredibly-rich-quick crowd. Their creativity and drive reap vast rewards in the stock market. Otherwise, they're just plain folks."

Like me! I thought. Let's go! Let's go!

The article ran down its list of winners and the value of their stock in their hot new companies that had just gone public. Andreessen, shown peering over his backyard fence with his bulldog and pretty girlfriend: $24 million. Steve Jobs, ice skating with one of his three children and riding his Pixar success: $728 million. Jeff Braun of Maxis, bouncing on a trampoline: $79 million. Doug Colbeth of Spyglass, playing soccer with his kids: $22 million. Bill Schrader of PSINet, grinning as he smoked a fat cigar: $86 million.

All young companies, *Time* pointed out. All riding high on the fabulous initial public offering craze of tech companies going public in a surging bull market.

"More capital was raised in IPOs by emerging high-tech firms in 1995 — $8.4 billion — than in any other year in history," offered the story. And the fortunes being made didn't take a lifetime to accumulate, like many fortunes in railroads, steel, and oil had taken, it pointed out. They were being made overnight.

Exactly! Let's go!

I tucked the magazine under the day's letters, its cover headline carefully positioned to show. Danielle couldn't miss it. She would read it. She would see what was happening, what was possible.

But she didn't read it. Not that night. Maybe not ever.

Dinner went well. We laughed together and had no squabbles with the kids over what they would or would not eat. We kept it light and easy. I read stories to Lauren that night for the first time in a long time and talked and wrestled with the boys, who were getting way too strong, and turned in early with Danielle.

Maybe we were calm enough now to talk about things, I thought. Maybe we had reconnected. Maybe in the morning . . .

Danielle kept a Valentine's Day tradition that went all the way back to our happy years just out of college in Hong Kong. It was sappy and funny and always made us laugh. No matter how late we turned in the night before, she was always the last one in the bathroom. And the next morning our bathroom mirror would be ablaze with cutout hearts of red construction paper, each with a funny Valentine's message — little quips and ditties in the silly, obtuse style of childhood Valentine's cards and candies. They were always deeply inside jokes, sometimes bawdy, usually playing off what had been going on in our lives, where we'd been, what crazy notions we'd played with lately.

The best of her goofy, affectionate Valentines I had saved like treasures. The year I had just come home from reporting for weeks in Vietnam and around Southeast Asia, she had inscribed one small heart "I'd be Laos without you." It captured our lives apart and a sweet, funny peculiarity of Vietnamese-accented English perfectly. It was corny and giving and intimately ours. I kept it in my wallet for years, tucked next to her picture.

This year, I didn't know what to expect. We were in strange, new territory. I hadn't delivered on my promise of quality time. Not even close.

But they were there in the morning light, taped to the mirror like a cloud of red butterflies. Sassy and silly as ever. Funny and touching mainly because she was willing to be so nakedly corny in sharing her affection. Having fun with references to a year of Africa and United

Nations peacekeepers. Generously acknowledging in ditties and silly poems my Internet startup dreams.

I stood in my underwear, reading them one by one, laughing softly. She was still there, still by me.

On the left-hand mirror was her Africa collection:

I Afrika out without you.

Tut Tut Tutsi Don't Cry, Tut Tut Tutsi Be Mine.

UN Me Against the World.

U NI SOM Good Lovin.

Q: Hutu is my Valentine? A: Tom.

In General Aidid always love you.

I give you my heart. Kenya give me yours?

They were absurd. They were sweet. I was unspeakably lucky to have somebody in this world who cared enough to dream them up and tape them to my mirror. Just for fun. Just for me.

Then came the startup riffs. These were the real gift. These must have been hard, even in jest. They were close to the bone:

Roses are red, violets are blue, I don't care about health plans, do you?

Even with no job, you'll always be a Steve Jobs to me!

I'll be internetally yours.

Roses are red, violets are blue, what's a 401K when love is so true?

You are so CD-ROMantic!

You'll always be a millionaire to me.

I'd invest in you!

I'm soft(ware) on you!

I'd like to sit on your board.

Click here!

Roses are red, violets are blue, who needs a salary when love is so true?

She was staring out from under her pillow when I stepped back into the bedroom. Her long brown hair twined behind her in the rumpled sheets. She had reached out to me in that red flutter of Valentines.

"Thanks," I said, smiling, pushing the pillow back and stroking her face. "You're funny."

"It was hard," she said softly, reserved.

Something was wrong. We should have been laughing and hugging already, each conceding the other's point of view.

"Everything will be okay," I said, wanting to stay appreciative, soothing.

She stared for a long time. Tears gathered in her eyes.

"Tom, do you have any idea what you're doing?" she said. It wasn't really a question. And already I began to bridle.

"I am trying," I said, wobbling between humility and insult, "to see if maybe there's another way for us to live. I'm trying to open my eyes and see what's going on, and not just trudge endlessly ahead on the road we happen to be on."

I should have left it there. I should have stayed humble and open and grateful. But I couldn't.

"Can you see that?" I asked, challenging, ever so slightly sharp, slipping stupidly toward anger.

"Yes, I can see that you're trying something. But I don't know what it is. And I don't know if you really know what it is either."

She was sitting up now, pulling her hair firmly over her shoulder in a twist, fighting tears, moving to the edge of the bed.

"Maybe if you paid attention, if you were willing to consider for one minute that this might be real, maybe you would understand!" I said, suddenly cutting. And all the glow was gone. Scorched. History. She was at the bathroom door, fists clenched at her sides, anger and hurt surging into her face.

"Tom, I am paying very close attention," she said. "I am paying attention to my children and my husband and our life, and I don't know what you are doing!"

"Well, here's what I'm doing!" I said. "I'm saying no to the *Newsweek* job. I'm putting ten thousand dollars into BuildingBlocks. And I think I'm *doing* this. And it would be nice if you could show me some tiny shred of support!"

"Oh, Tom!" Her voice was somewhere between fury and desperation. "I don't know if you're blind, but I know you are cruel!"

"Yeah? I'm cruel? Listen, the only thing I'm trying to do is get us ahead of the curve. You, me, the kids. Just a little bit ahead of the curve. And if you call my ambition cruelty, Danielle, then we . . . are . . . fucked!"

Oh, nice. Profane. Heartless. Brutal. Sorry, Heifitz, I flunked. There was no way back. Tears surged in her eyes again, tears of anger and fear and despair. I saw the cloud of simple Valentines over her shoulder — that she had made, late at night, by hand, willingly, for me — and the door slammed in my face.

I shaved that morning at a mirror covered with fuzzy red squares of empty tape. The red hearts were gone, ripped down, thrown torn and crumpled into the bathroom trash. When she was gone, I got down on my knees on the fading old tile and pulled them, one by one, out of the garbage. I gently flattened them and saved them in my dresser drawer, behind the kryptonite credit cards, where Danielle wouldn't find them and burn them.

This was bad. This was not our style. We had been through a lot together. We weren't melodramatic. And she had never called me cruel before. But this was new territory. Strange new territory.

What if my ambition was cruel or had the same effect? Maybe I should just go back to the *Globe* and forget it, I thought. Be true to my school. Stay put. Go with the flow.

And maybe not.

Someday, I prayed, we would laugh about this morning.

But it was hard to picture when it would be funny.

Chapter 8

Juice Guys

THERE WAS A NEW JUICE drink in the little deli where Rolly and I grabbed lunch whenever we were working together at midday. You couldn't miss it in the coolers. This juice came in beautifully sculpted bottles, not the old industrial-drab shapes. And it came in half a dozen rich flavors, all with deep, jewel colors and bright, evocative names. Nantucket Nectars, they were called. They cost a little more than other drinks, but at least half the time we bought them anyway. They tasted good. They were a little bigger than the rest. And they brought a pleasing touch of theater to an otherwise completely forgettable turkey sandwich and bag of chips.

Six months earlier, we had never heard of Nantucket Nectars, but they had made a splash in Boston with their novel appearance and a clever ad campaign by the two guys who had started the company from their boat off Nantucket Island. They were "Tom and Tom." Their homespun radio ads told the story of two guys who loved juice — pure, top-quality juice — and just wanted to share that love with the world.

"We're Tom and Tom," they always ended the ads, their sincere voices playing over a touch of surf that evoked sun-dappled harbors and the clean, open sea. "We're juice guys."

Rolly loved that ad. No matter how tough a problem we were wrestling with when it played in the car, he would stop and listen, then lean back with a big grin and a dreamy look in his eyes and repeat the parting line.

"Juice guys!" he would say, giving an up-and-at-'em fighter's shrug and clapping his hands. "We're juice guys!" And he meant us. Rolly and Tom.

He loved the line because it conveyed the kind of passion and fun we both wanted to bring to BuildingBlocks. And he loved it because it explained, in a phrase, our relationship in the business. Two guys, inspired by what they were doing and committed to making it great. Nothing complicated, folks. Just two guys with a dream and a passion to serve.

Of course, we were in home design, not juice. But the model tickled him and gave him a way of thinking about the partnership that had evolved between us. Simple. Good. Two old friends with a love of fine homes and fabulous new ways of making them happen. For now, it gave us a way to see our partnership internally. Someday, it might be the shape of our company's face to the world.

Ben and Jerry. Tom and Tom. Tom and Rolly. Rolly and Tom.

Juice guys.

I liked it, too. A lot. But from my perspective there was one little problem. We were barreling ahead as partners, and I only owned ten percent of the company. That would obviously have to change. But when? And how? And how would Rolly deal with it? We had already put a lot of sweat into this together, but he had sweated first. So what would be fair? What would be tolerable?

Very soon, I had to know.

There wasn't much time even to think about it. Spring term at Harvard was cranking up, and our work on BuildingBlocks was exploding. We had focus groups going, testing our ideas about the market, about how people made decisions about building and renovating homes. We had lots of new people coming into our circle. Bernice Cramer, my old friend from Japan, was becoming very helpful. Kathy Ahern was talking about coming to work for us. So was Stever Robbins, the Harvard B-school grad we had met through Len Schlesinger. And Rolly's original core of friends who had brainstormed with him on BuildingBlocks were heating up as well. Buz and Shawn and Megan were all on the phone these days, checking in on the excited noise coming from our direction. Peter Thorne got an update and offered to see if he could get us a meeting with Bill Kaiser, the top partner at Greylock, Boston's premier venture capital firm. BBDO, the advertising giant in New York, was calling to say that Carol Gee at Du Pont Corian had told them we should get together. Ham Shirmer had us scheduled to fly out to Detroit to meet with him at Masco. My own first money was in now. My neighbor Louise was making interested noises about investing. (Could she be serious? Did I have the nerve to take money from my own neighbor?) So was another VC we'd just met. And down in Greenwich, Connecticut, Rick Segal's investment gatekeeper, Scott Smith, the triggerman, was waiting for our visit.

Stone? Never mind Stone. It was wrong to pin that much hope on one friend. Anyway, our heads were spinning with attention. This was just the lift in the wings we had been pushing so hard to begin to feel. And it was there. It was happening. If we could just keep up with it. Between Harvard classes and road trips and Nieman seminars and flights and meetings, it was almost a blur.

"Wow!"

Bill Clinton made three syllables out of the word somehow, and the big crowd roared. He loved them, and they loved him. The president swung his hips in a playful Elvis curve up onstage, and the packed gymnasium at New Hampshire College rippled with the curve, like a summertime crowd at Fenway Park doing the Wave.

I'd organized a barnstorming bus trip to New Hampshire for Nieman Fellows to see American democracy up close. It was primary season, and they were all on the hustings. Steve Forbes's advance men had grabbed the Nieman folks from Namibia and my own son Dylan and pulled them onstage, right next to his wife and daughters, to get at least a few warm bodies behind their man for the cameras. He talked about an American "renaissance," but pronounced the word in such a Frenchified way that he was clearly doomed. Pat Buchanan shouted in such an apparent fury about the downtrodden American workingman that the foreign Niemans made politely frightened faces and muttered "Nazi." Bob Dole put everyone in the mood to go shopping for antiques.

Bill Clinton was hot that night, wowing a huge crowd with his President Elvis routine. He sparkled and emoted and wooed until my Nieman colleague from Paris, François, made little mocking kisses in the air and rolled his eyes. But it worked. And his theme was the same as every other candidate's we heard that day. The American worker was in trouble and the country had better do something quick.

Each had a different prescription. Clinton's very first thundering promise from the stage was to put an Internet connection in every classroom and public library in the country. On that cold February night, odds were that not one in ten, maybe not one in fifty, people in that gym had ever been on the Internet. But they all cheered wildly when he raised it. This wasn't the race to the moon or victory over Hitler he was talking about. It was the Internet. It was pipes and bandwidth and a little electricity. And they were going wild.

The stupendous bull market of the late '90s had not yet hit its full stride that night, or that season. The decade's earlier recession and economic restructuring were still resonating powerfully. Layoffs — sudden, unpredictable, *white-collar* layoffs — were the nation's fear. A few days later, the *New York Times* launched a massive seven-part series, "The Downsizing of America." The day-one headline: ON THE BATTLEFIELDS OF BUSINESS, MILLIONS OF CASUALTIES. The *Boston Globe* announced plans to lay off forty-one mailroom workers and cut the pay of fourteen top executives.

The Internet was a baby, but it was the future's baby.

Let's go, I was thinking. I'll take the future.

"Hope is much more a consequence of action than a cause of action. We must will ourselves by imagination into practical action that gives grounds for hope," Roberto Unger was saying from the dais.

I liked that. I wrote that down.

We were deep in Harvard Law School. Unger, the great Brazilian social philosopher, was standing now, snapped out of the catatonic trance he seemed to drift into when he listened to his co-teacher on the dais, Cornel West. Unger was lean, his close-cropped hair iron gray. When he listened in that trance, he pulled his head down in an old turtle's deep retreat.

West was just plain skinny. In his too-tight three-piece suit, flashing white cuffs, and oversize eyeglasses, the spellbinding black thinker and writer looked like a wise Jiminy Cricket with big hair.

They were teaching "Race, Nation and Democracy." I was listening, and drifting, and planning.

"There must be a pathway leading from memory to vision," said Unger.

Yes, I thought absently, trying to schedule the impossible days ahead. My datebook had become a tangle of crucial meetings. A pathway. From memory to vision. From Antelope John to my leap.

"A successful nation must be a pillager, roving the world and combining things never combined before . . . beliefs, technologies, institutions, practices. Each nation is in international competition. To compete each must be willing to eviscerate traditional customs."

Like what? I thought. Like marriage? Like patience and kindness?

"Nations are like King Lear when he said, 'I will do things, I know not what!'"

Cruel things, I thought. Or not. I needed to talk to Danielle.

"The self is not merely a creature of its context. There is more in the self than there is in a context."

And I'm thinking this is starting to sound like religion. Like my religion. I will find a way to keep it humane. I will.

"We must put all concrete elements of the past at risk, until perhaps all that is left is the trajectory, the pathway, to link past and present. And this is not just the American situation. This is the situation of the whole world."

Holy shit, I thought. Even the really big thinkers are telling me to put it all at risk.

Then Cornel West, replying, that afternoon and over weeks, not buying Unger's dream.

"Roberto wants to take off, and I applaud that desire," he said, eyeing the young hall full of bright, young students of every race and many nationalities. "But we must deal with what is! With what is."

We must look back and look around us, said West. At race, at injustice. He railed against "the straightjacket of market forces." He quoted Tennessee Williams on "the catastrophe of success." At length, and sorrowfully, he shared his skepticism of utopianism. In the end, he said, we must acknowledge the "tragicomedy" of life, and what remains is a "tragicomic" view of the world.

And there he lost me.

I know it's tragicomedy, I thought. I know it too damned well. But who wants to embrace that as a worldview? I'm looking for a better vista and I won't apologize for looking. Maybe it's Unger's vista. I don't know. I do know the past. I've filled notebooks and newspapers with it. I've tracked blood to the laptop keyboard and pulled tufts of massacred children's hair from my shoes while I organized notes. And I've cried and written and been done with it. But I'm looking ahead now. From memory to vision. To build something. And it's looking good.

"The mesomorphs," said Unger, shaking his head and laughing tragicomically late one night over beers at my Nieman colleague Regina Zappa's apartment. "They come to my classes, they listen, they leave and start businesses."

Yes, I'm thinking. Yes!

But what's a mesomorph?

Twenty-four hours.

They start like this.

Rolly and I are sitting in an underground parking lot in downtown Boston. It's a Thursday. Ten floors up, Bill Kaiser, national venture capital legend, is waiting to meet us in his offices at Greylock. It's our first formal sit-down with a venture capital company. Len may think they're all vulture capitalists, but they've got the money. And we need it.

And Rolly doesn't want to get out of the car.

"This does not feel right," he's saying, and he's breathing fast and he's flushed. "We are not ready for this."

"We've got to be ready," I'm saying. "Bill Kaiser is up there waiting."

"But we don't even know if we want VC money. And what does it do to our story line if Greylock says no?" he asks, his adrenaline-stoked brain doing a thousand calculations a second.

"Maybe they'll say yes," I say, taking his point, but not wanting to step into that river of fear. Besides, we've been told venture capital outfits move slowly, that it takes them months to make up their mind. By then we'll be ready.

"Come on, man. We're juice guys. Let's go get some money."

And he's shaking his head and grabbing his shoulder bag with the demo and we're out of the car and moving, almost running, cranked up on vague hope and real fear, across the underground lot and into the elevator, like doughboys out of a trench. Like Butch Cassidy and the Sundance Kid screaming off the cliff. Except we're going up.

Bill Kaiser is very nice. Polite. Craggy handsome. Pressed for time, he says. He's only got forty minutes.

He's joined by a junior colleague. We sit at a conference table overlooking the Boston Common. It's beautiful. It's starting to snow.

They lead off with a ritual we come to know well. I think of it as the recitation of the miracle of the loaves. In grave tones of muted pride they describe the depth of their very deep pockets, the splendor of their investment record, the famous entrepreneurs they have backed, the great companies they have helped build, the fortunes they have made. In Greylock's case, the record is truly impressive. Whether we get a penny from them or not, we will leave impressed.

And then it's our turn. Peter Thorne and Art Bardige had both told us to remember that we were the ones doing the shopping here. We were the ones squeezing the tomatoes. We were shopping for the right seed money, for the right investors, for good, well-connected, smart people who we wouldn't mind essentially being married to for the next several years.

But we don't feel like the shoppers. We feel like the tomatoes. Within five minutes we are selling like Bengali street peddlers. And Bill Kaiser is squeezing us good.

We paint the picture of the market, and its size. We have done some new research. It's a $300 billion market we are talking about now, annually, in new homes and renovations and home furnishings. We talk about how the market is broken, how frustrating it is for people who want to outfit their homes wonderfully but don't have the time or good ways to figure out their options. We show them the demo. We tell them about our warm reception in Houston. We show them our revenue projections — our very conservative projections, we stress — for the company.

And then we sit.

Bill Kaiser has three questions.

First, where are we in our fund-raising?

Rolly is in, and his mom is in, and I'm in. Fifty thousand in total.

Kaiser nods. I'm thinking it must sound pathetic to him. A mere pittance. And nobody but the two of us and Rolly's mom! Losers!

I'm wrong.

Greylock likes being in early, he said.

Wonderful! We are definitely early. Oh, yes. Early.

And if they come in, they will typically want at least thirty percent of the company for their first investment.

Terrible! We had already heard the stories of entrepreneurs who slaved for years to build companies with venture capital and ended up owning only one or two percent of all they had built. Not us! No way.

His second question is about our backgrounds. An energy consultant and a newspaper editor. Very interesting. He thumbs briefly through the business plan we sent, as though he's looking for something he's lost. But there is nothing else. That's who we are. There is no record of earlier companies taken public, no IPO, no flashy B-school degrees. We describe our track records in the worlds we come from, but they are not his world.

"I'm a student of business," Rolly offers gamely. A student of business! Kaiser nods very slightly. I check the time. The snow is really coming down. We have to drive to New York tonight.

Finally, Kaiser asks us to explain once more why people will want this product. And we do, leaping back in with full enthusiasm to explain how hard the current process is, how difficult and time-consuming it is for people to design and outfit a home.

"But why wouldn't these people simply use an architect or an interior designer?" he asks, polite but clearly not connecting with the picture we painted.

And at that moment we know. Bill Kaiser is the kind of man who doesn't think twice about these things. If his home needs a project done, he hires someone to do it. Period. And he enjoys it when it's done. We are aiming for an affluent audience, because that's the population that has home computers and will be first to go online. But Bill Kaiser has too much money. He can't relate. And the idea of people vicariously enjoying an electronic home design product even when they are not in the midst of a project is even more perplexing.

"You know," he says, playing with the demo for a moment, then putting the hammer down hard. "I would never buy a product like this."

Oooph. Not good. A long pause. And then we are right back up on our feet. Dazed but relentless. You're not typical, Bill, we say. Look at all the home style magazines Americans read every month. Twenty million of them! Maybe not you, but twenty million other people. And they're not all people who are building or renovating. A lot of them are dreaming. And we would help them dream.

But he is the wrong audience for our *Star Wars* pitch. There's not a visceral connection with the vision. And if there's a connection at some other level, he is being exceedingly discreet about it.

We pack up the laptop and thank him for his time. An hour and a half! We have held the great man's attention beyond our allotment. Take heart from that.

Kaiser walks us to the door. It's an interesting proposal, he says. He will take it up with the Greylock partners on Monday. We may have an answer that same day. Rolly pales. We are back in the elevator. Back in the underground garage. Back in the car. Rolly looks ready to puke.

"I would never buy a product like this!" he repeats, shuddering. It's cold. He's staring straight ahead into the gloom of the garage, hunched in his coat with the look of a man contemplating a death sentence. "And their answer on Monday? That's three days from now, not three months. It's too soon."

The vein is back in his temple. Pulsing.

"We've got to take the deal off the table," he says.

"What?"

"We have to call Bill Kaiser and take it off the table. Tell him we decline their consideration."

"Why?"

"Because we're not even sure we want VC money. And if Greylock says no, our story line is trashed. It will be a black mark right across our face that we can't escape. What private investor will want to invest if they know Greylock gave us a pass? And they'll know. Greylock says no and we're dead in the water before we even get started."

And so it came to pass that on a dark winter afternoon, with snow wailing down outside the bedroom windows, Rolly called Bill Kaiser, the audience for our very first VC pitch, the tallest tree in the East Coast VC forest, and told him we were taking the deal off the table. Little tiny BuildingBlocks was not available for the mighty Greylock's investment at any price. No need to raise it at the partners' meeting. No chance to render a verdict. We were off the table. Sayonara.

No time to think about it. We had to get on the road to New York. On Friday morning we were meeting with Glen Gilbert, a senior vice president at BBDO, the advertising powerhouse. We had an introduction from Du Pont Corian. BBDO was the big time. And then we were on in Connecticut with Scott Smith.

Carole and Danielle were appalled that we were going. The snow was turning to blizzard. The airports were closing. The radio was warning everyone off the highways. My tires were bald, but I had put off replacing them just now. I was starting to hoard my few resources for the way ahead.

"Is it worth your life?" Danielle asked at the door. But we were crazed. We were gone.

It took us almost eight hours to make the two-hundred-mile trip. We were alone on the highway most of the night, creeping through thick, howling snow. Uncertain even where the road was sometimes. Feeling our way on bald tires, trailing behind the taillights of snowplows whenever we could find them. By any sane assessment, we should have pulled over. But how could we? We were trying to build a fire under BuildingBlocks, trying to get it out of the third bedroom, out into the world, trying to make it real. We had two or three embers glowing now, but everything was so tenuous. Every tiny step seemed absolutely life and death.

And we had just blown off Bill Kaiser!

"What on earth do you think he makes of that?" I asked Rolly as we crept through the screaming mounds of snow.

"I don't know," he said. "It can't be good. I feel terrible about it, but we had to do it."

"Aw, let's forget it," I said. "We're a bug on his windshield. Anyway, what's he got that we need? Just money and power and all the experience in the world." We laughed.

"BuildingBlocks!" Rolly bellowed in his mock-profundo radio announcer voice. "Specialists in pissing off the mighty and blowing off millions!"

The snow came down in blinding waves. Almost no visibility. Who knew where we were? We were just moving, believing we would arrive.

"Hey, what's a mesomorph?" I asked somewhere in that night's endless trek.

"No idea," he said. "A big-boned, muscled something? I dunno."

We made it to Scarsdale by two in the morning. We were staying with Danny Schneider, a college classmate and dear friend, and his wife, Linnae. Danny was waiting up for us, in his old blue robe, grinning his cracked Buddha grin as we jumped through the snow to his door. He fed us and tucked us in. Linnae made a big breakfast the next morning, and Danny delivered us right to our destination in the heart of Manhattan.

The BBDO meeting was great. Glen Gilbert loved the demo, loved our approach, lavished compliments on us. He had seen a fair bit of what was going on with CD-ROMs in the home design area, he said, and ours was definitely "best of breed." Oh, we loved that. We quoted it for months. BBDO says best of breed! And we hadn't even rolled out an Internet product yet. But that would come.

We'll get you in front of our big advertisers in the home market, he said. They should love this. Absolutely.

We left Manhattan doing high fives, snow blind and sleep deprived, and headed for Greenwich. We got into town just after noon. The weather had cleared. The sun was out and the snow was sparkling. Greenwich was incredible. I had never seen it before. It was one enormous mansion after another. Grand. Venerable. Massive old homes with rolling grounds behind imposing stone walls and fences.

"Are these our customers?" I asked Rolly.

"They could be," he said. "But these might be a little rich for our target. We're aiming for the affluent. Not necessarily the superrich."

"A little rich," I repeated. "You know, no matter how rich I might ever get, I'm not sure this is quite the way I would want to live."

"When you're rich, Tom," he said, "you can do it any way you like. That's the point."

Scott Smith was in the paneled offices of Camelot Capital, juggling stocks when we arrived. The market was having an off day. Down a hundred and thirty points at lunchtime. We waited for ten minutes while he bought and sold over the phone, then settled down to tell him our story. His wife, Heidi, and their interior designer joined us. "World-class money spenders in this category," he said, with a nod to the pair. Scott had been a software analyst at DLJ in New York. Now he ran a software hedge fund and occasionally dabbled in early-stage investments. That was our tiny opening.

We revved up our presentation again, gave our analysis of the market, showed our financial projections, told them about Houston, told them about BBDO (best of breed!), even told them we had just spent an hour and a half the day before with Greylock (enough said). Then we showed the demo. They loved it. Heidi had tough, sharp questions but liked our answers. Even the designer seemed impressed. We were not out to replace interior designers and architects, we said. We were out to make their lives easier and their client service better.

"How much are you raising?" Scott asked.

Five hundred thousand dollars in a private placement, we said. Private placement meaning private investors, not institutions. Not VCs.

"And what's your post-money?"

All investment deals around startup companies have two main issues. The first is whether the startup has a good business model, a credible plan for entering and succeeding in the market. The second is how much the startup company is worth, its "valuation."

Valuation is where all the important negotiating goes on. There's enormous room for disagreement and conflict. If a startup is valued at $1 million, a $500,000 investment will buy you half of it. If that company is valued at $5 million, a $500,000 investment will buy you a tenth of it. That's a big difference.

A "pre-money" valuation is what one party asserts is the value of the startup before a particular round of investment comes in. "Post-money" valuation is the sum of the pre-money valuation plus the amount of the new investment. So Scott Smith was asking where we would peg the value of BuildingBlocks once this half-million dollars was raised.

"Post-money is five million," said Rolly coolly.

We held our breath. It was a ballsy number. By most traditional assessments, it made no sense at all. The company's assets were two laptops, a demo, a plan, and two guys insane enough to drive through a blizzard to make it go. That plus half a million dollars, we were saying, was worth $5 million. So a half-million-dollar invest-ment would buy ten percent of BuildingBlocks. Bill Kaiser might have wanted much more for the money, but he was Greylock. And anyway, anything related to the Internet just then was hot as a pistol. Who was to say we were not worth $5 million? This was the new economy, baby. And we had a story going.

Scott needed to get back to his damage control in the market. He liked what he had seen. It had the Internet in its future. Art Bardige had brought it to Rick. Rick had sent us to him. Why dicker?

"Five million post-money?" he said, weighing the number briefly.

We nodded slowly, as if it were the most ordinary thing in the world.

"Count me in for a hundred thousand."

Ka-ching!

The triggerman had spoken. Rick's gatekeeper was in.

Now the half million would flow, right?

Surely, surely our seed money was on the way.

From hell to heaven, in twenty-four hours.

"Next time, count to ten!"

Art Bardige could not believe we had blown off Greylock. He was running his fingers through his hair and staring at us as if we were madmen. "Sooner or later, you're going to have to deal with VC," he said, speaking slowly, as if to slow children. "Get used to the idea. Right now, you're turning an idea into a company," he said. "In the next six to eight weeks, it's time to become a real business. There's no reason to blow people off on anything. It's easy to get manic when you're getting something started. But remember, you've got time to think. Take it."

Then Art gave us his simple road map to venture capital.

"They're good salesmen," he said. "They're selling money. They tell you how great they are, how much they'll do for you, the connections they'll bring, blah, blah, blah. And you know, they don't always hit. Not near. Maybe one in ten."

He stepped to his beloved white board.

"Here's the VC math," he said. "It's simple."

10 VC-backed companies, he wrote, underlining in red and scribbling on.

3 die

"Three just flat-out die."

3 living dead

"Three just hang around and turn into money pits."

3 modest success

"Three more do okay, but the VCs aren't in this for okay."

1 big hit

He underlined that. He circled it. He stabbed at it with his red marker.

"This!" he said. "This is why the VCs are in the game. This is what they're looking for. This is all they really care about. This is where they make their money. This is where you have to be."

"And don't run out of money while you're looking for money," he said. "If you have to go out for money in a panic, you'll get killed."

Have you heard from Rick? we asked.

Yes, he said. Rick was feeling good about BuildingBlocks.

Harvey Cox was the most popular Divinity School professor at Harvard. He had a big swirl of white hair and a white beard framing the face of a well-fed, aging cherub. His heavy eyelids drooped over large, doleful eyes. He had written *The Secular City* when God was dead. Now, he was telling a seminar of Nieman Fellows, God was making a comeback, but in new ways.

The single most striking change in the personal statements of students applying for admission to Harvard, he said, was that these young people described themselves and what they wanted to do at

Harvard in explicitly religious terms. The baby boomers at the admissions office, he said, didn't know what to make of it.

"There's a sense that our lives are unraveling," Cox was saying. "There is a sense of wistful looking around. A sense of wanting something else. There's a sense among these very bright kids that this adult world isn't working.

"In the sixties, the line was, don't trust any folks over thirty. But we knew how to live. . . . Now kids are saying this whole thing isn't working, but they don't know what the answer is. Exodus is the central motif of liberal theology," Cox went on. "We find people economically, politically, and physically enslaved, and an exodus sets them free. God is the liberator. And Jesus picked up on that in a big way."

I'm drifting. Remembering Jesus, and sweaty sheets, and desperate tai chi in Africa. What a night. It must have been a thousand years ago, another lifetime. And the desperate, beautiful girl from Bujumbura. How she got me to the hotel, then camped in the lobby for days while I gathered horror stories outside. What future could she see?

But exodus, I liked that. Exodus meant feet moving. Exodus meant change.

I checked my watch. It was time to go.

Rolly was outside in a cab. I slipped out the back of the seminar room and we were tearing off to the airport. Off to Detroit, and Ham Shirmer and Masco.

The Masco headquarters was outside the city, a splendid corporate palace in a modest little town. The interior halls were lined with the impressive art collection of Masco's chairman emeritus, Alex Manoogian, who founded the company in 1957. Manoogian had assembled an enormous home products conglomerate encompassing some of the biggest names in the industry: Delta Faucets, Baldwin Brass, Merillat Cabinetry, and dozens more. The combined revenues listed in the annual report we thumbed through in the lobby's wide waiting area were $4.5 billion.

We could do business with these people.

We thumbed through the annual report while we waited for Ham, Masco's corporate head of marketing. The report was pointing at exactly the trends we were citing in our business plan: boomers reaching the age and income levels that would lead to greater spending on homes; two-income families spending more to create homes that serve as an expression of individuality; average home sizes growing as families sought private spaces for comfortable retreat, for accommodating aging parents and live-at-home children, and for increasingly prevalent home offices.

We met with Ham and Sam Cypert, Masco's director of communications. It was a good news, bad news, meeting. They were smart analysts of the industry and savvy marketers. We dreamed of their bringing dozens of Masco companies in as clients with the stroke of a pen. We sold hard. But it wasn't going to be that easy. They liked our product, they said. It looked like the future. They would love for their companies to be involved with it. But they could not just order that with a command from headquarters. Each Masco company would have to decide on its own. They would heartily recommend us. They would give us their blessing. But we would ultimately have to make the sales ourselves, one by one, all over the country.

This was a tall mountain to climb. And it was just one of many. On the way back to the airport I was feeling daunted, overwhelmed. I was a hairsbreadth away from leaving a great job to throw myself fully into this little sprout of a venture, and it was not going to be an easy road. I had to know what my stake would be. And it had to be bigger than it was.

Rolly and I were sitting in a garish, red plush bar in Detroit's hideous neo-Stalinist airport, waiting for our return flight, when I leapt in. We had to talk about equity, I said. About my stake in Building-Blocks. If I was fully committing, it would have to grow to reflect my role.

Rolly's face tightened. I felt myself tightening too, becoming formal. Oh, God.

I appreciated the deep work he had done in conceiving the company's roots and sketching out its original aspirations. In acknowledgment of that, and of how he had cut loose first from his old employment to dive in, I was not looking for a fifty-fifty split. I was thinking that a thirty-five percent stake might be appropriate.

Rolly had been perfectly still, following every word with his full-laser attention. When I said "thirty-five percent," he looked as if he had been punched in the stomach. He was stunned.

There are thousands of issues that a startup has to deal with. Equity, the distribution of shares in the company, is the nuclear issue. The x-ray issue. The one that opens things up right to the core. Rolly and I had sweated and toiled and struggled together on this company. But we could work together all we wanted, for as many days and nights and months and years as we liked. Until it came right down to discussing equity in hard numbers, our actual forward-going percentages of ownership, we did not really know each other's mind.

Now we would learn. Fast. And painfully. And we would each have a choice to make.

It took Rolly several minutes, an eternity, to recover his composure enough to speak.

"Apart from coming up with the idea, you're a fifty-fifty partner with me," he said. His hands were trembling. He was speaking in a slow, almost strangled voice, word by word, as if he had just been asked to surrender his child, or his religion. And in a sense, I suppose, he had.

"But the value of a company lies overwhelmingly in the ideas that make up its core," he said. "And those ideas, in this company, were mine."

He could not conceive of giving up thirty-five percent of the company to anyone. Not even to me. Not even close.

Now it was my turn to be stunned.

I acknowledged his role as original conceiver, I said again. I admired and appreciated it more than I could say. But I thought we were building a partnership here. I had reveled in the many ways in which my ideas were now also integral to the shape of the company. And now I was astonished and hurt by his response. I could not imagine leaving my entire career and throwing myself into a partnership, I said, unless that partnership, and my fundamental contribution to breathing life into this business, was acknowledged with at least a third of the company we were creating.

And there it was. A canyon. It opened in less than five minutes. It shocked us both. It took days and days to close. We fought. We shouted and raged. We insulted each other, and made up, and insulted each other again. Rolly laid out reams of calculations that expressed his mathematical analysis of the value of core strategies, and primary ideas, and initial hours invested. I made a gut argument that the company would not exist outside his mind, even in the fledgling form we had reached, without my energy and co-authorship of its development. He ridiculed my argument. I laughed at his. It was ugly. He budged to twenty percent. I budged to thirty. And we were stuck.

There must be a hell of a rumble going on in Rolly's mind right now, I thought. There sure was in mine. I began to yield toward the twenty percent, but in my heart I could not accept it. Our battle of perspectives continued to rage.

This couldn't be a true partnership unless he moved, I thought. And if it wasn't a true partnership, I could not leave my job, and this company, I believed, would fail. We were making it happen out of nothing because we were shoulder to shoulder. If we couldn't stay that way, it was no good going on.

And this couldn't be a true partnership, Rolly thought, unless I could acknowledge the essential truth of his view, that core ideas and strategy were supreme and had to be supremely valued. And if I couldn't do that, if his own partner couldn't share his profound reverence for the value of ideas, then he thought he might have a heart attack right now. And he wasn't kidding.

So we each had to suffer and decide.

And move.

Rolly handed over more of his creation, his safe haven from a uncomprehending world, his Xanadu, right out of the gate than he had ever imagined he would. He had to trust, let go of the fear of sharing his baby.

I swallowed my ego, acknowledged his point, and accepted in myself that I wanted this opportunity, and the opportunity to partner with his wild, uncompromising mind, enough to dive in for less equity than I had ever imagined I would.

Twenty-five percent. That would be my founder's stake. I knew that high-powered CEOs were being recruited to startups across the country for far, far less. And I knew something else. We could be partners, real partners. Twenty-five for me. Fifty-five for him. The rest set aside. And it was okay. It was good. We could build something great.

"Twenty-five percent of a billion-dollar company doesn't sound too bad to me," I said, when we finally shook hands in his little kitchen and the great equity war was over.

"Nope," he said, wiping a tear away on his sleeve. This was the nuclear zone. This was where you could see right through to the heart of things. We were there, and we were surviving.

"Juice guys?" I said as we shook, wanting to be absolutely sure his heart was in it.

He laughed, and looked free of a terrible burden, and smiled.

"Yeah," he said.

"Juice guys."

Chapter 9

The Last Commute

I T WAS MIDSUMMER already. My last months on leave had gone by in a wild blur. BuildingBlocks was still all but broke. But it was broke and alive. It was pulling me now like an invisible force. It had pulled on a lot of people in the last few months. Some it had grabbed and held. Some it had grabbed and lost. This startup path was not for everyone.

Shawn Becker looked like a keeper. In March, Rolly and I had gone back to the MIT Media Lab to track him down. We needed a technology heavyweight, we said. His work was the most compelling we had seen anywhere. We were just two guys with a plan, but it was an ambitious, interesting plan. Would he talk to us?

He would. He remembered us from the Media Lab's tenth-anniversary celebration. That first afternoon, we talked for hours in his little office. We poured out our vision to this brilliant young man we barely knew. And he listened to two impassioned dreamers he barely knew. And there was something special in the air right from the start.

Shawn was in the final months of finishing up his Ph.D. at the Media Lab. His work was at the leading edge of 3D visualization. He had been head of software engineering for the Media Lab's open architecture television project. He was no one's stereotypical software wizard. Shawn was a big, hardy Westerner in his late twenties, with an open, friendly face and a firm, pumping handshake. But he was a wizard in projective geometry and computer graphics and image processing and interface design. He and his wife, Linda, lived with their two young children stuffed in an MIT dorm. He was dying to get out, and he was being wooed on all sides. Hollywood's special effects giants were after him. The big computer-aided design companies were after him. Even the government was after him for the potential James Bond applications of his 3D modeling expertise.

And we were after him.

We got him. He could only work part-time until he finished his degree, but he was in. He loved the passion. He bought the dream. And BuildingBlocks suddenly had major technology chops in-house. It was a coup.

"You do think we're going to have money for paychecks, right?" he asked at one point.

"Absolutely," I said. Absolutely how? Down in White Plains, Rick Segal was taking his sweet time, making no promises, angling for a bigger piece of the company. We had met a new VC, Steve Coit, from Charles River Ventures in Boston. And he was excited, we thought. But that was too new a connection. He couldn't deliver in time. Never mind. Keep moving. We had had more great meetings with top manufacturers, top ad firms in New York, a giant insurance company interested in sponsoring the product. You'll find your money, your investors, said Tom Watson, the vice-chairman of Omnicom, the huge advertising firm. It's like catching eagles, he said. Be patient. You've got to get them one at a time. Go, go.

Katherine Ahern joined us. She was a filmmaker and former real estate appraiser who had dropped out to make handcrafted lamps of woven willow. She had little interest in returning to a "real job," she said, but this was exciting. We needed able bodies. Presto! She was our director of market research.

"A year from now, you'll have a whole new Rolodex," said Marc Meyer, a business professor at Northeastern University, one of dozens of people we were tapping for advice. "You'll do this, and your world will change. You'll rely on people you've never heard of today."

Steven Robbins had been raised by itinerant hippie parents who dressed him in a loincloth and lived in a dozen cities before he was fifteen. He went to Harvard Business School, he told us, "as an act of rebellion." He had a strong software development background and had worked for Intuit, our holy of holy startup models. We grabbed him as chief operating officer.

My old friend Bernice Cramer, a top-flight marketing consultant raising two sons a few blocks over, opened her home for our planning meetings, brought us industry insiders to learn from, and danced very close to joining herself. She brought by Rob Bruekner, a technocreative type who looked at BuildingBlocks and the dream and began quoting Wallace Stevens, from "The Man with the Blue Guitar."

"But play, you must. A tune beyond us, yet ourselves," he recited, and I loved it, the way it captured the homes we hoped to help people create, the open life we dreamed of building.

And Bernice? Would she join? We could use her brains and pluck. But no. We were very persuasive, she said. More persuasive than we had any right to be. But BuildingBlocks was ultimately too risky, too unformed then, for her and for others. Making the leap required such an odd combination of insight and blind faith. Some people, good people, just didn't have that peculiar mixture, and who could blame them.

I could. I did. Everything was still so personal, so urgent. We needed a team willing to form and work and commit even before there was money. We needed it right now, to show momentum, to begin producing. Some people, especially baby boomers, I thought, just couldn't seem to cross over. They could dream and get excited, but when they came right to the edge of the chasm, they wouldn't or couldn't jump. The closer I came to jumping myself, the more susceptible I became to serious boomer intolerance. In swimming through my own fears, I became a self-loathing boomer.

"We've got to get out of the clutches of these boomers and their angst and their aging parents and puking kids and their complicated emotional lives." I was ranting one morning, driving along the Massachusetts Turnpike with Rolly.

"With all the best intentions, they're dragging us down. They're making me crazy. They don't know if they even want to work at all. Or they can't work for any boss ever again. Or they're licking life wounds and projecting crappy experiences onto every prospect they come across. I'm fucking sick of boomers and all their fucking complications! Can they ever be free enough, committed enough, to do this? Can they ever be prepared or able to put a thousand other commitments on the back burner to give a startup the push it's going to need to make it?"

Rolly gave me a small, indulgent smile. Okay, I admit it, I said. I know I'm a boomer myself. And I'm ranting.

But when we got home, I decided to write down on a scrap of paper by the telephone the reasons that I, a boomer, could do this crazy thing:

i am excited by possibilities, by risk, by adventure

i have a high tolerance for conditions of uncertainty

i am unfazed by most pressures, especially by deadlines

i am unfazed by circumstances that require juggling several alternative perspectives or avenues until the last minute

my natural assumption is that things will go my way

i am an optimist

i am capable of self-delusion

That would do.

Angels. The bibles of the new economy magazine world — *Wired*, *Red Herring*, *Fast Company* — were jammed with talk of angels. I didn't know how literal that label could be. Or how close to home. Louise Citron showed me.

We had been neighbors for eight years. Louise and her husband, David, had a thriving audiology practice. Our boys were nearly the same age as theirs, and constant companions. We barbecued in the summer and shared Christmas and Hanukkah in the winter.

Louise's father had built a very successful fabric manufacturing company in Easthampton, Massachusetts. I had never forgotten how, at her son Eric's bar mitzvah celebration, the family had called on "the investors" to rise to be toasted. I assumed these aging men, standing in the candlelit hall, had made her father's success possible years before. And they were still part of his family's life. It was a striking image.

Louise was warm and bustling, brilliant and full of life. She missed nothing. She had met Rolly and had been watching our progress closely. She had seen Danielle's stark fear. She knew I was about to make the leap. She knew we were still dying for money, that we had prospects but no check, no guarantee. We needed the first outside investor — not family, but outside — to say "I believe in this" and put their money down. Louise stood up, almost unasked, and became that investor.

I was walking Sadie late one early summer night. Louise joined me with her white terrier, Duncan, out under the maple trees along our street. Her attorney had talked to ours, Gene Barton. Terms were agreed. She knew what she wanted to do, she said.

She handed me an envelope. There was a check for $50,000 inside, she said.

I almost fell down. The street was quiet, still. My face and arms were buzzing. We were standing close, but I heard her voice as if from far away, from heaven.

"I have tremendous confidence in you, Tom," she said, calm and clear, like an angel speaking. Like an oracle. A goddess.

"You've done well in your career. You'll do well with this company," she said. "You're going to have to work for it, but I can tell you, it is so satisfying when you build your own company. Every week when David and I do the payroll, I'm proud and satisfied at the livings our business makes possible for our little staff. Your staff will be much bigger, but you will know that satisfaction. And once the business is going, you'll do other things as well. You'll do charity work. You'll write. You'll leave a legacy for your children."

Whether there is a god or not, this was definitely an angel. Louise, standing next to me under the maples, our children asleep in our houses, our dogs wrestling in the grass, and her pressing that small white envelope into my hand and saying those things with such complete conviction. The money was a gulp of oxygen. Her confidence was the more precious gift.

There were no words sufficient for that moment. I stammered something, we hugged and said goodnight. I walked trembling into the house completely humbled and completely committed. Committed in my bones.

Bill Kovach leaned back in his chair, hands clasped behind his head, and ran his baleful, knowing eye over the two dozen Nieman Fellows sitting around him, plates on their laps, quiet. Our fellowship year was almost over. They called this the "reentry lunch." It felt like the Last Supper.

There was a familiar harness waiting for every journalist in the group. A world of expectations and routines and compromises that we all knew well. A job.

"Nobody's touching the wine," Bill joked.

"We're ready for detox," said David Bank, who would be heading off soon to join the *Wall Street Journal.*

Bill got us started. He had watched a lot of fellows go back into the world of work, he said. It wasn't easy. We had spent a year thinking, exploring, unfettered and free. Now we had to rejoin the world and our colleagues who had been working in harness, cranking out the news.

"Don't have an inflated idea of how excited they're going to be to have you back," Bill advised. "Your expectations are bound to be much greater than theirs. They haven't been at Harvard reimagining the world. But don't undersell yourself. You have no idea how much you've learned this year."

I looked around the room and knew he was right. I had watched these restless souls throw themselves ferociously into learning and growing over the last nine months. I had seen them scooping up new ideas, struggling with the meaning of our work as journalists, stretching the humanity and insight and perspective they brought to that work. They were good people. They would do good things, with or without me.

Nieman Fellows had a track record of going on to do great things in journalism, Bill said. They did great reporting. They became great columnists. The most typical path was a move into editing and newsroom management.

And about a quarter dropped out of journalism.

"That's not a bad rate," he said. "The people who apply are already asking if this is what they want to do with the rest of their lives."

I'm not dropping out, I said to myself in the back row. I'm just going to a very different end of the business. And I'll figure out this new medium, this electronic realm. And if there's any way to do it, I'll bring what I learn back to the mainstream press. In my little daydream, I saw glorious images of the entrepreneur coming home to save the village. But it was a stretch, and I knew it. I would still be moving information, but I was definitely leaving the high ground of the calling that Bill Kovach so fiercely championed. That world, noble and embattled, was a kind of secular priesthood, with strict vows of disinterested public service. I had worn that collar for a long time. And I was taking it off.

Upstairs, the summer issue of *Nieman Reports* was being prepared for the printer. It included this quote from Arthur Sulzberger, Jr., the publisher of the *New York Times,* from a staff meeting early in the year. His paper owned mine, but he could have been any top manager in brick-and-mortar America.

"These are tough times. I think it's a little extreme to say that everyone comes to work with their jobs in jeopardy, but I am the first to recognize that none of us has the same level of assurance that over the next twenty or thirty years, or however long it is before you choose to retire, that your job will be safe. Those days are gone. They are gone here, they are gone everywhere. You have to take more responsibility for yourself, make sure your skills are up to date, that your abilities are what they should be. Your career is in your own hands. . . . From management's point of view, we have the responsibility to give you the opportunity to enhance your skills and to make yourselves better and to give you the opportunity to get new job openings and so forth. But the old contract is gone."

And so was I.

My golden year at Harvard was ending. Just a few more events to attend. And one thing I needed to know. I bounded up the majestic staircase of Widener Library into the reference room, to the full *Oxford English Dictionary.* Mesomorph. The big volume quoted J. Z. Young: "In mesomorphs, muscle and bone predominate . . . and they are adventurous, aggressive, extroverted. . . ." See mesomorphic. Mesomorphic. More muscle and bone stuff, something about an embryo. And this: a state between liquid and crystal.

Between liquid and crystal. That just about caught it.

"Are you going to hear Gates?" a friend asked breathlessly, hustling with the crowd toward Sanders Theatre. And I was thinking Jesus again, and the old Sunday school stories of how he drew the wide-eyed throngs. "Are you going to hear Jesus? Have you heard the Word?" Echoes of childhood and children's Bibles and the sandaled feet of Israelites flipflapping as they rush, buoyant and expectant, to hear the Good News.

Bill Gates!

He will proclaim!

He stood just where Robert Coles had stood, in the same great Victorian hall. But this was the living word, not the bound word. This was the word made flesh. Oh yes, believers! Hitch your cart quick. Harvard was throwing an Internet conference. The university president, Neil Rudenstine, had opened the gathering with talk of revolution and "the verge of something . . . profound." Now waves of growly world music rumbled exotically in the old hall. Marble statues of early American aristocrats stared down at Harvard's most famous dropout, the world's richest man, the great Alpha and Omega, Jesus and Lucifer, Genghis Khan and Napoleon of the information revolution. William H. (Bill) Gates. He was forty. Forty! My age! Mister follow-your-bliss-and-suck-the-toes-of-life-Joe-Visa-bill me! Shit! This skinny-assed little earth mover had dropped out in his freshman year to start Microsoft — Microsoft! — in 1975, when I was off playing dharma bum love child in India. He had driven personal computers into millions and millions of homes. He had come late to the Internet. Very late. Only a few months before this very morning he had seen the light in a vast way, instructing the sprawling apparatus of Microsoft to embrace the Web, to engulf the Web. Now he was its single most powerful promoter. Standing spitting distance from my twitchy heart, grinning like a ten-year-old.

"It's great to be back," he said, pushing his big glasses up his nose, a geek in total triumph. "One of the few classes I actually attended was held here. It was Professor Finley teaching *The Iliad* and *The Odyssey.*"

The crowd roared with laughter. Raise my sail, Homer, I thought. Raise my soul. I may be slow but I'm ready, big guy. Let's go!

Gates was standing at a low table, his left hand planted on his hip, his right hand gesturing continuously. And he was already doing his famous forward and back rock, heel to toe, heel to toe, nonstop. A big screen had been stretched behind him by an obviously well-equipped Microsoft advance crew. It announced in huge letters THE ARRIVAL OF THE INFORMATION AGE above a pictorial timeline that soared like the ascent of man: pen, printing press, telephone, radio, television, personal computer.

The Internet had already acquired a critical mass of core users, Gates was saying. Next would come the explosion. Of users. Of online content.

"The amount of content we have today is fantastic, but it's nothing compared to what we'll have a year from now, two years from now," he said. "Content is breaking down the resistance of users with no technical interest."

BuildingBlocks users, I thought.

"The marginal cost of publishing in this industry is close to zero."

Thank God, I thought, because that's just about what we've got.

"If you have a PC and a modem, you're as empowered as Time Warner."

Let's go! Let's go.

"We are in a frenzy right now," Gates said, preaching to his First Church of the Future. "Almost a gold rush."

That pretty much caught it.

"The very mechanism of capitalism is being greatly improved. . . . Finding a lawyer, a consultant, even a baby-sitter — these transactions are not well mediated. They will be."

And outfitting a home, too, I thought. My vine to the future.

Let's go!

I made peace with Danielle. It wasn't easy. It was peace like the Gaza Strip has peace. But it was peace.

It took a full day of nothing else to find it. Time with her, time with the kids. Overdue time. I nuzzled late in bed with Lauren and a pile of her books and toys. Breakfast with Dylan, almost a man, with new birthday presents: a lacrosse stick, a big glider, a huge CD rack, a man-sized bathrobe. Fourteen. A soccer game with Ben, a victory. And hours with Danielle. And many continents of concern. And tears. In brief:

There was the money issue.

Did I really understand all I was walking away from? There was that salary, the overwhelming mainstay of our tight finances. Bonuses, stock options, health insurance, expense account, seniority, world travel, retirement plan. Did I understand I was about to leave all that? Did I really understand?

Yes, I understood.

Well then, could I assure her that this new thing was going to work? Could I say to her, right now, that I was seventy-five percent sure?

I was quiet.

Fifty percent sure? She sounded sick to have to ask that.

It's not about certainty, I said. It's about a chance. It's about a change.

Did I understand that I was forty now, not twenty-four? That Dylan would be going to college in three years? That there would be tuition to pay?

How much have we saved for that so far? I asked. Bupkis. Almost nothing. This way we'll either be rich or poor, I said. He'll have no problem or a full ride, financial aid, loans, I don't know what.

Okay. She was rocking slightly in her chair, like a nervous hostage. She changed her tack. Was it just about money? she asked. Was this all just about making piles of money? Because if it was . . .

No, I said. Money was embedded in it, sure. It was hard to disentangle. I would be happy to have it if it came. But in the end, I didn't think it was about money at all. It was about wanting to feel really, really alive. Wanting to be at the hot heart of what was going on in the world. Not just in the churn of headlines, with their plodding, rearview mirror presumptions. I wanted to be part of building something new, to be on fire again with dreams, and maybe to show our kids the way of the world in a new century, how things worked in the new economy.

This drew a long level stare. Danielle's bullshit meter was acute, but this thicket of yearning and grandiosity was too much even for her to pick apart. I'm not sure I could have dissected it myself.

She sighed and simplified.

She couldn't personally relate to this product I was working on, she said. She knew that Americans bought millions of home style magazines every month, and that was great, but she wasn't one of those Americans. Covering a coup d'état she could relate to. Covering home design didn't grab her in the same way. And when did I get so into it, by the way?

Look, Rolly's the true architecture head, I said. I do love great design. Great homes are inspiring. But the main thing for me here is figuring out how to use this new medium to move information in a way that makes a difference in the quality of people's lives. Okay, it's not great affairs of state. But it's the path I've found into this new world, and this world is what I want to see. Anyway, people are into their homes. Homes shape lives. They want to make them better, unique. We'll help them do that. And to me, that's cool.

Danielle accepted that. Then she got to her real issue.

She wanted to be home with Lauren. She wanted it so badly she could taste it. She was ready to walk away from her dean's post to be with her daughter. To quit. But that depended on my bringing home my salary. Now I was cutting off her retreat. She would live with it. But did I understand the tradeoff that this was forcing. My dream for hers.

I hung my head. I understood. But she would not avoid working if we just slogged ahead. Not unless we changed our lives in ways we had not yet found. This was our last chance to change in a way that really stepped up, not down. We had lived a wonderful, full life so far, with love and travel and excitement. We have all that at our back to draw on, to remember, if this is hard, I said. But if we wanted the rest to be as good, to be even better, this was the time to go for it.

But how long will it take? she asked, granting for a moment that it just might work at all.

I had no idea how long it would take. The news was full of overnight successes, but I was starting to see that most overnight successes had years of spadework buried in them somewhere, all the thinking and work that made them suddenly blossom in the public eye. I couldn't pretend otherwise.

Give me five years, I said.

She looked stricken.

Maybe less, I said quickly. Lauren will still be young. So will we. And we'll be more free than I can ever foresee on the path we're on now.

But five years, Tom!

Five years!

And that brought us to us. It was evening now. We had moved inside and fed the kids and put Lauren to bed. And the conversation went on, epochal, to our own bed.

We had been together since we were sixteen. We had married three times, to each other. Twice for fun. Once in India as students, when we were nineteen and couldn't live together at Andhra University unless we were wed. Once in Hong Kong City Hall, when the Indian union was forgotten and local mores again made their demand. And once for real, the only one our parents knew for years, in the pasture where I grew up raising sheep.

We lay together now, miles into a conversation that could have no easy end, and laughed at the pasture vows we wrote in 1979, so nudgy and oblique, in the fashion of that time, about marriage and commitment itself. "Bless our oneness in our twoness!" we hooted in parody, and we laughed again at how we had danced in Balinese masks from an old friend and with a big Red Meat Congo watermelon that Bob Murphy had hauled up from his patch in Mississippi, and how the wild core of the wedding party had leapt into the back of our old pickup truck on that hot summer night, full of champagne and sweaty joy and wind in our hair, and tumbled out to run skinny-dipping into Hank Falb's blue gill pond.

And now what about us?

The week before we had said good-bye to our best and oldest friends in Boston, Sue and Tom. They were moving west. Tom was helping to lead a union drive in Nevada with the AFL-CIO. Helping dishwashers make a decent wage while I chased moonbeams. The irony was not missed. He was rolling up his sleeves and diving into the income gap. And I had looked into it and was racing to jump over. Who knew which would finally matter more? Fixing an old world or building a new one? West or Unger? Dealing with what is or chasing what might be? Minimum wage battles or a new universe of economic growth?

But the issue was friendship, Danielle said, coming to her point.

Companionship. Sue was leaving town. And that left me for her to count on. Only me. Not just as lover, she said, eyes glistening, brimming over, but as deepest friend. I was her best buddy in the world, she said, and in the past year I had been too distracted to fill the role. I was so focused on this new thing that she felt alone. All alone. She had signed on for better or worse. And she meant it. She would stand in that pasture again anytime, by the redbud tree my parents had planted where we made our vows. And she would swim naked again in that pond, anytime. And all the rest — money and work and pensions — could be damned, she would stick with me, she said. But she couldn't stand to feel so very alone.

And that cracked me. The day's trickle of tears had been hers, but now they were mine. Not soft like hers, but messy tears in tortured, gasping sobs. Because I knew that loneliness, too. And I could see the pain she felt. But I could not stand down.

"I'll be back," I finally choked out, hunched and slobber-faced on the edge of the bed. "I promise. And it will be better, Danielle. I swear to God that's why I'm doing this."

She reached across the bed to me. I bent my head into the curve of her hip and choked the words into her side. I didn't deserve her face. I was reckless and obsessed.

"But I will be back. Completely back."

She took my head in her arms.

"And I will be your buddy forever."

We clung to each other, not daring to let go. She pulled me into the covers, and cleaned my face with her nightgown, and stroked my head long into that night.

I would do things, I did not know what. But I would finally be with her, I prayed. Always with her. Whatever happened.

"Oh, my man in the clouds," she whispered, rocking softly in the bed, surely wondering where we were going now. "My man, my man.

"My man in the clouds."

Rick Segal was cagey. Careful. That was his job. We negotiated up and down for weeks. The ground kept shifting. He would put together $1.5 million for us, he said, but would want forty percent of the company for that money. Our stake would be hugely diluted right out of the gate. We didn't want the deal. But we needed the money. We kept the conversation going. We're catching eagles, we said now. Slowly, slowly.

But we really needed the money. Get money when you don't need it, Rolly liked to say. Because needing it makes you vulnerable. You can't let on how much you need it. But we needed it. We had people coming on. We were busting out of Rolly's house, spilling out of the extra bedroom into the living room and everywhere. We had found office space in an old church building. A lease was being drawn up. We needed money.

Art called us to his house one afternoon. He was on the treadmill when we arrived. I could see the strain in his face. He had grown attached to us, spent family chits for us, stood up and voted for us, and somehow it wasn't coming together. Get an experienced CEO, guys, he said, huffing. Right now. That would do it. You can be the vision guys, but get a manager in here with a track record.

And we would not do it. This was our baby. It was too early. No professional gunslinger would understand. We could do it. We knew we could do it.

But we needed money!

And it was clear to me now that we would not have it when I resigned. The one promise I had made to Danielle a year ago I would now break. I would leap without a net.

It's coming, I told her. The money's coming.

But it wasn't there.

And there was no guarantee.

None.

The radio spoke at six o'clock, like it did every morning. NPR, like every morning. Must be Bob Edwards. Danielle stretched next to me. I lay still, listening. The radio was talking about two *Baltimore Sun* reporters who had traveled to Sudan to expose the modern slave trade there. They had actually bought two young slave boys.

What a story. I hazily pictured the dusty trucks they must have taken, the village headmen they must have sat with, the sweaty beds and exhaustion and traders and bargaining. The notebooks and flights and stories they wrote. The headlines. I rubbed Danielle's back and let my mind slowly creep up on the notion that I was leaving that world.

Today.

The resignation letter was written. It was on the chest across the room. But don't hurry to that thought. Stay half asleep. Remember. Remember walking out of Tibet through the Himalayas when the king of Nepal had closed the roads, walking in those endless mountains and how good it was. And Malacanang the night Marcos fled his palace, and the big machine gun under the grand piano and the bonfires of burning documents, and the strange stillness in his abandoned bedroom before the mob grew brave and poured in behind us to see, to see Imelda's ivory inlaid Ouija board and tall magnums of perfume and those infamous racks of shoes. Remember Daniel Ortega, campaigning on horseback in highland Nicaragua, and swimming in the volcano outside Managua, and how good it was. And tens of thousands of Japanese standing in the snow, screaming "Banzai!" on New Year's Day for Hirohito at his balcony. Ten thousand years! And the crazy knifepoint kidnapping in Moscow, and Dan Rather, standing on a wooden box for height, reporting live from Red Square when the laughing young Russian boy took a bead on the camera and dropped his trousers and mooned America and was swept up in seconds by a tiny Russian police car in front of Lenin's tomb. And Delhi in flames when Indira Gandhi was assassinated, and the rows of blood-soaked Sikhs guarding the ramparts at the old Imperial Hotel, and Indira on her funeral pyre, crackling on sandalwood ten feet from my hot face, and half a million angry Hindus in the surging crowd around us, and the garlanded priest with flowers in his beard who leaned down close to knock a tiny hole in her head upon the flames, to set her spirit free. And the Amerasian girl who led me, stumbling drunk at 3 A.M. from too much vodka with Russians on the roof of the old Rex Hotel, down the empty streets of Saigon, the primordial stage set of my American century, and the former Vietnamese captain who leaned close in the little restaurant in Hanoi to ask what I had named my first son. Dylan, I said. And you? Victory, he said.

Enough said.

I was leaving that behind, a thousand days and nights in the world, for a new way. Today. I crawled out of bed but could barely function. I couldn't decide whether to brush my teeth or my hair, which pants to put on, time for shoes or not. I was in a daze with Sadie at the field, trying old John Peng's tai chi to collect myself, losing my way in the routine.

Comb the mane of the wild horse, I could hear him say. Grasp the peacock's tail. Move with cloud hands. Be full of energy, but calm. Be focused. Be free. My God. What was I doing?

I had called David Greenway the night before, tracked him down with his wife, J.B., on vacation in the Austrian hills. I woke him from a dead sleep. Me. An old foreign editor who should know time zones.

"David, I'm so sorry to wake you." My voice was thick with emotion. When I was younger, I had dreamed of a career like his, circling the world in search of great stories. The world had changed, but I still knew that dream. "David, something important. You're my oldest friend and constant mentor at the paper and I want you to know first. I'm giving notice of my resignation tomorrow."

A long silence. I rushed in to outline, broad stroke, what I was going to do. Internet. Publishing. All new.

"I'm only forty, David. I've got twenty-five more years, anyway. I need green fields to charge around in."

And the phone at Pension Steffel Bauer crackled back. "Gosh, I think that's great, Tom. I'm excited for you."

And then the call to Helen Donovan, on vacation on Cape Cod. I would miss her humor and her steel.

"Wow, that's quite an update," she said when we had talked it through. "Well, you are forty. I suppose this is the time."

She was not much more than forty, I thought. And she was staying.

"I've got to do it, Helen. It's like when people were jumping on boats for the New World. Europe didn't go away. It's still there. It's fine. But I'm a New World kind of guy."

"Yeah," she said. "I think you are. It sounds terrific."

And I had fallen asleep thinking maybe this wouldn't be so bad.

* * *

There was business to do this morning before going to the *Globe*. Andy Markuvitz at Matrix Partners was seeing Rolly and me today. Matrix was another VC kingpin. We were still new to the game. I still imagined, hoped against all hope, that we might somehow soar out of this meeting with piles of money on the way, that I would not have to resign today into a perfect void. That there would be a bridge, a hint of gold, at least some vine to grab.

Matrix was out on the old Route 128 in a palatial hilltop office complex that was home, it seemed, to half the venture capital firms in the Boston area. The complex was serene and august on its tall bluff overlooking a wide reservoir. The Magic Mountain, I thought, as we wound up its side. Be magic today.

Andy Markuvitz was so cerebral, he looked as if he had a few extra lobes tucked in. He got straight to the point. Matrix had lots of money, but he only got to invest so much of it at a time, in just a very few companies a year. And he was very, very picky.

"I get three arrows a year to shoot," he said, gazing out over the idyllic reservoir and pines. "I've got to be sure I use them wisely."

There was a formula he followed, he said. A simple formula. First, find good founders, people with great track records, and get them onto a great idea. Second, help them put together a great team. Ideally, they come alone. Naked. And Matrix builds the team around them. Third, bring the right money to bear and get a big piece of the startup, maybe fifty percent, right from the get-go.

Great. Our track records were from left field. We had already begun putting together a team he was absolutely certain to find checkered, at best. And we were in no way looking to give up fifty percent of our little sprout of a company, our dream.

Never mind all that. We made our pitch. He listened closely, had good questions, good suggestions. He bored in on exactly how we were going to make money. Was advertising a sufficient model? He looked doubtful. And how would we scale up this product? How could we structure it so it took advantage of the Internet's unique characteristics? How could we make our database of home design products grow and grow without a groaning, impossibly expensive effort?

They were good questions. We talked for more than three hours. My appointment with Matt Storin, the *Globe*'s editor, was approaching. We had to cut to the chase. Andy had the brainpower to investigate all day.

"So, Andy, bottom line," I suddenly blurted out. "Are you interested in what we're up to?"

He made a steeple of his long fingers in front of his chest.

"I would rather have met you before you got going," he said. When we hadn't plunged in, started assembling a team, started swimming in our own direction. That hurt. It would have been better, he was saying, if we had not been busting our hump all these months to build our little fire.

Well, we said, we were sorry about that. But we were already moving. We couldn't help it. Our show was on the road.

He looked quizzical, something like caring.

"You know, if I look at it and Greylock looks at it and maybe Highland looks at it, and none of us is interested in doing it, why would you be interested in doing it?"

Wow. Another perfect sting to the heart. I was resigning in forty-five minutes! The letter was in my pocket. The die was fucking cast! And this very smart guy is asking why we were even interested in doing it? Well, I thought, in a flush of irritation and hope and fear, we were doing it because we believed in the vision, whether Matrix Partners saw it on this day or not. We were doing it because we didn't have a thousand freaking options, and this is where we had driven our stake in the ground. We were doing it because someone was going to figure out this excellent corner of the Internet, and it may as well be us. And yes, God dammit, we were diving in and we would twist and turn and scrape and struggle and do whatever — whatever — it took to figure it out, and old King I Will Do Things Lear would have nothing on us! Nothing!

Now excuse me, I thought, while I step outside and burn my bridges.

We said polite good-byes and ran to the car. I still didn't know if he was interested or not. But I had a pretty good idea. And it wasn't good.

"We are rash!" I yelled, windows down, music cranked, as we tore toward the city. "We are two rash, rash yahoos on a complete tear."

"Look, he talked to us for three and a half hours," Rolly yelled, and I thanked God for his relentlessly positive interpretations. Because I was quitting my job, my calling, today. In about twenty minutes, in fact. And a little something positive, just a thin little thread at least, would be very welcome right now.

"We clearly got his attention," Rolly yelled against the wind. "He can say whatever he wants, but if we're building something that's working, he'll come around."

I careened off the turnpike, dropped Rolly at a bus stop, and tore on to the *Globe*. I had wanted to meditate on this moment, to come in slow and ready and composed. And now I'm roaring down the highway and there's no way to be composed. No time. Just have to do it. I've driven this commute probably two thousand times. And now it's over. The last commute. Maybe anywhere. Maybe ever. I turn the radio way up and fly along to John Mellencamp, something about "Ain't That America," and by God it does feel like an American moment. All-American. I'm pushing eighty now, too fast, but I don't care. I'm flying. Where to, I don't know. But this is the day I bust out.

I'm sweeping past Chinatown, looping onto Route 93, past the carcasses of old industrial junk and new construction on new highways, past the dead power plant south of the city with its ugly dead cigars of smokestacks that I've thought were ugly two thousand times, down the exit ramp that I've descended in drizzle and sun and snow, and into the front lot of the paper. It's an elegant building, no doubt about it. But it's bricks and mortar to me. And I'm in, and past the towering old gilt-framed portrait of Eben Jordan, the *Globe*'s first money, a century ago, glowering down over his muttonchops. Pray for me, you wise old coot. I wish I could hit you up for money. But right now all I'm thinking about is the knife in my pocket. My resignation letter. I forgot envelopes, so I've folded the signed one, for Matt, into my left jacket pocket and put two more copies into my right. For Ben Taylor. For Bill Taylor. Who knows. An old mainte-

nance man who's been my pal for years spots me as I'm heading upstairs. Hey, geez, it's been a long time, he says with a big handshake.
Where the hell have you been? I've been off the reservation, I say,
flash a smile, and keep moving. I want this clean. I don't want to talk
to anybody on the way to the corner office. I want this to go straight
to Matt. I don't want to tell any lies. Not now. I want it out on the table. His table.

Is he going to rage? Take after me with a baseball bat the way he
did to another reporter at a company game years ago? We'll see. He's
got a famous temper. I'm sweeping through the newsroom. Strong
pace. My usual. Everything is a blur. Nods here and there, but I'm all
forward focus. Robbie, the metro editor, spots me coming and gives
a big hallo from the city desk. Handshake. Eye glint. He's a tough
piece of leather. I keep moving. Matt's secretary, Eileen, is smiling
brightly, a sheaf of papers in her hand.

"Is he in there?" I ask. He's there, she says, and I'm through the
glass door. And the knot of fear begins to melt from my very first
glimpse. He's just a man with a whole newspaper on his shoulders.
And I can see it's heavy today. Deep creases run down his cheeks
now. He's more gaunt than I remember. Thinner. Still with those intense eyes, but there's something hurting in them. He looks weary.

"At last we get together," he says, tidying up his conference table. "I
was afraid I wasn't going to see you before you got back. We've been
meeting all day today with the directors . . ."

A shadow crosses his face, then the big pro forma smile and the
big handshake. We'll talk about my return.

"Was it great?" he says, sitting down. "Was it terrific?"

He's asking about the year, the fellowship, I think. And I don't
want to get into that. I don't want to get into any chitchat at all. I'm
feeling light-headed.

"Matt, we have to have a serious talk," I say, sitting down, feeling
my own face draw tight, my eyes surge with the load of extra tears
that has been my curse at big moments since childhood. He's peering
over the top of his glasses now. He must wonder what the hell is up.

"I came to the *Globe* when I was twenty-four," I say clumsily,
speaking evenly but heavily, my voice veering embarrassingly toward

the low registers of hysteria. "Now I'm forty. There's a lot I want to do in life. I'm resigning."

"Oh! . . . Ow!" he mutters as I reach into my coat pocket for the letter. "To another paper?"

I don't say anything, not trusting myself just now. I hand him the letter, nodding at it as if to say "It's all there."

He unfolds it and reads slowly down the page. I don't know where this is going to go. I feel weightless, just hanging in space. It's done. The letter is in his hands. He's reading. And I know what he's reading. That I'm leaving to start a new media company with an old friend. That it's heart-wrenching for me (and it is). That the *Globe* has nurtured and taught me in a thousand ways (and it has). That I believe we're at a rare hinge point in history, and I want to be directly engaged in the change. That I'll always be grateful to the paper, and will always wish the best for everyone there.

And I know what it means. It means I'm gone. I've cut loose from a whole community and its familiar structure of demands and deadlines and battles and rhythms and paychecks. I'm out of there.

His eyebrows shoot up, way up the way old-fashioned cash registers did when they totaled a sale. It means he's taken it in. He looks up across the table slowly, tired and more kindly than I ever expected.

"The first thing I have to say, Tom, is congratulations," he says, reaching over to shake my hand.

"I'm glad for you. Really glad," he says. "And envious too, to tell you the truth. You know, I just came from a board of directors meeting and it was seventy-five percent bad news. Some of that seventy-five percent we can deal with, we can change. But no small part of it we can't. . . . The world is changing around us.

"You remind me of how I left the *Globe* eleven years ago myself, and that was the best thing I ever did. And not because I came back, but because of all the experiences and learning along the way. I tell you, I really am more than a little envious. Much more than a little. I've got to say congratulations."

This all threw me off my track. I was ready to be treated like an ingrate. I was ready to talk about all I had given the *Globe*, how I had labored in the vineyards and written my guts out and been steadfast. And he wasn't asking for any of that. He wasn't asking for justification at all. He was reminding me that I was the second-highest-ranking editor ever to leave the paper, and he was the highest. He'd been there, in his own way. He was just saying yeah, go for it.

I stammer something about how much the *Globe* means to me, how much I love the paper. And it's true, I realize, sitting there. I do. For all its warts and pimples, it's a grand institution, a great place.

Matt cuts in. "You don't have to say that, Tom. I know what you feel. We all know it. You've given good measure here for a long time. You were the best foreign correspondent we ever had. You've been a leader. It's going to make a lot of people sad to see you go. But I understand it. I wish you well."

I tell him I'm prepared to pay the *Globe* back for its support during the Nieman year. He says no way, he won't consider it, that I'm a special case and he'll tell Bill Taylor so.

"You've paid your dues, Tom," he says. "You've been a mainstay. We don't forget that."

I've also been a third wheel, I think to myself. A maverick, upstart pain in the ass sometimes. But never mind.

He asks if I can stick around a few weeks more. There are a couple weeks when people are trying to get vacations, he says. Maybe you can step in and help run the place for a couple of weeks.

Sure, whatever you need, I say, with no idea how this summer is going to proceed.

"I wish you all the luck in the world," Matt says as we stand. "And if it doesn't work out, remember, your star is always high here."

I have no idea if he means that as an honest invitation to return. But I file it away.

We shake hands, and my eyes begin to tear up again. And then I'm out of the office and soaring through the newsroom. Settling on no faces. Moving. On to see Ben. And Bill. Ande Zellman falls in beside me.

"I just resigned," I whisper to her as she quicksteps alongside.

"Whoa!" she says. "Are you serious? Well, congratulations!"

Congratulations. Everybody is saying congratulations. Everybody.

It's as if I won the lottery or bought my freedom or something. It's weird.

I stop in to see Mike Larkin, my old pal. He is cooling his heels, as usual. Making it happen without breaking a sweat.

"I don't want to spend the rest of my career fighting a rear guard action, praying that the newspaper industry will limp along at least until I retire," I'm saying, hands between my knees in his office. And he's nodding slowly, Mister Cool.

"A lot of journalists are thinking and living with just that assumption. Prominent journalists," he says. "Go for it. You'll have fun."

And now I'm sitting with Bill Taylor. Chairman and publisher of the *Boston Globe*, heir to empire, pillar of the community, Yankee paragon, employer of thousands. He is at his fine desk in his elegant office. His familiar, chiseled features are welcoming, calm. He is God in this domain. He has turned the *Globe* into a billion-dollar property. He has seen a dozen Pulitzer Prizes racked up by the paper in his time. He has sent a warm, personal note every time I have been promoted. His signature has been stamped on every paycheck and company Christmas card I have received for fifteen years. He is the last stop on the exit ramp. Point of no return. Resign with Bill and you've resigned.

And he's waiting.

I feel suddenly as though I'm in a dream, floating in midair in this fine office in front of this good and principled man. I have been lucky to work here. It is a good place, with a complex, human heart but a good heart.

"I'm resigning, Bill," I say. And his hawklike old eye flashes up and he sucks in a short cluck through his teeth. He listens while I give him the quick story. Top level only. He's the top man. But I see he's really listening. Closely. I'm walking out of this palace, the palace he built, for a bedroom office so crowded now you can barely turn around. And he's not looking angry or even dismayed. It's something else completely. And I finally stop talking for a second just to wonder what it is.

And the great man speaks.

"Golly," he says softly, clearly. "I wish I were in your shoes."

* * *

For the op-ed page a few weeks later, my last piece for the *Globe:*

Figure this.

I'm 40. I have three kids, two car payments, one fat mortgage on a house that needs paint, an all-American stack of credit card bills, and I'm quitting my job.

After 15 good years with one good employer, I'm walking away to start a company of my own. I'm taking the leap from the old economy to the new economy. From paper and ink to digital magic. From major corporation to tiny start-up. From automatic deposits, pension plan and 401K statements to big dreams, white knuckles and prayer.

The leap is thrilling. Terrifying, too. It's hard on a marriage and hard to explain to a financial planner. But it feels so right. So free. So full of promise. And somehow, so intimately connected with an American legacy much older than the vanishing 9-to-5 certainties of mid-20th-century work.

Americans are turning entrepreneurial in record numbers. Is anyone surprised? Years of layoffs and corporate "restructuring" have led most of us to weigh our own resources and imagine how we might rely on them. Dreaming is the beginning of doing.

We're told that we'll all have seven or eight careers in the new economy — the fluid, digital, no-guarantees economy that's lapping at everyone's hips by now. Maybe some of us just get tired of waiting to find out what the next career will be. When nothing is forever, why pretend? Maybe now, to leap is to live.

But some part of the urge to jump feels almost genetic, a seed of history and blood just waiting for the climate that calls it up. In all my life, I've never felt closer to the experience of immigrant forebears than I do now. They sailed from old world to new. Now it's my turn.

The new economy is, in its way, like a new continent in our midst. It has its own rough shoreline, its own excited vocabulary, its own rambunctious ethos, heroes and hustlers. It has its staked territories, its uncharted wilderness, its mythical streets paved with gold and its dreams of manifest destiny. Some people go to it voluntarily. Some arrive against their will. Almost all are changed in passage. Human nature isn't upended in the new economy, but human relationships and assumptions and identities surely are. It is a new world.

By 1996, the economy of the cyber era has already named its visionary explorers and brave pioneers. I make no claim at all to those ranks.

Now comes the big migration, the waves of settlers. And I'm sailing to make my claim.

Was it the same in 1682 when my family's first American came ashore as an indentured servant in New Jersey? Had his mother sighed and asked him the same unanswerable questions on the pier? Was he sure? We don't know just what prompted him to sail from Belfast, only that he mortgaged seven years of his life to do it. Now I'm paying my price for passage, to investors, to venture capitalists, to the new patrons of transformation.

There were Germans later in our line, fleeing famine all the way to the American prairie, settling unsettled Illinois, facing down wolves with pine knots and no options. They built a farm that lasted across centuries. Will I, without starvation at my back, be as bold?

Our Swedes came last, leaving poverty and despair behind. Their mother threw herself down the well when they had gone. They changed their names to fit America's sound but never lost their easy tears or their love of birch trees in snow. What will I lose on the way I'm taking? What will I keep?

The old world didn't go away. It still stands. But the energy and edge of history are migratory, and my people moved with them. Now I'm raising my sail and listening for the echo of their voices on the wind. What did they think as they crossed the water? Were they confident? Afraid? Brash? Certain? Until today, my interest was dispassionate, just idle curiosity when I wondered at all. Now I really want to know.

Chapter 10

Space Shot

I T FELT LIKE a touch-and-go shuttle launch.

First came the roar and smoke and flames, of emotion and decision and tearing loose from life's old gravity. The moment when you wonder if the whole thing will break apart before it's even into the blue.

We signed an office lease, personally guaranteeing the rent, before the seed money was in. We had to. We had to keep moving. Up, up, or die. We went round and round with Rick Segal. BuildingBlocks was taking off, we said. This little company was hot as hell. We were absolutely confident we would raise at least another million dollars before the next six months were out. Did he want in at half a million for ten percent now or not?

We were the team. This was the deal. What did he say?

And then we prayed. Almost on our knees. Our little band of staff milled around Rolly's bungalow, charting plans, keeping their heads down, clinging to hope. It's coming, Rolly and I told them. The money's coming. And our eyes would lock for a split second and widen with the sickening, private awareness that nothing was certain here except desire. It is coming, right? Somehow. Soon. Soon! This was a new kind of vulnerability to me. Complete vulnerability. For our immediate needs — salary for the staff, computers to work on, telephone lines — there was no time to find other backers. There was no distant headquarters to squeeze. We were it. This was it.

Our steadfast attorney, Gene Barton, wrestled the paperwork and worked the phone. Rolly's eyes were puffy, red-rimmed, resolute, almost wild with the strain of holding the line. Salamander eyes, Carole called them. We had all read the warning of risk that Gene had insisted start right on the front of the private placement memorandum, the draft of the document that would solicit the money and seal the deal. The warning was right out there in capital letters, in hideous bold type. It was boilerplate for a deal like this, Gene said. Absolutely standard. But wicked cold. Stone cold sober, no bullshit whatsoever, so that no investor, nowhere, no-how, could ever say he or she hadn't known.

You are stepping straight into the land of naked risk, it announced:

THE SHARES OF COMMON STOCK BEING OFFERED HEREBY ARE SPECULATIVE AND INVOLVE A HIGH DEGREE OF RISK AND SUBSTANTIAL IMMEDIATE DILUTION. THE COMPANY IS IN THE DEVELOPMENT STAGE, HAS A LIMITED HISTORY OF OPERATIONS WITH NO REVENUE TO DATE AND IS SUBJECT TO ALL THE RISKS INHERENT IN A BUSINESS THAT IS IN THE DEVELOPMENT STAGE.

And for anyone who still wasn't getting the picture, there was this charming icepick of a postscript:

INVESTORS MUST BE PREPARED TO LOSE THEIR ENTIRE INVESTMENT IN THE COMPANY.

Got it? In legal terms, this is a flat-out crapshoot, a big fat lottery ticket, and you've been warned. And dilution? You bet. Lots. The minute more money comes in behind yours, your stake shrinks in percentage terms. The pie gets bigger and your percentage will be less of the whole. So pray the thing is a big winner. Pray that less is still more. Don't whine if it's not. You are fully, richly, one hundred percent warned. Good luck to you.

Still the noises from Rick were positive. He liked what he saw. Scott Smith was on board. Art was in there for us. The noises were good, they were strong. But there was no substitute for the money. The money in the bank. Our bank. Soon. Please, God, soon. Rolly was starting to cover a gap now. He fed in $2,000 to keep us going. "Out of the chute and dead in the water!" he would mutter as we pushed blindly ahead. The roar of the takeoff was shaking us wall to wall. Up, up. More fuel!

And then it was there. Half a million. In the bank.

We held the little bank slip carefully in our fingers, as if it were the commutation of a death sentence. Breathing shallow. Reading it again and again: "Your balance: $503,103."

We had closed our first money. Our seed round, in startup speak. We were launched.

I sat alone that afternoon in our new, almost empty office, tucked into the top floor of a grand old Methodist church, with six folding tables from Staples and ten stacking chairs, and I thought how quiet it must be in the spaceship once the roar of the launch dies away.

We were up. We were out there. On our space shot.

Now we actually had to make it all happen. We had launched the leap. Now we had to make the landing.

And the real education began.

There were a few last odds and ends to wrap up at the *Globe*. A slab cake came down from the cafeteria cooler for the ritual newsroom sendoff. White frosting, blue trim. There was a slab cake waiting up there for each of us, they said. I was glad to have mine done with. There were sayonara parties. Heart-to-heart conversations. And e-mail to answer, from friends who asked how it felt to be going. Thrilling and terrifying, I always responded. "Yeah," came one response. "Like staying here. Terrifying."

Then there was the mandatory checkout with the Human Resources Department, down in the bowels of the building. My severance pay after fifteen years, the HR guy told me, would be $35,000. My stock options I would have to cash out within a year. My accumulated pension would be waiting for me at retirement, he said, "even if this digital stuff washes the newspaper away." But since I was checking out early, at age forty, I shouldn't count on the *Globe* pension for much, he said with a tight grin that suggested he didn't know whether I was brilliant or crazy. When I was sixty-five, he said, this pension "might just be enough to cover groceries."

Swell.

I took the $35,000 and bought Danielle a new wedding ring the next day at Shreve, Crump & Low. Nothing too expensive, but nicer than the little one I had bought her in Hong Kong years before. The old one was falling apart, and who knew when I would have a few spare bucks in my pocket again. With the half million in, Rolly and I were drawing BuildingBlocks salaries, but they were less than half of what we had made before. For Danielle and me, like Rolly and Carole, that left a combined income that did not begin to cover our household costs. We counted up my severance pay, and the profit we could expect from the *New York Times* stock options I had accumulated when the *Times* bought the *Globe,* and our modest savings. It looked respectable. Not huge, but respectable. Surely more than enough to take us through this temporary cut in pay. BuildingBlocks would soon get fully funded, and the business would take off, and we would be fine.

But just in case it doesn't quite go that way, I thought, let's mark this moment with a ring. Let's remember when we were embracing and full of hope.

The new ring had three diamonds, one for each child. We laughed like newlyweds when we bought it. I slipped it onto Danielle's finger just like on the pasture hillside. The saleslady cooed. Danielle stood by the glittering display case and leaned her head against my chest, laughing, and maybe crying too. It was hard to tell.

We had started a new chapter.

Out in the quiet of space.

We didn't yet know how quiet it really was. BuildingBlocks Interactive Corporation, the company name we settled on before the seed money came in, was funded in the very last hours of an Internet investment frenzy that had gripped the country for almost a year. Many of the first Internet companies that had been funded with venture capital were already failing. They hadn't known how to succeed in this new arena, and while they were trying to figure it out, they died.

The early die-off had hit especially hard at Internet companies offering content online. And hardest of all at companies offering content for consumers, the Internet's most elusive constituency at that time.

In other words, companies like ours.

Investors were still ready to put money into companies developing the technical infrastructure for the Internet. That looked like a no-lose proposition. Everyone believed the Internet would be used and used heavily someday. It would have to have infrastructure, the nuts and bolts systems that would make it work.

The question was, how would it be used? What kind of content would Internet users want? And how would anyone make money providing it, especially providing it to consumers? Plenty of early efforts had already failed. Now, the wave of Internet investment euphoria that had supported them — and us — was crashing.

And we didn't know.

We had sworn to Rick Segal that we believed we could raise at least another million dollars within six months. He didn't forget. Right in the middle of the documents that brought his group's investment was a tough little clause. If we did not raise another million within six months, our seed round investors automatically got fifty-one percent voting control of the company. Raise the money, that clause said, or lose control of your company.

Leafy Newton, eight miles from Boston Harbor, was a long way from the real hotbeds of the Internet industry, in San Francisco and Silicon Valley. We didn't hear the investment door slamming. We were fired up. We were amazed and thrilled just to be in business, to be in the middle of the world's hottest new thing. The "Year of the Net," *Newsweek* would call it. And young as it was, we were there.

On the day our seed money hit the bank, fewer than ten percent of American households were online. Maybe far fewer. The groups that published estimates all seemed to have some interest in pushing the Internet story. We were completely undaunted by that small penetration. For starters, we told anyone who would listen, the Internet was going first into the country's affluent households, which made it a good channel for marketing even if it didn't yet have television's reach. Second, we always said, you had to look at the hockey stick.

The beloved hockey stick.

New "enabling technologies" — electric light, telephone, television — tended to seep slowly into acceptance with the public when they were first introduced, then suddenly soar into widespread use.

Graph that pattern above a timeline, and you get the shape of a hockey stick, the graph line only creeping up at first, then suddenly turning skyward in an almost vertical climb. Television was the perfect example. From 1940 to 1945, its penetration into the market barely crept above zero. Between 1945 and 1950, it turned the corner, reaching adoption by twenty percent of U.S. households. And then television penetration exploded, the chart line zooming almost vertically to reach eighty percent by 1960.

We knew we were still in the slow years of Internet adoption. But everyone believed we were heading for the hockey stick explosion. Which was a beautiful thing. It meant that business plans for startups like BuildingBlocks could project revenues exploding in a hockey stick pattern, too. Small at first, sure. But when Internet use climbed the hockey stick, we would soar with it. Exploding revenues. Exploding stock prices. Exploding company value.

Rolly had roughed out a chart that showed how the value of BuildingBlocks stock, assuming we eventually took the company public, could ride that lovely hockey stick. The numbers were just back-of-an-envelope estimates, but they brimmed with the excitement that hockey sticks produce. If we hit our projected sales — our "very conservative" projections, we never failed to point out — a two percent share of founder's stock in this tiny company, with its six folding tables and ten stacking chairs, would be worth more than $2 million in year five. If we hit our real goals — more ambitious, of course, than our very conservative projections — that two percent stake would be worth more than $10 million. And if the Internet hockey stick really went wild, who knew what those shares might be worth. Who knew!

This was the Internet's golden joy juice. It made people crazy. We tried to sip it sparingly. The point was to build a great company, we said, and let the chips fall where they would. But you couldn't avoid the nostril-flaring scent of potential fortune.

"If you guys play this right, in five years you'll be so rich, the only work you'll have to do the rest of your life is roll out of bed," a new industry friend told us that summer. And we pooh-poohed the comment. Who could tell what would happen? we said. No one could see the future. We tried not to think about the business in those terms.

But with seed money in the bank and our little team growing, I couldn't help extending Rolly's math to my own founder's stake. Let's see, if a two percent stake could turn into a $10 million pot in five years, then my twenty-five percent stake could turn into . . . $125 million!

Now, that was fuck-you money on a grand scale!

It was also purest speculation, built on assumption after assumption of difficult achievements. And even if we did ride the hockey stick's ascent, there would be slumps along the way.

We were headed straight into one.

As the year rolled on, a news story on HotWired, an online news service born in the Internet's first go-go flush, described a San Francisco Internet investment conference as "half empty . . . desperate, even depressing," a shadow of the raging investment festivals of a few months earlier. The cash gusher was being capped.

And we didn't know.

But we found out.

"Dreaming about beautiful homes = safe sex on the Internet," I wrote on our gleaming new white board. How was that for a marketing approach. We all laughed. People loved homes, and we would help them love homes in a new way. Our little BuildingBlocks team was gathered on the top floor of the church, and we were giddy. This was no palace, but it was an office, at last! No more tiny bedroom for us! And just five minutes from my house! We had money to buy computers and Post-it Notes and even a white board. We ordered business cards, with our new address, that said "CEO" for Rolly and "Publisher" for me. Wow! This felt like the real thing.

And we were growing. We had just hired Eric Westby to work as a graphic designer. And we had hired Gwen Simpkins to come in two days a week as our Home Style Editor. How grand! Gwen was a longtime home style maven for the *Boston Globe* and for *Boston Magazine* who also had her own business building million-dollar homes. She was a high-spirited, no-nonsense beauty who knew how to get things done.

And we had so much to do!

There was software to write. There was the CD-ROM to build.

There was the Web site to create. There were home tours and design settings to photograph and program. There was marketing, and sales, and all the organizational growth and gelling we would need to move ahead.

And, of course, there was fund-raising. That would have to start again right away. Outstanding bills had already bitten into the half million. And now we had a payroll to meet.

"So what's your burn rate?" Rick Segal asked in his first call after the money came in. It was already heading toward $75,000 a month. It was easy to do the math. We had six months at the outside. We had to hurry.

But the more we hurried, the clearer it became that we had not yet really figured out this business. Our summer product development schedules, which had looked so crisp and manageable before the seed money came, now looked impossibly ambitious. Our CD-ROM product, which could do so many things that the bandwidth-constrained Internet could not, was at the center of our planning. But investors were backing away from CD-ROM businesses even faster than they were fleeing from the Internet. CD-ROM sales had bombed that year, and firms that published them were collapsing all over. The Web would have to come to the center of our planning, but we had not yet worked that through completely. Everyone was beavering away, staying long hours, digging in. But within a very few weeks it began to feel as though we were playing house. The vision was great, but we didn't really know yet how to get there. And the clock was ticking.

We were scouting for beautiful homes, and shooting design scenes, and talking to architects and builders, and programming away. And it wasn't coherent yet. We knew it. And the pressure was building. I had wanted to feel the steel, to be out on the edge. The steel came.

Stever was the first to bolt. He had been thinking about his life goals, he announced. They didn't match with what he was doing at BuildingBlocks. What's more, he had understood we would have more money in by October, and he couldn't see that happening. Things were too fluid, too undefined. Anyway, we didn't really need him yet as a manager, he said, and he didn't want to do programming. It was time to go.

"The bottom line is, I don't have faith in the schedule, and I can't work on a schedule I don't have faith in," he said.

We couldn't wave a wand and make the schedule work, but we begged him to stay long enough to help us finish the prototype. Shawn Becker was still finishing his doctorate at MIT, so Stever was all the full-time technical horsepower we had. He agreed, honorably lashed himself in long enough to build the prototype, and was gone.

"Don't sweat it. It's no big deal," Gene Barton counseled us when we called, groaning to have already lost a team member. It happens, he said. Get over it. "He won't leave a hole. Move on."

And we did. But the giddy days had passed very quickly. And the pressure moved in, bigtime.

"How would a divorce work into this picture?" Rolly joked grimly one night when we were back at the office after dinner, working late as usual. He and Carole had fought the night before, he said. She had ended up sleeping alone in their new guest bed, in the bedroom we had just vacated. Not good.

And then he told me a story about why we had to succeed.

We had to succeed, he said, because this was a gold rush. And if you went on a gold rush, you had to come home with gold, or else everyone thought you were a feckless fool. Worse than that, he said, come home without gold and you were positively offensive to people.

The day before, he said, he had run into the parents of an old day care classmate of Kendra's. They knew he was starting a new company, and they asked how it was going. Rolly usually answered with an enthusiastic "Things are great, things are terrific." But Stever had just resigned, and Rolly was feeling low, and he had glumly launched into a little spiel about how hard it was getting started, how many hills there were to climb, how success was so very far from guaranteed.

"And you know, I looked at their faces," he told me, "and none of that registered. None of it. They didn't want to hear it. Nobody wants to hear about an entrepreneur that doesn't make it. It fucks up their myths. It's not the story line they love.

"God help any poor bastard who does fail."

Fail? In all the time we had been working together, I had never heard him use that word before. And we sat quietly for a minute in our church office, with its folding desks and stacking chairs and midnight coming on.

Jim Righter, Rolly's old architecture instructor, was designing a "camp" off the coast of Maine for Ed Anderson, a partner at North Bridge Venture Partners. Jim had seen our demo, liked it, liked Rolly, and suggested we talk to Ed and get his advice on raising money. Ed met us early one October morning in his sleek offices above Route 128. Bill Geary, another of the four partners in the firm, joined us.

Both had boyish features. Ed had the lilting clip of Yankee aristocracy in his voice. Bill was an edge-of-the-chair type, lots of energy. They introduced North Bridge in a warm, easygoing tone. I knew this was just supposed to be an advisory meeting, but I liked these guys. As they talked, I began to imagine that they had read our business plan and were overwhelmed with an urgent desire to invest in us.

North Bridge did active, early-stage investing, they said. They got their hands dirty with the firms they worked with, really got involved. They were just closing a new $80 million investment fund. They always came in as a minority investor, rarely owning more than twenty percent of a company. They came in expecting to work with a company for four to six years, until a "liquidity event," the sale of the company or a public stock offering that would make the company's value liquid and let them take their profits.

We listened with interest, then gave an overview of what we were up to. Consumer expectations in housing were changing. People wanted unique, high-quality homes. Manufacturers were making the best products ever but couldn't get them in front of consumers effectively. Home Depot and the big warehouse stores had come in and killed a lot of showrooms. Most consumers were seeing only a fraction of the great product options that were available. In the nick of time, here comes the digital revolution. Affluent consumers are getting wired up, ready to learn, communicate, and buy online. That's the situation we were addressing. We would bring greater efficiency and convenience to choosing products in this big industry.

Ed and Bill nodded along politely, but they were clearly listening for something they were not hearing.

"What is the value-adding proposition of your product?" asked Ed. "Give it to me in one sentence."

I glibly gave them the line on the front of our latest business plan.

"We're creating the digital destination for home design decision-making and commerce," I said.

They stared quizzically, as if to say "Is that it? Is that as concrete as it gets?" I shot a hopeful look at Rolly, but he offered no miracle line to plug the gap.

"Well, let's look at the demo," said Ed, still all avuncular and friendly. We showed them. And Ed leaned back in his chair thoughtfully.

"That's a great UI," he said — UI for "user interface." "In fact, that may be the best I've ever seen. But don't assume that the reaction your great interface gets from people like me means you've got a great business proposition."

Then he laid it out for us. We weren't going to get anything like a $5 million valuation from our next investors in BuildingBlocks, he said. Maybe $3 million, tops.

Advertising-based schemes on the Internet weren't working out, said Geary. To him, it looked as if we were an information aggregator. He said it with a sympathetic look, but it sounded as though he was describing something just above garbage collector or tin scavenger.

They could see the disappointment in our faces.

"Maybe you really don't want to go the VC route," said Ed. "But if you do, don't feel bad about what you have to give up in equity. We've built plenty of companies that ended up with values of six or seven hundred million dollars, and the founders go away with ten percent feeling very good indeed."

Ten percent! We shifted uncomfortably in our chairs. The meeting was ending. They were smart and experienced and kind. But they couldn't see our value-adding proposition. God help us.

"Maybe you should raise another million from friends and family," Ed said as we packed up the laptop. "You could get your product built, then come back to the VC channel."

We walked to the car in silence. Another million from friends and family! Exactly what million would that be?

"I feel like I just got hit in the back of the head with a two-by-four," Rolly said. "We can't even articulate our value-add!"

We drove back to the office, parked, and slumped into the sub shop for lunch. Stever was already gone. Shawn's Ph.D. work was taking longer than expected, so he still wasn't around much. Rolly and I were working every night and every weekend, but the money was dribbling away faster than we could work. It wasn't clear now that we had the resources to get the product built. And Ed Anderson couldn't see our value-add, the essential value-adding proposition that would make BuildingBlocks a moneymaker.

This was not a pretty picture.

"I'm ordering lunch," Rolly said, "and I feel like I should be throwing up."

From the next table I heard a familiar riff of Internet babble, about servers and GIFs and download times. Two young guys, Dag and Tak, with their own new Internet company around the corner. My God, I thought, everybody's starting an Internet company. You can't go out for a sandwich without running into another crew jumping into the gold rush. Dag mentioned he had been married for a year and felt as though he had almost never seen his wife. Life was work. Just work.

I knew the feeling, I said. And I was diving in with three kids. I had just missed most of Ben's school concert the night before, the latest of a quickly mounting heap of missed moments.

Tak looked over. I knew he was trying to guess my age.

"It's a risky business," he finally said. "I don't know if I would have the guts to do it in your shoes."

Pass the barf bag.

* * *

It got worse before it got better. It was October. Our burn rate was still $75,000 a month. We had a quarter million left in the bank.

And there was another burn rate, too, that we began to sense early on. A burn rate isn't just the speed of money burning. It's the combustion of time, of stores of energy, of hope, of belief, of hours that might have been spent with a child or lover or a spade in the garden. It's the combustion of one's body and soul being fed willingly into a goal, an undertaking, a mission, being fed into the flame. Sometimes that was a great feeling. We would blaze and feed the flame, and with it we would forge something excellent and new. And sometimes it just felt like burning alive, like all that remained at last might be ashes.

We were new to this. We were learning on the job. We were struggling. The strain started to show. Rolly and I were working nonstop — seven days a week, all hours — struggling to turn the key in the lock, to find the right way ahead. We were tired and alarmed and beginning to feel cornered. Rats in a barrel. Frustrated. Fuming.

One rainy morning, we were doing a photo shoot at a huge new house Gwen had just finished building in Newton. It was pristine. Buyers were already lining up. But it was still empty. We were trying out a complex new formula for photographing scenes that would let our users later manipulate them, integrating different products to create the look they wanted. It was difficult, painstaking work, and Rolly was holding most of the math in his head, working with his photographer brother-in-law, Randy, who had agreed to help out.

Gwen was giving me a tour of the house, with its enormous kitchen and old-fashioned pantry and palatial master bedroom. And I was learning more about her, too. How she had been the first female "copyboy" at the *Globe* years earlier, how she had spent large stretches of her youth in Italy, how close she came to marrying a fiery young Italian before she quailed, a month before the wedding, and eloped with an American twelve years her senior, Marshall, now her husband.

We moved back into the empty living room, talking animatedly about Italy and impetuous love and how we might shoot different rooms, different homes. Rolly and Randy were deep in the calculation of a particularly difficult shot. Our conversation was intruding. Rolly got pulled into both conversations, losing his train of thought.

"We've decided all this before!" he suddenly barked, too stressed and tired for tact.

"I don't think so!" I barked back, and we were at it. Chest to chest. Flaming over completely forgettable details of planning, schedules, priorities, over nothing and everything. I couldn't believe his bitter tone. He couldn't believe my muleheadedness. It was spinning out of control.

"Asshole!" I muttered, and turned on my heel. Maybe it was time to take a drive. Get some distance. Cool off.

Rolly followed me out into the car, and it went right on.

"Sometimes I feel like breaking your fucking nose!" I seethed, gripping the steering wheel, turning to him. "What the fuck is up with you, exploding like that?"

"And sometimes I feel like breaking yours right back," he said.

"Look, we're working ourselves silly. I know it's stressful," I said, trying to step away from the flame. "But we have to be civil with each other. We have to."

It wasn't that easy. The night before we had sat with a new acquaintance, Nick d'Arbeloff, talking about how we could simplify our product, our business model. Nick had suggested we move to a simple online catalogue of products for the home. Clean. Quick. Get it out. I had nodded along casually. We clearly needed to think about simplifying. But Rolly had taken that nod as a full readiness to jettison our vision of a grander context for understanding design tradeoffs and making good choices.

"I saw you agreeing with Nick, and I couldn't believe it," he said now. "We have to simplify, but not like that."

"And I'm not suggesting we become just a catalogue company," I said. "But we do have to simplify, because nobody's getting this. Not the VCs, not Nick. We've built this elaborate palace in our minds and it's got dozens of wings and splendid rooms. But it's too big, and we've got to whack it down, no matter how hard that is."

"Don't say that like I'm the only one adding wings!" Rolly shot back. "Jesus, you're always throwing out some wild new idea, with no idea what the technical implications are of accomplishing it. It makes me nuts sometimes! And then I saw you nodding along with Nick, and I felt betrayed."

"You are not betrayed. We are in this together, about as deep as we can be. But we cannot clash like this. What is our staff supposed to think if we're duking it out in the middle of everything else we have to deal with? It's impossible."

And we breathed deeply and went back and put our heads down and kept working.

One after another, people helped us through. People like Nick d'Arbeloff.

Nick was a tall, rangy, high-intensity marketing pro, a little younger than we were, with a cool laser stare and an analytical approach to business. He came from a famous family of Boston entrepreneurs. His father had started the Millipore Corporation, an early high-tech success in Massachusetts. His uncle had founded Teradyne, a leading high-tech testing company headquartered in Boston. Nick had been part of the founding team of Wildfire, a local startup funded by Greylock and Matrix that produced an electronic telephone assistant service. Now the management at Wildfire was "evolving," new economy style, and Nick was beginning to look for a new company to get involved with. We had met him six months earlier through a mutual friend. Then he called out of the blue.

Nick got us back to basics. Back to our customers: consumers and manufacturers, and the design professionals who worked with them. We weren't ready to buy his first suggestion, an online product catalogue. So he rolled up his sleeves and took us back out into the market. To talk again, in depth, with consumers, our primary target users. And to talk again, in depth, with manufacturers. He disciplined us to listen and to think coolly about what we heard.

And the messages came up clear and compelling again in interview after interview. Consumers wanted an easier, more convenient, and effective way to learn their product options and act on what they learned. They were frustrated by the scavenger hunt they currently faced in trying to figure out what products were available and how to get them. Even architects and interior designers, experienced professionals, had trouble keeping up with the gusher of products and product information.

On the other side of the equation, manufacturers wanted a better way to get their products and product information in front of consumers who wanted to learn about them. Physical showrooms were great, necessary even, but they didn't begin to show all the options. And they didn't give manufacturers a way to get their message to interested, or "prequalified," shoppers. We could.

Another thing we heard again and again, especially from consumers and professionals, when we were done with the interviewing and let them see the demo, the prototype, what we were doing. They loved it. They wanted it, in full-blown product form, right now. Simple as that. They needed it. It was exciting. How soon could they have it?

"There are your marching orders," said Nick. "Don't pursue a vision so elaborate that it saps resources and is complicated to use. You've got a great concept here. Rein in it. Get a single focus."

And another thing, he said. Boot the name New American DreamHome. It's not what people are asking for. He was right. Everyone we talked to wanted a way to find the right products and save them to a scrapbook for planning projects and purchases. That original insight was resoundingly confirmed. We would let them do that online and call the product something relevant.

We had been working with Jennifer Karin, a public relations consultant, on the right name. Scrapbook seemed too rough, electronic showroom too cold. We needed something personal, something that acknowledged the importance people attached to these decisions. What about portfolio? Home portfolio?

We ran to the computer and pulled up the Internet to see if the domain name was already taken. When we had started chasing this dream, almost every domain name had been available. Now, even the most obscure names were being snatched up.

We waited impatiently for the answer, maybe a full minute.

It was free!

So there it was. Home Portfolio. It would help consumers find and save the products they wanted and help manufacturers get deeper information, instantly, to people who wanted it. We shoved the words together to leave no doubt about the Web address.

HomePortfolio.

At www.homeportfolio.com.

Awesome!

Art called, inviting us over for lunch. Just seeing him, rippling with experience and warmth, lifted our spirits. He listened to our concerns tumble out, then made it simple.

"It's hard. I know it's hard," he said. "Just focus on the product. Get it built. Sell it. You need your proof of concept. Build the product. Sell the product. You can do it. You're closer than you think. Keep going."

"The gods are trying to soothe and calm us," I said to Rolly as we left Art's office. It was the closest we had come to talking about our near fistfight.

"Yup," he said, shaking his hair back and exhaling big. "I do believe they are."

Then Len weighed in. He took us to lunch at the B-school Faculty Club. It was gleaming, all elegant carpets and rich paneling and proud, highback chairs and huge birch logs at the ready in the fireplace. He sat us down at a table overlooking the Charles River and fixed his blazing eyes on us. There was more fire than twinkle in his eyes that day.

"Fellas, it's time to come to Jesus," he said. And he proceeded to lay out story after story of young companies that had lost their way, been blinded by distractions, failed to focus on the right questions.

"Here's the question for you," he said, locking eyes on us hard. "How will you really and truly make money? Don't give me all the big picture stuff. Just tell me this: What is the little engine at the heart of BuildingBlocks that will go and go and go and make . . . the . . . money?

"I believe it's in there," he said. "You go figure out what it is. Right now. It's time. And you'll be fine."

It was early morning after another late, fevered night. The elevator to our fifth-floor office in the church was dead slow. The slowest I had ever ridden. And when the door finally creaked open, it opened straight into our office. No vestibule, no reception desk. Just boom — smack into the middle of the office.

And there was Rolly, already pacing and whirling in mad scientist mode, hair pushed high off his forehead, looking like Mozart after a wild night of composing. He had taken our July version of the business plan, our most recent version, and marked it up until after midnight, then gone home and marked it up some more. Now he was striding under the big old industrial skylight in the center of the room and waving the plan and bellowing.

"This is so rinky-dink!"

He slapped the plan up against the wall and slashed at more lines with his pen, laughing and shaking his head and groaning, scribbling more notes in the margin.

"We've been shipping out mush! Lots of pretty words that never said what we are really creating, never said straight out what it is. And so we didn't know!"

He had been devouring Geoffrey Moore's *Crossing the Chasm*, the bible of high-tech marketing. We took Moore's "elevator test": Could we explain our product in the time it takes to ride up in an elevator? No.

So we dived in again on the product description and the plan, boiling everything down and down to its essentials. We slashed and burned and cheered when we threw out entire passages. And something far cleaner began to emerge from the rubble.

The first thing consumers wanted was not 3D modeling and lots of technical bells and whistles. The first thing they wanted was a better way to go shopping, to know their product options, and to have a context for making choices. They were busy people. They didn't want to schlep to showrooms all weekend, wait hours for sketchy sales help, and still feel they didn't really know their options. Home-Portfolio, we said, would not be a mere catalogue but a system for finding, selecting, and learning how and where to buy — maybe online and maybe not — the world's best home design products. It would be a service for finding everything consumers chose visually for the home, from windows and wallpaper to faucets and fixtures and furnishings. We would show them all the best products on the market, independently chosen by our own editors. And when they found products they liked, we would let them save them to their own online portfolio, and let them ask sponsoring manufacturers for more information electronically, and receive it instantly, online.

Simple, we said. Shopping. Shopping for the complex "considered purchases" that outfitting a home required. This was the little ring through which everything would flow. Other features? Sure, we had imagined plenty. But first we would nail this. It was ambitious enough.

And we wrote our elevator pitch:

"For consumers and trade professionals, HomePortfolio is the first online guide to premium-tier home design products. It's the fastest, easiest way to find the products people want for their homes.

"For manufacturers, HomePortfolio is a new direct marketing channel. It helps them reach and prequalify sales prospects online."

And the little moneymaking machine at the center of it all? We would charge manufacturers for helping them deliver deeper product and purchasing information to consumers and professionals at exactly the moment they wanted it. If they made a great product, we would show it and describe it at no charge. But if they wanted to be able to offer deeper information, instantly, within HomePortfolio, they would pay for that new marketing channel. We were offering a brand-new way to get their product information to people who wanted it, at precisely the moment they wanted it, at a fraction of their current costs of responding to requests for information.

There was our value-add.

And we believed manufacturers would pay gladly. Paper-and-ink brochures were punishingly expensive to produce and mail and difficult to keep in stock and up-to-date. Individual company Web sites were hell to surf through one by one, presenting consumers with a cacophony of different voices and formats — if consumers could find them at all. The people we surveyed tried going from company site to company site, and they hated it. HomePortfolio would give them a one-stop destination on the Web for finding the products they wanted. We would focus on premium-tier products only, because those were the most difficult to find and learn about in the physical world. And when the market was ready to move to online ordering, we would be ready, too. Manufacturers could fill orders directly or through their local retailers. Either way, we would take the order. Everybody would win.

Excellent! This would work. It was a far cry from the grand vision that had made us run howling and punch-drunk through the woods in the early days. It was a long way from capturing all of Xanadu and the glory of the *Star Wars* page. But we didn't live in Xanadu. Not yet. We lived here. And we had to eat here, and raise families here, and hold marriages together here. The glorious big picture would have to wait. This was a clean, simple approach that investors would surely understand. And none too soon. We had a big VC meeting in two days.

Steve Coit of Charles River Ventures had been tracking us since the spring. Calling. Meeting. Keeping up. Steve was a whirlwind. He thought fast and talked fast and skipped so many mundane steps in the process that you had to pay very close attention to keep up. Sculpted Scandinavian features with a sharp touch of Russian steppe around the eyes. Hello Attila. On the side, he told us, he was an avid painter. I pictured him at his easel, painting, very fast. Sharp strokes.

And today we were presenting to his board, the partners of Charles River Ventures. We had covered our white board from side to side with a huge planning exercise outlining our presentation. Tom Timko, Rolly's old pal, had come to work it through with us. He loved the new business plan.

"It looks great, radically improved," he said. "Investors don't want all the flowery stuff. It makes them think somebody's trying to take them. They want the essential proposition. And I think you've finally got it."

We hoped so. We were on our way. Back to the Magic Mountain, the same serene hilltop office complex above the reservoir and Route 128 that housed Matrix and Andy Markuvitz.

"Refuse to lose!" said Rolly as we headed in.

"Grin to win!" I answered.

And we gave them our new story. Top to bottom. With overhead projector slides, our new elevator pitch, the demo, the works. We

were looking for $3 million to make it happen, we said. They nod-
ded. They asked lots of questions. They bored in hard, but we felt
ready.

And we came out feeling good. Solid.

Very interesting, they had said. Quite intriguing. They would decide at their next partners' meeting, in four days.

And this time we weren't pulling anything off the table.

I liked talking with Arthur Walworth. He was ninety-four. He had
won the Pulitzer Prize for his biography of Woodrow Wilson before
I was born. He lived now in an exclusive retirement facility that must
have cost him a fortune. It was populated with a remarkable concentration of distinguished writers and thinkers and former business ti-
tans. Like me, Arthur had spent an important piece of his youth in
China. He was wise and well spoken. His mind was brilliantly clear,
with a long perspective that I found deeply comforting. He invited
me for dinner to talk about my new venture, and I ended up looking
for life advice from a man born at the turn of the last century. Who
else could I share my uncertainties with?

"It's such a big change, Arthur," I said. "I don't know if I'm doing
the right thing. I'm full of optimism, but it's impossible to know how
it will turn out. Here I am in the middle of my life taking a flying
leap. Am I crazy? Did you ever have the urge to do it?"

He took his time answering, thinking quietly before he did.

"These times of great change always bring out the entrepreneurs,
the risk-takers," he said. "And they leave winners and they leave losers. Losers because things are changing so fast and are so unsettled
that you can't know which path really leads ahead and which path
will end up a dead end."

He paused. No dead ends for me, please, I thought.

"My grandfather invested an enormous amount of money in a
project of Thomas Edison's that ended up a total bust. He lost everything. And I remember growing up with Edna Stanley, right here in
Newton. When automobiles were becoming popular, her father invented the Stanley Steamer. Oh, it was a wonderful thing. But it depended on horse troughs being around for its source of water. And

of course the more popular automobiles became, the fewer horses there were. And the Stanley Steamer just faded right away."

He was lost in memory for a moment. And I was lost in the notion of a Thomas Edison project going bust. Damn. It could happen to anybody! Then Arthur turned back to me.

"Look at your life, Tom," he said. "You've been an adventurer from early on. Off to India, to Alaska, to Hong Kong, and all the rest. Maybe it's from growing up on the farm, longing for wider horizons. I don't know. But it looks to me as though it may be in your blood."

He chuckled and sighed.

"Fact is," he said, looking right into my eyes and laughing softly, "you may not have much choice in the matter."

"Oh, that's a hoot, Arthur," I said. "That's just a hoot."

Chapter 11

Splatto

I FELL IN LOVE with FedEx.

Its truck always came on time. Its stacks of big, bright envelopes were so smooth and crisp and businesslike. And free! FedEx was efficient. FedEx was dependable. FedEx was always there. Some days, in the rush and frenzy and messiness of starting up, FedEx was the only crisp, clean, calming thing I knew.

Every day now, in the middle of everything else going on, we would rush and sweat to prepare a fresh stack of business plans to go out to potential investors around the country. We would line up the FedEx envelopes on the big table in the main room, and get all the shipping labels filled out just so, and, always on deadline, slip our plans — our lives! — into those fine, crisp, cardboard envelopes that sealed so very perfectly, and run to the FedEx box at six twenty-five on the dot to slide that beautiful stack of neatly packaged hope into the mouth of the pickup box like a temple offering. And it was the best moment of every day.

FedEx would deliver. Absolutely. And tomorrow those recipients, in their gleaming, paneled offices stuffed with money, would not see a desperate little band of wild-eyed visionaries sweating and praying on the top floor of an old church by the turnpike. Not at all! They would see a clean, crisp FedEx envelope that said efficiency, that said certainty and dependability. It was magic. I loved FedEx.

We weren't just waiting for Charles River Ventures. We were showering the plan on other VCs from New York to California. We were pulling Shawn Becker away from his dissertation every moment we could to bang out software code for the very first version — the alpha version — of HomePortfolio. We were designing and planning and testing and talking to professionals and consumers and manufacturers, getting their advice and feedback, sixteen hours a day.

But we were also waiting for Charles River. They were our best hope. On the morning of the day their partners were deciding what to do with BuildingBlocks, we were headed north to a meeting, driving up Route 128 right across the big, pine-ringed reservoir from the Magic Mountain where they would sit behind shining glass, debating our future.

"I bet they're up there talking about BuildingBlocks right now!" Rolly said as we sped along in traffic. And we lunged for the car windows and leaned out, laughing like maniacs, yelling at the top of our lungs, waving and punching thumbs-up across the wide, wide water.

"Pleeeeeeease!"

"Hoooooockeeeeey stiiiiiiiiick!"

"Sell it, Steeeeevieeeeee!"

Steve Coit called three days later. He had a response for us, he said. It was positive, he said, "but not the full bite.

"I'm going to suggest we formalize a relationship around a small amount of money," he said. Our phone connection was a little crackly. He was on his cell phone, as usual.

"We want to see whether you really need the Nantucket sleigh ride, big harpoon-sized chunk of money or not."

Nantucket sleigh ride? Full bite? Harpoon-sized? I loved the way these guys talked. I shot a laughing glance at Rolly, but he was completely focused on the speakerphone.

"We think there's something here, but we're not sure what yet. Why don't we loan you $250,000 and take three to six months to hammer out exactly what's here. If we decide to go ahead, we'll pull in another VC to do the valuation. Right now, you look to us like a publishing venture. We can imagine that turning into a very profitable $25 million company. But publications don't usually go public. They saturate a market and reap profits, but their growth is intrinsically capped. We'd like to see you develop the service side of your plan more fully. Then we can imagine a much larger upside potential. No cap. Which means you can go public and there's much more money to be made."

He hung up for half a minute to pick up his daughter. A loan? For small money? Steve was right back on the phone.

"I like the idea of a future that includes transactions," he said. "Pick a category. Don't try to boil the ocean. Look at wallpaper. Something you can ship. We'll work with you to get a plan together. And if we succeed, we can raise $5 million for you in two weeks. Nothing simpler."

A fat crackle of static broke in and we lost him.

"I haven't heard anything that's a vision-killer," I said tentatively, hoping that Rolly saw a big silver lining in here somewhere.

"Yeah, but it's making me sick," Rolly said.

Steve was back.

"So look, you're on our hot list," he said. "At the same time, I want to make it clear there is no guarantee in this. If it doesn't work out, it's a loan. We won't be unctuous about it, but it is a loan. But let me tell you, I don't embark on one of these things unless I'm awfully sure we're going to get there."

And that was it.

Jesus.

We put on our coats and went for a walk. It was gratifying to finally have some positive VC feedback. We were on Charles River's hot list. Yes! That sounded good. But this deal! The pits! It meant our committing to them without their committing to us. Getting engaged with no promise of marriage. If it all worked out, great. But if anything went wrong and they didn't end up investing, we would have blown critical months. Our seed money would be gone and we would owe Charles River money! We might not be able to survive.

We couldn't risk it. We waited over the weekend, then called Steve back to say no thanks. We'd like to work with you, we said. We know Charles River is a top-tier, first-class VC. We respect that. But we don't want to take the loan. We're confident we're going to be funded soon, we said. (And by whom? I wondered.) We felt that taking this deal would be a step backward.

Don't decide that too quickly, Steve said. Charles River was ready to roll up its sleeves and work with us. We shouldn't take that lightly.

Okay. We'd think about it.

"We can't take this deal," said Rolly when we hung up. "It would look completely weak. We're beyond that, and we've got to make that point. There's no telling what directions this deal could take us off in. We're much better off drawing our line in the sand."

"Yeah," I said. "As long as we don't die on the sand."

Now the FedEx packages went out in really tall stacks. We shipped business plans to every investment outfit where we had the thinnest thread of an introduction or connection or just a good vibe from something we had read. This was getting serious. Shawn was still finishing his thesis, carving out time for BuildingBlocks whenever he could, but struggling to get the degree wrapped up. And we were spending so much time trying to raise money that we couldn't sink ourselves into building the product. Katherine and Eric were struggling along, beginning to build a database of great home design products, but we were so wrapped up in fund-raising that we weren't giving them much support. Katherine was stressed. She wanted to be off weaving birch and willow lamps. She was here out of personal loyalty to Rolly, but Rolly was getting mighty prickly some days. Gwen was pitching in gamely too, but we didn't really have the resources to make our goals. It was all getting to be a nasty chicken and egg salad: not enough money to develop the product and not enough product to raise the money.

Some days it was so bad it was funny, and Rolly and I would drag Katherine into the big room and grab empty bottles from the water cooler for drums and dance and drum and sing around her like idiots while she turned like a Maypole.

"Katherine, queen of the birch and willow!" we would hoot and sing. Into the void.

Between crazed bursts of activity, we were despondent. Rick Segal was going to call one day very soon, and what were we going to say?

"They're going to ask us what the fuck we did with half a million dollars," I groaned. "And what are we going to tell them? We blew it trying to figure out what the hell we were doing?"

"Yup, that's us," Rolly intoned, banging away at the product designs piling up in his computer and wearily spoofing the marketing slogans we had been working to craft. "BuildingBlocks," he said, "the company that talks about making things."

I got so desperate, I even shipped a plan to the top guys at the *Globe*. We were hardly their kind of business, but who knew? We knocked everywhere. And the echo that came back was everywhere the same: we looked like Internet content, and Internet content was going nowhere. So scram.

"You know, we're not really content," Rolly said one afternoon when we were laying out the Web site and another raft of "no thank you" letters had come in the mail.

"What we really are is objects. Why can't people get that? It's the central theme of our time. The falling of the wall between content and structure. Content fused with functionality. Object orientation. It's going to change everything. Why is that so hard to get?"

"Maybe it's not," I said, knowing full well that nine out of ten people I talked to had no idea what object orientation was about. "Let's run with it!"

I riffed off in a space adventure sendup. "We are objects, beamed here from a different galaxy, more advanced than your own!"

It wasn't funny, but we needed to laugh at something. We were marooned in some dark corner of the universe. Rolly sat bolt upright and spoke into his fist.

"Greetings, earthlings! This is your Star Trek commander speaking. Speaking about objects. Hello? Hello? Our signal is breaking up!"

And it was.

"I'm still trying to figure out how to get off the dime with you guys."

It was Coit again. On the cell phone. Charles River had just met a high-powered woman who was in charge of personal online services for AT&T. A real hotshot, Steve said. One of the core team that had built CNBC. Background with King World and JC Penney. A big wheel at AT&T, but antsy there.

Her name was Caroline Vanderlip.

VCs are always doing matchmaker work. Charles River had met her, been impressed, and thought of us.

"We told her you were a couple of real smart guys with a very interesting idea," he said. "She's expecting your call. Maybe she'd get involved somehow. She's marrying a guy in Boston. Maybe she'd be interested in something up here. Maybe with you. She's the CEO type. I can tell you, having her involved would certainly help with funding."

Caroline Vanderlip. What a name! Sounded like Jackie Onassis. We hadn't heard of her, but a quick check of Nexis by a journalist pal pulled up tons of stories. Keynote speaker here. Quoted authority there. She was big stuff.

I called. It was the Tuesday before Thanksgiving. Her secretary in New Jersey acted as if she were taking a note for the president of the United States. An hour later, Caroline Vanderlip called. All business. Very uptown New York. Almost brusque. Yes, Charles River had mentioned us. She was in Boston for the holiday. I asked if we could get together. Glad to, she said. Tomorrow morning. Ten o'clock.

"Jesus! Tomorrow morning?" Rolly jolted when I told him, as if he saw a thunderbolt coming. "We've got to clean up this dump!"

I hadn't thought of it for weeks, but the office was a wreck. Papers strewn everywhere. Computer boxes still stacked where they'd been unpacked. Teetering piles of product catalogues. A little too much creative ferment. We raced around that night putting books on the shelves, watering wilted plants, freaking out. Here we were, two guys and a tiny team in a sty of an office, and she was from the corporate big leagues!

Caroline Vanderlip! Coit had spoken of her with such reverence. Was he suggesting we try to woo this senior VP at AT&T to be our CEO? Assuming she would even remotely consider it, what kind of trip would that launch us on? We had never heard of her before yesterday!

On the other hand, said Rolly, if she somehow didn't like what we were doing, thought it was dumb, we were screwed forever with Charles River and maybe other VCs, too. If Caroline Vanderlip gave us a thumbs-down, think how that would ripple out!

We clearly hadn't been getting out enough. Our nerves were frayed. We were starting to hyperventilate.

"Look," I said, groping for any calming thought. "She's, she's . . .
lucky to be talking to us! Yeah! Any bigshot would be. If you want
to earn the golden nimbus these days, you've got to do it with a
cool startup. So what if she's been with AT&T? No bigshot manager really earns their stripes these days unless they propel some
smart startup into a hot item. That's the only thing that counts.
Look at Jim Barksdale and Netscape. Hell, Caroline Vanderlip needs
BuildingBlocks! She needs to make some whippersnapper great.
Why not us? We shouldn't be kowtowing. We're in the catbird seat!"

Rolly was staring off, listening, taking some comfort, it seemed,
from my chest-beating tirade. It was time for sleep.

She called the next morning at quarter of ten. Caught in a conference call. Running ten minutes late. We dithered and cleaned up one
last time. It was shaggy but presentable. Good enough.

The elevator door gave its gasping ding, and Caroline Vanderlip
swept in. Long gray coat. Looked tailored. Red scarf. Medium-long
blond hair, a little wiry and clearly lightened. An attractive face
with an appealing smile of straight teeth and probing blue eyes. But
not the face of a sweetypie. Not close. This was someone who had
crossed the Badlands, had stood in front of demanding boards, had
fought in the world. A force. Good, I thought. Perfect.

We said our hellos, took her coat and scarf. Rolly ran out to Appassionato for coffee. Four months here and we still didn't have a
coffeepot. God, we were out of it. Caroline and I sat down and I slid
her our standard nondisclosure agreement. Three pages of legal lan-
guage promising that the signee would not rip off our ideas. Caroline was an Internet executive on the prowl for new turf. She couldn't
sign lightly, so read attentively for a few minutes. I watched her face.
Clean. Calm. Determined. Better than FedEx. Way better.

Rolly stepped in with her coffee. She cracked the lid and it was
showtime.

"Okay," she said. "Who are you guys? And what are you up to?"

And we gave her the whole story, all the way back to college room-
mate days. And our accidental reconnection. And our restless paths
intertwining. And the vision, the dream, of using the Internet to remake the way people dreamed about and planned and acted on new

homes and home improvements. We showed her the demo, and the prototype, and the alpha version that we were crunching to finish. We told her about all the learning we had done in Boston and across the country, digging in with consumers and professionals and manufacturers, listening to exactly what they wanted, refining our product design to match their needs. And she turned everything inside out and upside down, probing, challenging, testing.

We'd been going for three hours straight when she pulled up out of the conversation, leaned back in her chair, crossed her arms on her chest, and set her jaw. A verdict was coming. If she shot us down, we were whacked. Stripped. Cooked.

"Guys," she said, staring each of us full in the face. "The thinking you've done here is incredible. Fabulous. You're aggregating content that's never been aggregated before. You're targeting, creating even, a great community around that content. And you're doing it with lots of personalization. That's your answer to churn, to differentiation, to loyalty. I think this can be huge. Enormous."

"Is it something you might consider getting involved with?" Rolly asked tentatively.

"That would depend . . . ," she said, glancing at her watch. "Oh my God! Three hours! Mark is going to kill me!"

Her fiancé was waiting in the car.

"Listen," she said, scooping up her coat and a copy of our business plan. "I love it. I'll call you. We'll talk."

And she was on the elevator. The instant the door slid closed, we broke into a war dance under the big skylight. Yelping and whirling. Loud high fives. We weren't crazy. This was a good idea. Smart people would get it. Caroline Vanderlip got it! She could have been our executioner, and instead she loved it!

The rest of the day was bathed in rosy hues as we basked in the afterglow of her attentions. What a Thanksgiving gift! Maybe we were turning a corner here.

Eric Westby quit. He was hired away by a big magazine with a real payroll and other staff to talk to. It hurt whenever someone bailed.

"And then they were five," Rolly said. We were shrinking!

But not everyone was cut out for this walk through the bush. We understood that. And, it trimmed our burn rate a welcome bit. Shawn's brother Chris was a designer and came in to help us out. We kept slogging.

We needed the alpha, the first, version of the product desperately. We hadn't abandoned the CD-ROM, but instead had linked it to the Internet. A company called Marimba in Palo Alto had come out with a great software product called Castanet, one of the "push" products so hot that season. We weren't using Castanet to push content to users, but rather to let them update a desktop version of HomePortfolio over the Internet. Drop in the HomePortfolio CD-ROM starter kit with Castanet and it would engage your hard drive and call out to the Web for updates. Very cool. We would have a straight Web site version of HomePortfolio and also offer Home-Portfolio in a full-blown desktop software application with a more elaborate interface. Just as soon as we could get it all built.

Rick Segal's secretary called. Could we come down to White Plains on December 23 to bring Rick up-to-date?

Sure. No problem. We'll be there.

Help!

"We need a million dollars," Rolly said. "We need a million dollars to bring this product out. We need a million dollars or Rick takes control of the company. It's right there in the deal."

A million dollars. No problem. We'll just call up the million-dollar shop and order a million dollars. Done.

We had just over $200,000 left in the bank. We kept pushing.

Jeff Hurst was coming in, from Commonwealth Capital. Another VC. Gene Barton had hooked us up. Jeff was a big fellow with a big laugh and a blunt way with words. He roared in with the December cold still in his big coat, looked around, grunted, and made himself at home at our Staples folding table.

Commonwealth had looked at four hundred Internet business proposals in the last year, he said, skipping the formalities.

"And let me tell you," he said, "we usually just pee all over them. Everybody walks in and says they'll need $3 million to $5 million and they'll put up the Web site and it will work. For eighteen months, that's what we've been hearing. And I'm not saying some of them didn't find funding. And some of them got revenue from American

Express or Coke or some other giant with a budget to dabble in this stuff. But it's not real. It's just play money. Ninety percent of these guys will go to the end of that false revenue and that will be the end. Poof. Gone."

He gave a big laugh and slapped the table. It rattled.

"I saw your plan and gave it a quick scan and, I've got to tell you, I didn't get too focused. But I passed it on to my partners, and to my surprise, two of them came back and said, 'Hey, let's take a look at this.' Now, that's a very unusual development for a Web plan these days. Very unusual. So I looked again. And you know what? This is a great fucking idea. Great. It can work. I don't doubt it for a minute. The question is, when will it work? Can you get the manufacturers to buy in? How many of them? Which ones? And, more important, can you get eyeballs?"

You need to test it, he said. Throw $750,000 into a test. Get it out there. Get some data. See if the "eyeballs" — an Internet audience — will come. Get the money from somewhere to test it. Maybe AOL. Maybe Apple. Who knows. Somebody.

Not from a venture capital outfit, he said. Not this money. It was too early. It would come too dear.

"To get this money from a VC to do this test is going to cost you your body, your wife, your children!" he said, slapping the table again with another big belly laugh.

Wife? Children? I vaguely remembered them.

"I love it," Caroline said when she called back. "I read the plan. I played with all the related products on the market. You win hands down. There's nothing out there that does what you're trying to do. I love it as much now as I did when I talked to you."

Excellent. Would she consider joining us? We needed "critical mass," Steve Coit had told us. Caroline would add a lot of critical mass, he had said. Rolly was not eager to give up the CEO role. What about a position as president and chief operating officer?

She would think about it, she said. She and Mark were deciding whether they were going to be living in Boston or New York. She liked us. She liked the company. If they decided on Boston, she would be very interested. Very. She would start putting out feelers for us for money. But we'd have to wait a little bit to learn where she and Mark decided to land.

And we were headed back to White Plains, to our date with Rick Segal. December 23. Scott Smith would be there, too.

The roads were jammed with people heading off for the holidays. Not us. Mile after mile we rehearsed how to present the situation we confronted. We didn't need them just to understand. We needed them to put in more money. There was $180,000 left in the bank now. Our burn rate was $60,000 a month. There was precious little time for us to find another backer. We would chase down every prospect, but things were getting tight.

What if they agreed to put more money in? We hadn't even thought about terms. We pulled off the highway. Rolly stood at a battered outdoor phone with the wind whipping his coat to call Gene Barton back in Boston for advice on how a further investment from Rick and Scott might be structured.

We could have saved the thirty-five cents.

The view from the big corner office was gray, but wintry crisp. Rick was polite, cordial. Scott's baby had been up all night, and he had been up with it. He looked as if he was almost nodding off. And Art was there, subdued. There wasn't much chitchat.

Rolly bravely jumped in.

We've been making great progress and we are very optimistic, he said. We've built the HomePortfolio prototype. We're well into product development. We've honed our business model. We have a strong conversation about funding going with Charles River Ventures. We're on their hot list. And we're out to a substantial list of other good VCs. Charles River has been good enough to connect us with Caroline Vanderlip, and she is very interested in joining BuildingBlocks if her new marriage brings her to Boston. We believe the market is ready. The technology we need, like Castanet, is coming onstream just as we need it. Our target niche remains wide open. It's time to accelerate. We really ought to be feeding some more money in right now to crank things up.

Then he breathed.

Good man, Rolly, I thought. Good, brave man.

Scott and Rick nodded approvingly, furrowed their brows thoughtfully. Scott asked the first question.

"Have you signed up any paying manufacturers?"

That cut to the heart of things. We squirmed and danced. Our business model and proposition had been changing so rapidly, we said, that we had not been working at selling lately. Everything was too fluid. And we hadn't had the bandwidth to both build and sell.

Lame, I thought. True, but lame!

Scott listened patiently, then gave his response.

"There isn't a proof of concept here yet," he said, and the meeting could have ended right there. "You need your first vendors to jump in or a major distributor to pick you up, to get you eyeballs. One or the other, to prove this is something people really want. Something they'll lay money down for.

"I know it's a chicken and egg thing," he said. "But somebody has to kick in first."

Rick joined in. We had to have distribution for this product or it wasn't going to work. We needed to strike a deal, right away, with AOL or Microsoft or somebody. Sell them on our goods. Let them worry about distribution.

"Actually, our hope has been to establish our own brand and Internet presence independent of the big guys," Rolly came back. We didn't just want to be cranked through someone else's sausage machine. We wanted to shape our own face to the world.

"That's a tough road," said Rick, clearly not buying it. "You're going to have to hitch up with somebody fast. You're going to have to sell your soul to somebody."

And there it was. The heart of the matter, as sharply drawn as the view out Rick's big windows, as the superrealist paintings on his walls. We had come down this road to find our souls, not to sell them.

"We're not saying you're on the wrong track," Rick said. "You've raised your first money. You've worked hard. You've made good progress . . .

"But right now, you're on a path like this," he said, slanting his flattened hand down from his elbow. This was not a hockey stick. It was a nosedive. I hated looking at that downward slant. Hated it. A distant continent of Buddha statues flashed across my mind, holding their hands in expressions of mercy, of teaching, of welcome. And now this one, with its forearm slanting down in front of its chest. An expression of demise. We had carved this Buddha. It was ours to carve again.

Refuse to lose, I thought. Refuse to lose.

"You've got limited time and limited money and your position is not likely to get a lot stronger without taking these steps," Rick said. "I'd sell out to everybody. I mean, the market's so big, what does it matter?"

Rolly had looked comatose next to me. Now he roused. And he picked up our rehearsed agenda to make a last, vain charge through the day's smoke and ruin. I couldn't believe the nerve it took. He ran straight into their guns.

"So, Rick, the question is, would you guys be interested in coming in with another round of investment? We don't buy your characterization of BuildingBlocks as on a downhill slope. We think we're making great progress and have great prospects. We hear what you're saying today, and we will respond. But we'd like to know if we might look to you for more investment?"

Scott gave their response. It was completely reasonable. It was positive, even generous, in its way. And it left our butts completely in the cold, cold wind.

"I would consider putting in more money if there was a concept validation," he said. "Get customers, or get picked up by an Internet network, and I would certainly consider it."

"That's the silver lining," Rolly said as we headed back north for Christmas Eve. "That's the takeaway. They'll consider putting in more money."

He was incredible. He would refuse to lose.

We took a day off after Christmas. Danielle and I loaded the kids into the van and drove out to central Massachusetts, where our friends Harry and Mary had a cozy little lake cabin in the woods. Harry's sleek woodstove was roaring along with lovely Danish efficiency. A big lunch was over. Our kids were sprawled across the warm floor with theirs, reading, playing chess, staring off at the great mound of Tully Mountain across the lake. We lingered at the table, talking about losing everything.

I had no idea how the next three months were going to play out. Anything could happen. And Harry, a neurologist with a big Boston HMO, had just narrowly missed being laid off. For the first time in his life, he was grappling with the possibility that he — a doctor! — could lose his job. That's something he had never imagined in med school. He wouldn't have believed it six months ago. And then, boom, there it was. Almost on him.

He had just bought sixteen acres of rough land in the woods up along Butterworth Ridge, near New Hampshire. He and Mary had in mind a dream house for the spot. But now he was imagining a different scenario. Not a dream house but a low-cost retreat if his job in Boston should come crashing down. Sell the condo in Cambridge. Cut back on all fronts. Retreat to the woods.

"So that's your Plan Z?" I asked. "That's your survival scenario?"

"That's it," Harry said as we sat in the winter midday candlelight with Mary and Danielle. "God forbid, but if the worst comes, that's what we'd do."

"What's your Plan Z?" he asked, and I immediately wished he hadn't.

"Yes, what is our Plan Z?" Danielle asked, glad somebody else had leaned on the door she had grown wary of touching.

"Well, let's talk about Scheme X first," I said. "I hitch up with journalism again. Maybe in New York. Maybe in Washington. I'll always have that bug. It wouldn't be fun uprooting the kids. And it would feel like a hell of a retreat right now. But if it came to it . . ."

"And what about Plan Z?" Danielle asked again, noticing I hadn't gone there. "And don't tell me it's back to the farm."

"Sorry, sweetheart, but that's what it is. That's Plan Z. You know that nice old shed behind Cynthia's place? I've always liked the way it felt inside, so stark and clean. Almost Japanese."

"Oh, God," said Danielle, gazing off toward the mountain in the mist. She didn't know when I was joking anymore. I didn't either.

"You see, it could be messy," I said. "Unlike your situation, Harry, where you're either employed or unemployed, and the change will be quick and clean when it comes, I will be in a situation where there is always a temptation to hang on a little longer and a little longer in the hope that we might still pull it off. So that if I do have to bail, there may not be much time for the parachute to open. And there may not be much parachute."

Harry grinned across the table, eyes laughing at the vaguely unhinged tone of the conversation.

"Splatto!" he said.

"Splatto," I said, less jovial but somehow in good humor.

"You know, it's strange to admit, but there is something about all this uncertainty that I almost like," I said. "It makes the air feel cleaner. It makes possibilities seem nearer. It makes my soul feel less encrusted, less on autopilot. Sometimes I even feel attracted to having nothing, the monk thing. Do you know what I mean?"

"Definitely," said Mary, who had just left a job at the public television station. "I feel much more open to the world since I left." And she talked about Buddha dharma or something, and we drank more wine. And Danielle stared into the mountain.

The company had $150,000 left. We built the product. It was awesome. We took it to the Builders' Show in Houston again. And they loved it again. But it would take time to close our first deals. We had proposed that manufacturers pay on a performance basis for sales leads. They didn't know how to budget for performance-based pricing. It didn't fit their routine. But they were coming around.

"We need to be spending faster," Rolly told Steve Coit when he called. "It's time."

"I wouldn't," Steve said. "Entrepreneurs always want to build fast. But it's far more important that you know exactly what you're doing, exactly how you're going to win."

But without cash we couldn't crank up, and without cranking up, how could we move ahead?

We were flying west, on another sales call. We had seven weeks of money left, but that hardly needed saying. We sat across the center aisle from each other, heads down. We both saw with brutal clarity how close the bottom of the sugar bowl was. So much clarity that I, at least, found myself almost unconsciously fuzzing up the outlook a little, fogging it with humor, with the immediacy of eating or kissing or anything that was satisfying in the moment, that was attached to nothing farther down the road than the end of the moment. The night before, I had taken Lauren for a walk, and she stuck out her tongue to feel the crisp, cold air, and I stuck out my tongue too, wanting to feel nothing more than that crisp air, with her, right then and there.

But those were only moments. We had worked seven days a week for five months now, until almost midnight every night. I knew we were drawing on every reserve we touched. I was thinking back to a subway ride we had taken in Atlanta almost nine months earlier. I had struck up a conversation with a lawyer on the train. We were so proud to be starting a new business that we started puffing up, telling our story, right there on the train. He must have done it once himself or seen it done up close.

"Just two things I can tell you," he had said, gazing steadily at us across the subway car. "Don't run out of money. And don't run out of enthusiasm."

I remembered thinking then that his comment was so obvious, it was almost ridiculous. Not anymore. I was getting a head-on view of shrinking supplies at close range.

"I'm so deep in debt," I said to Rolly, across the aisle of the plane. "And not just money. I've drawn down my accounts with Danielle, with the kids, my friends, my own sagging body. It's quite a hole we've dug here, huh?"

This was not helpful.

"And you know, the scary thing is, I believe in this business. It will happen. Somebody will make it happen. And I've got this fear that if it's not us, we'll spend the rest of our lives half nuts, babbling about lost chances on a park bench. And nobody else will really understand what we're talking about, how close it was."

This also was not helpful.

Rolly grunted, eyes red-rimmed and closed.

Refuse to lose.

Nick d'Arbeloff was in the office again. He had been pitching in while he checked us out and had been a lot of help. A godsend. He

had looked closely at twenty companies he had considered joining, he said now. He had a whole checklist of metrics he was using
to judge opportunities. Nick was amazingly meticulous. He laid out
his list:

The company he joined had to have a great core team.

It had to be consumer-focused, because that was his first love.

It had to be focused on a tight, definable market, because that's
where success lay.

Its product had to have sex appeal, to be capable of making a big
splash.

It had to create a new category of offering, something a lot of people would care about.

It had to be related to the Internet, because that was the frontier.

And, ideally, it should be a must-have product, something people
could not do without.

"So how do we stack up?" I asked.

"Fantastically," he said. He was sold on every point except maybe
the last one, the "must-have" requirement.

"You know they'll want it, Nick," I said. "You've seen how people
respond."

"Yeah, you're right," he said. Which left one issue not on his list.
Why was it taking so long for us to get going?

"It's been so much fun working with you," he said. "It's been a
blast. And I've got to tell you, there's no other opportunity out there
that I've found that excites me as much. But every once in a while I
do ask myself, are you guys two great minds who can't get the rubber
to the road?"

In half a second, Rolly was peeling rubber all over that.

"Well," he said, and I could see immediately he'd been pondering
this one himself, "we could have taken VC money last summer instead of private placement and given up thirty or forty percent in the
first round and been under way. But would that have been the right
way to go? I don't think so. We're much better off having the focus
we have today."

"Let's get the money, then," said Nick.

The clock was ticking.

Maybe we would have to go back to Coit. We tried it. What about a loan, but a bigger loan? we asked. Like a million dollars. Or half a million.

"The two hundred and fifty thousand doesn't creep," he said.

We tried another local VC. Back to the Magic Mountain to talk with Polaris Ventures. We had talked with their West Coast guy, Steve Arnold, and Steve had been warm. We took Nick along as our potential VP-marketing-in-waiting. It was a short, impassioned meeting. We had honed our message to just the key points we knew the VCs needed to hear. No bullshit. Steve seemed, to our eye, to be taken with the BuildingBlocks plan. His partner, John Flint, was not. After fifty intense minutes, he put his foot down hard. Content and consumers were not part of the Polaris focus on the Internet, he said. Period.

"This is not the profile we are looking for, nor is it the profile our investors want us to be pursuing," he said with finality. "We wish you good luck."

Nick was seriously bummed.

"You guys were great in there," he said in the cold parking lot. "Truly great. You really made the case. And what I find so depressing is that we were flatly rejected in spite of that, and on a point of principle that we can barely respond to. If content is out and we're selling content, there's only so much we can say. It may be insurmountable."

February was ending. The pressure was terrible. Nothing was moving fast enough. I came in one morning and heard Rolly mumbling that he had a numbness in his left arm and a pain in his chest.

I sat at my computer, banging away in a daze. Denial. Go, go. Refuse to lose. Had he said what I thought he said? Shawn heard him, too, and sent him straight to the doctor's office. And he didn't come back for hours. I began to surface from my daze. What if he had actually had a heart attack? Given everything we were wrestling with, would that be the least bit surprising? What if he was in a ditch somewhere right now? And a little light was finally coming on somewhere deep in my mind. He could be dead. He could have broken himself over this dream. He could have died for it this morning, a long way from hockey sticks and crystal palaces.

I was checking my watch every five minutes, waiting for the phone to ring. Beautiful, dangerous dreams, I thought. Maybe they can kill.

But not that day. Rolly walked back in, ashen. They had shaved his chest and given him an EKG. And the same light had gone on in his head as he lay on the examination table, waiting to learn what was up. We had been pushing awfully hard. The test did not indicate a heart attack, the nurse told him, but the results were notoriously unreliable, she said. He should take it easy. Right.

"I really don't think you've had a heart attack," the nurse had said nonchalantly as he dressed. "At your age, they're usually fatal."

Have a nice day.

People helped us, again. In ways they didn't even know and probably couldn't have understood if we had told them. The pressure was hardening us and making us more emotional, all at the same time. Small things meant a lot.

My neighbors became a little rooting section. Marion left cookies and encouraging notes. Soto, who ran his own business out of his house three doors down, gave me soothing counsel. Ruth Burns, almost as old as Arthur Walworth and a career banker before women had careers, doted on my children when I couldn't. She knew what it was to start a business, she said. She prayed for me every night, right across the street. I would make it, she said. She could see that I would make it. And I took her words as a blessing.

Louise came to the office and we showed her the alpha version. Her eyes sparkled when we put it through its paces.

"I believe in you guys," she said. "You'll do it. Don't give up."

Give up? How could we give up? She believed in us! And we had taken her money.

Danny and Linnae fed us and housed us every time we trekked to New York, and Danny would debrief us with that wild grin that never ever doubted, even when we swam in an ocean of doubt. That grin didn't promise we would succeed. It promised we would go on, we would live and see the sun come up whatever happened, which was easy to forget sometimes.

Danielle and I had dinner with Jonathan Kaufman — my friend

who accused me of being a serial adventurer — and his wife, Barb. And afterward he pulled me aside.

"I didn't get a chance to tell you over dinner how much I admire what you're doing," he said. "As long as I've known you, you've had this pattern of appearing to bite off more than you can chew, and then succeeding wonderfully. I'm sure you'll do it again."

I wanted to kiss his big black beard. Because belief took on an extra weight. Heavier than gold. And we needed it. We needed it like oxygen.

It was March. I heard Rolly answer his phone, full of spunk and energy. There was still no money, but the product was really coming along now. Shawn was finally through defending his doctoral thesis and was working wonders with HomePortfolio. And it buoyed us.

"Hi, Steve! We're doing great! How 'bout you?"

It was Coit. We had scheduled a meeting with Charles River to make one more run at funding. We had called Steve to set up the meeting, vowing not to grovel. Then we had groveled, anyway, and got a date. Now, in his usual tone of breathless, burning insight, Coit was calling the meeting off.

"I would buy your product. I think you have the makings of a very profitable business here," he said over the speakerphone when I came in. "But I'm not convinced it's got the right model for a venture capital investment."

There was a long pause.

"Hey, Tom," Steve said cheerily. "I've never heard you speechless before."

I passed out the next-to-last paychecks our dwindling account would cover. It felt like a religious sacrament. Like communion wafers.

"I don't know about you, but I don't have a whole lot in the way of resources at this point," I told Rolly over lunch, doing a quick tally. "Just from covering things so far, I've got about twenty thousand in credit card debt. My home equity line is maxed out. I'm not prepared to lose the house. That would be the end of Danielle's support. I mean, the end."

I had been at a parents' meeting for Ben's soccer team the night before, and the coaches had made their standard little speech at the end that if anybody had any trouble covering their son's tournament fees — a hundred here, a hundred there — they should just let them know. I had always wondered what it would be like to have to approach the coaches after a meeting like that and say I couldn't cover a hundred-dollar fee. Christ! I was staring at it.

"Well, there's always the credit card route," Rolly said. And I knew he was talking the kryptonite pile. I shuddered.

We kept pushing. We talked to Bessemer Venture Partners, just the other side of Route 128.

"You guys have that visionary feel," they said. "You'll probably get a thousand manufacturers in. The problem is the *Waiting for Godot* problem. How long will you have to wait for a critical mass of users?"

We kept pushing. We had a dozen more lines out, in Boston, in New York, in Chicago, on the West Coast.

We had lunch with Matt Lindley. Matt and his pal Tom Aley at Ziff Davis in Cambridge had been great sounding boards from early on, full of ideas and enthusiasm and high, good humor. Now they were busting their own humps to launch the first television show devoted to the Web. *The Wild, Wild Web,* they were going to call it.

Matt was always a fresh breeze, droll and wickedly funny. He would be a perfect host, I thought: Jerry Seinfeld meets Netmeister. He and Tom were still working full-time at Ziff Davis, but they had been flogging an eight-minute demo of the show all over the place, and the response was heating up. It looked very promising. But you never really knew.

Matt had just spent the weekend in New Orleans, at a big convention where TV shows were bought and sold, sitting in a booth near Bob Vila and Martha Stewart, explaining his plans for *The Wild, Wild Web.* Prince Albert of Monaco came through, he said, and spent a long time talking with him.

"It's wild," Matt said. "Like one of those dreams where a face looms up very close to you, with big eyes bulging out, and the background recedes a thousand miles, and you're talking to Prince Albert of Monaco. About your big TV show on the Web. And how it might play in Monaco. And just last night you were sitting at your desk, at the office, where everybody shows up and has coffee and calmly repeats their daily routines. And you walk out and grab a plane with some wild idea in your pocket, and the next morning you're sitting in la-la land, talking about millions and zillions and everything is rushing. Talking about your lightning in a bottle, and how it's going to explode any second, the hottest thing ever. And then you're home again. And you haven't heard back, and it feels dead in the water, and your wife asks you how everything is, and you say fine and sit in front of the TV, at eleven o'clock, staring right through that TV, right through the wall, right into the pit."

I could relate to that.

Lincoln Millstein came by from the *Globe* that afternoon to see our stuff. Very interesting, he said. Really cool. I was feeling great. The meeting ended, and Rolly pulled me aside.

"Katherine just came to talk to me," he said. "She forgot to account for one of the January payrolls. We actually have seventeen thousand less than the books have been showing. We can't make Thursday's payroll.

"We're out of money."

Chapter 12

Death Valley Days

T HERE IS A GAME that I called startup solitaire. It doesn't have a rule book. It just comes to you, usually late at night. It's simple. It goes like this.

You're alone in your bedroom at midnight with a tall stack of credit cards. You've taken the stack and you're slowly spreading it out on the bed, turning the cards over and over, checking them against your monthly statements, looking for the ones that still have a few dollars left to borrow.

It's important to play this game alone. Not many people can stand to watch it. The bigger the stack of credit cards, the more gripping the game. And it's a progressive game. The more months you play, the harder it gets to win.

There are variations, different styles of play. Maybe you're quiet, thinking about a job you left, about your son's canceled guitar lessons or your daughter's overdue nursery school bill. About the money you've taken from family and friends.

Or maybe you're mindlessly muttering as you flip the cards. Muttering is common, in the vein of "she loves me, she loves me not." Maybe you're muttering, "We'll make it, I'm insane, we'll make it, I'm nuts."

Now you're playing startup solitaire!

Late at night, when we had finally locked up the office or left Shawn there, still programming at midnight, Rolly would lay out the plastic. Kendra would be asleep across the hall. Carole would be downstairs on the couch watching Jay Leno. And Rolly would be playing startup solitaire.

The credit cards covered the bed like a hideous, glittering quilt. So shiny! So colorful! So richly trimmed in silver and gold!

So nauseating.

Their bed was just about the only flat surface in the house big enough, and private enough, to hold this load. Uncle Visa, I called it. There was a shiny annex to that quilt in my bedroom at home, where I would play the game when I was damn sure Danielle was not around. But Rolly's credit card quilt was the staggering mother lode of plastic. A quarter-million-dollar credit line of pure kryptonite, patched together from the "Special Offer!" mass mailings of grasping, grinning banks all over these United States.

There was Citibank. Citibank Visa. Citibank Preferred Visa. Chase Visa. Chase Credit. Choice Visa. First Card. First Union. First USA Bank. There was the Corestate family of cards. And the Fleet family. And the BankBoston family. And the HCS GM Card, and the HCS Classic Visa, and Advanta and Travelers and the MBNA family, and on and on and on until you could almost go blind staring at that winking, twinkling, evil, glittering quilt of cards.

At first it was easy playing the game. Pick a card, any card, and there was available credit on it. Five thousand. Ten thousand. Fifteen thousand. Twenty thousand. No problem! "Use these convenient checks!" the mailings begged.

But it got harder. Much harder. Until you could spend half the night flipping those damned cards, reading down monthly statements in the yellow light, searching for just a little more cash to squeeze, a little more credit, while your wife slept alone in the guest bedroom and you juggled everything you owned and all this bright, engulfing quilt of plastic, too.

Only a fool would like this game. I had to work myself into a cursing, sweating frenzy to play. Launching a startup was, in part, about delaying gratification, about sacrificing time now for time in the future. But the credit card game was about betting the future, too. And if it didn't work, you could be Uncle Visa's galley slave for a long, long time.

Rolly had a special constitution for this extreme sport, a world-view that kept him going. For him, the world was not, finally, a random, chaotic, absurd place. It had structure and logic, and the consistency of human motivation supported that structure. Everything would change except human nature. If our analysis was correct, if our ideas were right, and we worked like hell, we would ultimately prevail. This was not a crapshoot. This was the destiny of right thinking and iron will.

And so he flipped the cards.

When the seed money first ran out, Rolly's mom bailed us out. Gee, a check in the mail might be too slow, Mom, I heard him saying. Could you possibly wire the money? Maybe this afternoon? Or right now even? Then my parents and my sister stepped up. Twenty thousand dollars. A lot of money to them, invested in this crazy son and brother without a question, without a moment's hesitation after Mom and Dad drove out from Illinois and saw the passion in our little office and the tension at home.

"Tom," said the note my dad wrapped around the checks. "Last week was great. I hope this helps."

And you wonder where that kind of love comes from. And you pray you'll pay it back a hundredfold because they need that money, because there's an issue here about succeeding that goes way, way back, because you're carrying some family flame now, some longing to believe. But you can't take time to think about it. Not now. You've got to push. Everything is on the line. All your senses are heightened. Adrenaline runs like everyday blood. A week feels like a month, a month feels like a year. You're running naked.

There was a goofy movie moment that flashed in my mind often in those months. An Indiana Jones film, where Indy confronts a bottomless chasm and there's no bridge in sight, and the little book in his hand says he's got to walk across if he wants to find the Holy Grail. But there's no bridge! But he's got to walk across! So he closes his eyes and steps into the abyss. On faith.

Is that stupid? Or brilliant? Or just a fairy tale from the movies? Whatever it was, I was relating.

Our challenge with BuildingBlocks was trickier now than before.

We needed to do all the things that we had always needed to do, but with no money beyond what we could shake out of the nooks and crannies of our lives. Rolly and I stopped drawing salaries. There wasn't much alternative. We counted up our last resources, took a deep breath, and stepped ahead. We'd be fine. It wouldn't be long now. We'd find water soon.

"Above all, we cannot look desperate," Rolly said. Right. We are on track. We are bound for glory. We are moving ahead, just a little slower than before, because above all, we have to survive to keep fighting. Sell the product. Build the product. Find the money. Survive. And when people ask, never say you're broke. Say you're "running on fumes." It sounds better. Not good, but better.

Shawn was moving mountains now. We pulled together photographs and information and interface designs, and he cranked out miracles of software code that sewed it all together, made it dance and run. I would stand watching over his shoulder sometimes as he composed line after line of code down the screen of his big monitor. He would patiently walk me through a few pages, giving me a glimpse of the logic and systems that made it work, but this would never be my homeland. On the white board, where visions were laid out and organized, our worlds met. But Shawn turned visions into glowing green lines of software code. He was the man. We had sworn we would not get ourselves out on the bleeding edge of new technology, where so much was untested and unpredictable. But we got there anyway. Our vision was too hungry to resist. The alpha version of HomePortfolio that Shawn programmed was immediately pushing Marimba's Castanet software to its limits. And that was for the relatively high bandwidth format you could approximate with a "push" channel. How would we deal with the slow, low-bandwidth world of the ordinary Internet?

Don't worry. Keep moving. Remember the stories Dad used to read. Jack London. To build a fire. Go, go. Sign the next year's office lease on a personal guarantee. You'll make it. You won't have to pay it off with your last dollar of retirement savings. Naw. Go, go!

Good things were happening. Rick Segal had spared us the takeover that our failure to raise a million dollars within six months had entitled him to. He could still do it, but he hadn't. He was holding his

fire, giving us a chance. What a man! Of course, he needed us fully
motivated here, too. And we had our best VC meeting yet with Paul
Maeder at Highland Capital in Boston. It was brilliant, we thought,
and Paul seemed impressed. Rolly and Nick and I celebrated with a
quick stroll along Boston Harbor, and a beautiful, dark porpoise
rolled up out of the water right in front of us by Rowe's Wharf. None
of us had ever seen that in this harbor before. It had to be a good
omen.

We flew out to the big Kitchen and Bath Industry Show in Chicago with Gwen and Katherine and Dorian Adams, a wonderful
sales guru from Santa Barbara that the e-commerce manager at
Masco had sent our way, and we got our first little industry commitments. We needed industry beta testers, a few companies that would
come in as trial-run clients, for us to work with in shaping Home-
Portfolio. Carol Gee at Du Pont Corian had seen our potential from
the beginning. She agreed to dip her toe in. And so did Al DeGenova
and Jeff Carney, the bright-eyed marketing guys from Grohe's U.S.
offices, outside Chicago. These weren't real sales. Scott Smith would
not call them proof of concept. But they were investments of brain
cycles, as Nick liked to say, and brain cycles — people's mental time
and energy — were gifts, at least.

And there were more good signs. Jim and Barbara Conen had
built one of the most innovative bath and kitchen showrooms in the
country, called Splash, just a few miles from our office. We knocked
on their door and they listened to our plans and became real enthusiasts, opening their store and minds to us with a generosity that
pushed our detailed understanding of the industry we were embracing miles ahead.

Then we started hearing from Marimba. We had put our Castanet
Channel up on the Web, in beta form, and Marimba had found it. It
was the sexiest application of their software anywhere, they said, and
they loved it. When their photogenic CEO, Kim Polese, went on TV
to show off Castanet, she used HomePortfolio. She didn't name us.
But we saw our little creation on the flickering computer screen between Kim and her interviewer. We saw the beautiful homes and
products we were showing, our cool interface. But what did it matter? On the day Marimba first e-mailed us, BuildingBlocks had $300

left in the bank. And Highland Capital declined to invest. We had "too many moving parts," they said. Still too many moving parts. Still not simple enough.

So we simplified some more and kept crawling forward.

It was getting hard on Nick. He needed a paying job. We could barely cover Shawn and Katherine and Gwen. Sometimes, now, even Gwen was waving off her paycheck. Later, she said. When you can.

But Nick didn't have a construction business on the side, and he was slipping away from us. He had pitched in a lot. He wanted to believe. But this was too high-wire. Running on fumes was not his style. We had a potential investor in one afternoon, and Rolly described our situation with brutal honesty. The empty kitty. The growing debt. And the guy noted that some of his friends, not him of course, would see this not as a venture opportunity but a "vulture opportunity," a chance to come in and grab a hunk of the company for next to nothing. It was happening to Web companies all over, he said.

"This Internet industry is a wasteland!" Nick moaned late one night in the parking lot across from the old church, when we were finally heading home and he knew his path was leading elsewhere.

"It's like Ethiopia. A very few people drifting around with a little wad of food in their bellies, and everyone else lying on the ground starving. I'm sure it's going to be great eventually, but you're going to have ten years of constant flux. And you can't even really get started without money. What the hell are you guys going to do?"

"We're going to win, Nick," I said. "We're going to win because we have to win. Our asses are completely out there now."

"Yeah," he said wistfully.

We looked up at the stars over the church. They were bright tonight. And far away.

"But when are you going to win?"

When. Always when. Time is such a bastard.

"I don't know."

Nick brought us an investment banker, a friend of a friend named Jeff Nixon. Jeff's business was helping young companies find investors. If he succeeded, he got a cut of the investment. We didn't want to have to build that cut into a deal. We didn't want a go-between. But we obviously needed something. We had approached three dozen VCs now and had been turned away, with varying degrees of interest and elegance, by every single one. Maybe it was our rookie status, our inexperience, that was insurmountable.

Jeff Nixon was a whole new face for BuildingBlocks. We were two raw dreamers, a big-picture tech wizard, a displaced basket-weaver, and a part-time editor. Jeff was flashy cuff links, good suits, keen intelligence, lots of experience, and contacts everywhere. He was a beefy Connecticut social set kid who had followed his own dreaming instinct early on into a high-tech venture that struggled and ultimately folded, but not before he had gained a deep education in startup capital.

He sat at our folding table, big gold cuff links in the shape of fat anchors, listening and weighing. Hiring him was a risk for us. We couldn't know exactly how it would play with investors. But taking us on was a risk for him, too. He couldn't afford to pour his time and reputation into ventures that didn't have strong odds of success.

"Everybody's hair is on fire with this Internet stuff," Jeff said when we had laid out our plans and shared our tale of fund-raising woe. "It's exciting. It's incredible. It's going to be huge. But not everybody's going to make it." He would think about our situation, he said. He liked what he had heard. He liked the grit we had shown in sticking with it. He would do some poking around.

And the next time he called he was ready to go. He liked the plan, he said. He liked us. Let's do it. We negotiated. There were bells and whistles in the deal, but the heart of it was five percent for Jeff of whatever funds we raised in the next round. We hated to give up that slice, but we would die without the round.

Jeff hit his Rolodex, and the FedEx envelopes stacked up again every night with fresh, clean business plans, and VC meetings started up again in earnest. We'd have a handshake on money by the end of July, Jeff predicted. Three and a half million dollars.

Yes, please.

It couldn't come fast enough. The office was tense, and life at home, when I got to see it, was on the edge. If we cashed out everything, the household could scrape by for eight more months, I figured. Until January. And that would be the end. But could I possibly consider taking things that far? To the bitter, flat-broke end?

We would go back to the office after dinner to update the business plan, the endlessly evolving business plan, and sometimes, late at night, the whole thing would start to seem so very unlikely, so ephemeral. Just a pile of paragraphs and charts floating up off the page, pretty thoughts and assertions drifting away, out of reach.

There was so much to be done, and only our tiny band to do it. We needed to debug the channel, to get up a Web site for direct Internet use, to put a corporate identity kit together, to feed in thousands of products and product descriptions, to get more manufacturers involved as beta testers, and a hundred other urgent things. Rolly kept a to-do list on his computer that had grown so long, I hated to scroll down to the bottom. Who was going to do all that? We banged away at it every day, but it grew faster than we could knock it back.

I wasn't the only one intimidated by the pile of work and uncertain prospects. The market for top technology talent was blazing hot. A Seattle company with lots of money and a proven market took a hard run at Shawn, and he wobbled. They offered to double his BuildingBlocks salary, move him back west, treat him like a king. And we had no money, and no real customers yet, and thirty-nine-dollar Staples tables for desks. He wobbled hard, and who could blame him? He had school debts to pay off and two young kids, and his wife, Linda, had just been laid off from her job. I watched Rolly get down on his knees and beg Shawn to think again, to consider what we were building here, how great it would be. And I heard him double Shawn's salary on the spot. And I knew that raise came straight off the midnight quilt of credit cards. What a will!

"What do you think, Tom? What should I do?" asked Shawn, so young and smart and earnest.

"I think you'll look back one day and be proud you went the distance with this company," I said. "I think we're all in this together."

He stayed, and we thanked God every day that he did.

"Another bullet dodged! A big one!" said Rolly, shaken and relieved. "This is quite the ride we're on."

My own mood swings were like the Bay of Fundy tide. Vast and fast. One morning I'd picture myself a broken forty-two-year-old wreck with a mountain of debt, putting on a brave face as I trudged back out into the ordinary world of work, strapping on someone else's harness — if I could even bear to do it. In the afternoon of the same day, with the right sequence of completed work and promising phone calls and encouraging signs, I would conjure up an entirely different picture. I'd see an accomplished man of means who prospered in the great migration, all good fortune and gravitas, the happy father and husband, lord of his domain, a gentleman geek. My wife could work or not, as she pleased. My children had a model of success to see and learn from. I had the means and leisure to cultivate obscure interests, to address the world easily, to watch sunsets with my daughter and sing all night if I felt like it.

And the mail would come, and I'd snag another credit card application to add to the quilt.

Danielle was mildly unhinged by the strain. "I'll think about that tomorrow," I heard her whispering to herself as she struggled to pay bills, like Scarlett O'Hara in the ruins of war. We had to talk, she told me. Soon.

So we made a date for Saturday night, our first night out in a long time. We sat at the bar at a favorite restaurant. She looked good, but stressed. I'm sure I looked worse.

"I hate to do this, but we've got to look at the numbers," she said right away, with the long, steady look she used when she was in such turmoil that she couldn't afford anything jumpy. "I mean, how long does this go on? How long can we survive? When do you pull the rip cord? I want some warning, some time to respond. I don't want you to just come to me one day and say, 'Well, Danielle, we can't make the mortgage, we're moving next month.'"

So we looked at the numbers, scribbling on the paper placemat at the bar, and she agreed that if we emptied every pocket and watched our pennies, we could make it to January. But that would take us to the very bottom of the barrel. No leeway for job-hunting time. No leeway for anything.

"And then what?" she asked, working to keep her composure.

"Tom, I'm already cutting and cutting, but we have to buy clothes for the kids. Dylan needs new shoes. So does Ben. We're going to have to drop his guitar lessons. You tell him. And I'm paying for Lauren's nursery school with the credit card! I don't think you really understand how much debt we're in. The equity loan, the credit cards. If you take it to the very end, Tom, how do we live?"

There had been a time when the slightest hint of doubt on her part sent me flaring with anger. But not now. We had to look straight at this.

"Well, at some point I guess I have to cut loose from the company if it's not going," I said for the first time.

"When?"

"I don't know. Maybe the end of the summer. Labor Day."

"Does Rolly know that?"

"We don't talk about it, but I've told him the one thing I cannot do is lose the house. So he knows there's an endpoint somewhere."

She stared closely, searching my face. "Will you really walk away from it?"

I hesitated too long. There was a huge neon fish over the bar. It was blue, a beautiful cool blue. You could lose yourself in a beautiful blue like that. The chasm was so big. Could we cross it?

"Tom!" Danielle was not comforted to see me drifting off. Her voice was stern. "Just tell me this, at least. Do you think you've got a better than fifty-fifty chance of making this company go, of succeeding?"

How to answer that? I believed we did, but I didn't know we did. I couldn't know we did. It was all about not knowing. It was about hunches and best guesses and best efforts and the most complete planning you could do. But you couldn't know. No one could know. That was the definition of the game.

"I don't know," I said at last. This wasn't a VC I was talking to, with a hundred million more dollars to draw on if we tanked. This was my wife. "I think so," I said, "I really think so, but I can't know."

Danielle twisted her wedding ring slowly on her finger, then sighed and laughed softly. She ordered another glass of wine. She leaned close and put her arm on my shoulder. She wasn't strangling me yet, but she wasn't giving me a walk either. She had made some kind of decision, but I couldn't read her. It was good just to be with her like this, I thought, even if nothing made sense. We leaned against each other and clinked glasses to I don't know what. Experience? Blue fish? Love in a hard place?

"I guess you have to be a little crazy to start a new business, huh?" she said, leaning closer.

"Yeah," I exhaled. "A little crazy."

"You know, Tom, our friends don't have the courage to ask you what the hell you're doing. But they ask me. They ask how long you're going to give it. They say they're sure we have fallback resources in case it doesn't work out. They ask what makes you so confident it's going to succeed. I never know what to tell them, but I want you to know it's not just me asking."

"I know," I said. "I'm sure it's not." She was so reasonable, so gentle with her big fool of a husband. But there was something she wanted me to hear. She delivered it evenly, softly, in the dark of the bar, close to my ear, like a trainer whispering to a difficult horse.

"Tom, this whole thing has been so much against my grain that I've had to make a fundamental decision. I'm walking out on the wire with you. I'm not looking down. I'm trusting you. But remember, Tom, we are all in your hands now. You've done what you wanted to do, but in the process you've taken on a huge responsibility. You have to realize that. You have to act in accordance with that."

She leaned away now, and stared at me.

"Labor Day," she said. "You've got until Labor Day."

Three months.

Danny's son, Eli, was turning thirteen, having his bar mitzvah, formally becoming a man. We took the whole family down, our first time really together in months. My boys were getting big, too, and Lauren ran everywhere now, no longer a baby. Was it possible that I had worked all these nights and weekends for so long, away from these treasures? That was the tradeoff, and with every week now it became more stark: How much irretrievable time are you willing to trade away now in the hope that it will buy much more free time later?

It was like startup solitaire — easy at first, hard later. Would you

give up a week now for a life of more ease and time with your children when the week was over? Of course. Would you give up ten
weeks? Probably. Ten months? And if you were game enough to give
up ten months and had not quite succeeded yet, but had invested
that much, would you give up just ten more months to succeed? And
soon you're into years.

Lauren had started sitting by the bathtub now just to have time
with me. Whatever else was going on, I had a daily soak. And whenever she heard that water run, she would come, even from the midst
of sleep at midnight, to sit by the tub, wrapped in towels, and talk. It
was our time, sometimes our only time, together. Ben, I managed an
occasional basketball game with. Dylan, I saw briefly over breakfast
and when I drove the carpool to school. This wasn't my style. They
deserved more. I missed them.

Eli was already on the bima at the front of the temple, ready to
read his portion from the Torah. We filed into a row of seats near the
back. Stone sat down beside me, as easy as breathing. I hadn't seen
him since my desperate, unanswered phone calls more than a year
before. Now we were shoulder to shoulder in the temple, in skull-
caps, and our friend's son was becoming a man.

The praying began. We shared a book of prayer and song and philosophy across our knees. God, how we had laughed as young men.
Free and happy. What funny paths life took. We turned the pages of
the book, reading as the music and prayer rolled on.

"All journeys are destinations of which the traveler is unaware,"
we read, from Martin Buber. Danny and Linnae stood by Eli and the
rabbi.

"Cherish your doubts, for doubt is the handmaiden of truth.
Doubt is the key to the door of knowledge," we read, from Robert
Weston. Eli was giving his speech, about learning from adversity. The
parking lot was full of fancy cars. We were sitting in Scarsdale, a
tower of wealth. But never mind. Adversity travels.

"Our prayers are answered not when we are given what we ask,
but when we are challenged to be what we can be," Stone and I read,
from Rabbi Morris Adler.

The temple was full of light, and it was good to sit with an old
friend and hear the music. I had been so madly steeled and braced,

I had grown hard. I had taken things too personally. And sitting there in the temple I let all that melt away. I remembered the night Danielle and I had sat years before with Stone and brainstormed names for our first son. Dylan, it became, for the songs of tangled youth and dreaming, for the poetry of longing and joy. Dylan, to live with Victory. We each had our journey. So flow. Accept. Friends at the beginning. Friends at the end.

We read from Vaclav Havel: "Hope is an orientation of the spirit, an orientation of the heart. It is not the conviction that something will turn out well, but the certainty that something makes sense, regardless of how it turns out."

"I'm sorry about last year," Stone said back at Danny's house, during a long, lazy afternoon of family and wine. "It just seemed so risky, I didn't know what to say. Maybe I'm too conservative."

"Oh, I don't think so," I said. "I was the one who was out of line. I was just so stoked. Can you believe that?"

"Yes, I can," he said. And we laughed.

"How's it going now?" he asked.

"It's going great," I said, and in that sweet hour I meant it. "Hey, we're here and we're alive, aren't we?"

We were approaching full bungee, the point at which it feels as if the cord can't stretch much farther. But Jeff Nixon was working our case hard now. We would make it. US West, the big Colorado phone company, flew its man out from Denver to see us about investing. It looks good, he said. It looks very good.

We talked with Hearst's venture investment arm in New York. Much excitement ensued. This was hot, they said. They needed a demo right away, to show the bigwigs there and speed their consideration. So Rolly and Shawn spent the weekend updating the demo to ship on Monday morning. No problem.

We met with Cathy Agee, who flew out from Oak Investment Partners in Minneapolis. It was a great meeting. She liked our niche, she said. We would talk again soon.

Our meeting with Flatiron, the New York venture fund, was strangely flat. We tried and tried, but there was no energy in the room. Was it us? Them? I found myself weirdly sympathizing with the partner hearing our pitch. How many pitches did he listen to in a year? It must be hard. Announce you have money to invest in the future, and the world rushes in with an ocean of dreams and fantasies. And soon, surely, you long to be spared the monotony of raw yearning.

But the meeting threw us off our stride, and the last meeting that day in Manhattan, with Scripps Ventures, had none of the fire we usually brought to the table. I was in a foul mood. Rolly droned catatonically. Only Benjy Burditt, the turbocharged Scripps partner, kept the room alive. He liked what he was hearing, he said. His parent company, E. W. Scripps, owned Home & Garden Television, HGTV, the industry phenom that had brought twenty-four-hour home and gardening programming to cable television. He needed to check in with them to see what their own Internet plans were.

"But I liked him," Rolly said as we headed with Jeff back into the Manhattan traffic, rolling our eyes at how morose we had been.

"Yeah," I said. "Wouldn't it be ironic if we hit with them. Like nobody will love you until you just don't give a damn anymore. Then they'll love you."

But good things were happening.

Caroline Vanderlip agreed to join our board of directors. She had watched us plow ahead. She had been pitching for us from the sidelines. She and Mark were not moving to Boston, but she was ready to get more involved. That could only be good.

Then we got a call from Larry D'Onofrio. Larry was one of the earliest crew members of *This Old House*, the public television show produced by WGBH in Boston. He had been a construction hand on the show who became a *This Old House* producer and then head of underwriting for all of WGBH. He had been working with big home product companies for years. He knew homes and home construction. He headed a team that sold millions of dollars in sponsorships each year. And he was interested in us, maybe even in working for us.

"I've got a great job in many ways," he said over coffee at Appassionato. "I'm at a place that has been very good to me. But maybe I'm not done growing."

Hey, that was our theme song! And he was terrific. This could be good. Very good.

And then Marimba called, from Palo Alto. HomePortfolio had become the centerpiece of the worldwide sales presentation for their Castanet software. Now, they said, Netscape was coming out with a new component of its Web browser that would let millions of users get access to "push" channels via the Internet. It would be called Netcaster. They wanted to get HomePortfolio onto it. Would we be interested?

Would we be interested? We felt as if we'd been asked out on our very first date. We would be on Netscape, beside the channels of ABC News, CBS Sportsline, USA TODAY, Lycos Direct, Quote.com, and Capitol Records. Yes, we would be interested. Oh, yes.

"Ooooweee!" Rolly shouted, both arms high when he got off the phone. "We are a Netcaster channel! We . . . are . . . a . . . Netcaster . . . channel!"

Who knew what it would really mean? Nobody. But it sounded damn good. HomePortfolio featured on Netscape. An audience of millions. Let's go!

We went back to Scott Smith in Greenwich and laid out our progress. Jeff Nixon said he was confident we would have a handshake on big money by the end of September — never mind the promise of July — and Scott was warm. He talked to Rick. They had seen us survive some desert and keep moving. At the end of July they put in another hundred thousand. A gulp of oxygen. We kept moving.

Hearst said no. They would not invest now. They were very hot on HomePortfolio, but the company was too young for them to invest in. Please come back in six months.

Six months! We could be dead in three!

US West said no. They couldn't get agreement between their Colorado and Boston offices on whether this was a priority for them. They were undergoing their own corporate reorganization. Maybe later. Ciao.

Oak said no. At least not yet. We weren't sufficiently "consumer-ready" for them. A very fair point. Despite our star turn on Netcaster, we knew we were not really ready for prime time. But how were we going to get ready without resources?

Here were three big rejections in a row, and that didn't even count the investors who hadn't been interested in the first place. I had eaten more rejection in the past twelve months than in all the rest of my life put together. This rain of blows was grinding me down.

"What is it?" I ranted, sitting in the wild clutter of the office. I was losing it. We couldn't wait forever. Our great vision was starving to death. "Do we smell bad? Is our cosmic fly down? What exactly is the problem here? Do we sound stoned to these people?"

"Not at all," said Rolly, pushing right back. "We're on the right track. And the proof is in the hearings we're getting. These aren't brushoffs. These are real hearings. Visits. Serious consideration. It's just that we're not quite there yet."

This guy was amazing. He had a point. I got it. But I also knew his reflexes now. Put him in a corner, and he would spin stories of imminent success all night and all day. He would turn that big brain on and scour every angle and tiny crevice for hope, for light, for tools of rebuttal. And he would find them.

But behind that reflex he was hurting, too. We had walked away from careers. We had worked seven days a week until midnight for a year. We had put everything on the line. We had nearly abandoned our families. And his bed was the one groaning with the mother lode of plastic.

"Okay, maybe they're right, then," I said. "Maybe the company is too young. But how do we get older without money?"

Our little operation had gulped Rick's latest hundred thousand down like a snack. We had bills stacked up all over. Just keeping the telephone service turned on was a challenge.

We sat in silence for long minutes. Rolly's eyes clouded over.

"Well, the reality is, everything has its clearing price," he said. I knew what he was thinking. We could slash our asking price for equity in the company. Forget the $5 million valuation we had won in the seed round. Take whatever we could get. Let Rick and Scott be crammed down, let their stake in the company be gutted by a fire sale valuation on the next round. I pictured us selling to some ruthless, bottom-feeding investor looking for a distress sale. Vulture capital. I pictured us lashed into the deal, working like slaves for a tiny share of our company.

"Even junk gets sold at yard sales," Rolly almost whispered. I had never heard him talk like that before.

"You don't want that," I said. "And I don't either."

The phone rang. It was Jeff.

"We're going to have to aggressively pursue a bridge round," he said, meaning a smaller investment that would tide us over until we could get a big one. "We're just too early for most of the people we've been talking to. The question is, how do we keep going until we're ready for the big money?"

I loved this guy. I really did. He was as crazy as we were. He was hanging in. Another can-do dreamer, smart and crazy all at once, just like the rogues in the old all-American storybooks. Lock them in a room and anything seems possible. Slap them around with some sharp reality, and five minutes later they've brainstormed their way back to the dream, like bobbers that just won't go down. They're like ecstatic worshipers, like coal walkers. They chant the words, they caress the idea, the vision, and it makes them high, makes them impervious to pain. It's their cocaine, their khat, their peyote. And ruin is the snake they handle. Look, it won't bite me, they say. I can wrap utter ruin all around my neck and lay its fangs on my throat and howl, and it won't bite me. I am armored by belief, made imperishable by vision. Even ruin is not ruin. Only my flesh is vulnerable, and I am not flesh. I am one with the vision. I will walk on water, I will pull the sun up with my bare hands. I will be immortal. I will make new worlds. I will rise above all ordinary cares and fly.

But he was also retreating. Forget the big money for now, guys, Jeff was saying. Squeak out what you can.

"How far could you get on a million dollars?" he asked.

"We could make it to launch. We'd make it to January," said Rolly.

"Would you take it at five million pre-money?" asked Jeff, meaning no increase over our seed-round valuation, no bump for all the work we had put in.

"We'd do it at six million pre-money," Rolly said, and then he remembered all the desert and wasteland around us. "Well, okay, we'd do it at five million."

We'd be lucky to get that. We were in deep shit.

"Chin up, guys. I'll talk to you tomorrow," said Jeff. And he was gone. And our $3.5 million dreams were gone with him. A bridge round! It would be just as much work as a big round, maybe more, and then we'd still have to get the big round.

We sat like statues for a long time. We didn't feel like heroes. We didn't feel anything. The road was getting way too long. And it just got harder. We were going to have to go back to Rick on our knees. This was supposed to be a gold rush. It felt more like building a railroad through the Rockies with no shovel. Like walking naked across Death Valley.

Rolly threw his head back in his chair and flung his arms out, wide and beseeching.

"Why do people do this?" he moaned. "How do they survive it? It's just too hard! And then it's humiliating!"

"Amen, brother," I said. "And if you screw up, you're bankrupt. You're a stupid, pathetic overreacher, a penniless fool."

Whoa! Things were getting a little shaky here. It was my turn to steady the boat.

"But look, we're doing it," I said reflexively. "We're on the path. We're still standing."

In a manner of speaking.

Labor Day came with astonishing speed. I worked, came home, took Lauren for a walk around the lake, and came back to overhear Danielle on the phone with her parents.

"I'm in a tough position," she was saying upstairs as I helped Lauren take her shoes off. "How far can you go before you say, 'Okay, we tried, it just didn't work out'? Even with a billion-dollar idea, at some point it has to work out, right? If only my salary could cover our essential expenses. I wish, I wish it did. But it doesn't even come close. It's hard, you know. Some people need to take risks. I know that. But how far can we afford to go?"

And then it was our turn, hers and mine. Ben watched Lauren in the backyard. Dylan was off with a friend.

Danielle began. She had listened for a year and a half now to my excited accounts of the progress we were making and the investment money we were anticipating. And so many of those anticipated stepping-stones had not panned out. People who were going to join and bolster us came and went. Potential investors became imminent saviors, then vanished from conversation. Dates by which we would certainly be better situated came and went, with new dates, further down the road, further down our dwindling bank balance, talked up to replace them. She couldn't find money for Dylan's karate lessons anymore. She wasn't signing Lauren up for dance classes. We couldn't afford them. She knew this wasn't starvation, but at this rate groceries would be an issue soon, too.

"This has been hard for me, Tom. But I've hung in there. I've gone through big changes of attitude, changes of outlook and expectation to deal with your dream. And I want it to work. You know I do. But I need to know how far we are going to push this. I don't want to be a dream killer, but I am practical. We're coming down to the wire. I can't even cover the mortgage and car payment with my salary. And you don't have a salary."

She paused. It was my turn. We would have to get down to numbers, but they were so stark and simple now that we both knew them perfectly well.

I knew there had been lots of unfulfilled expectations about when and how this business would take root, I said. They had been difficult for me, too. But through all those ups and downs, I believed we had built something here that was valuable. And this whole project, which I had started out holding at arm's length and trying to treat as a risk-limited experiment, had become a major life marker. A test I could not fail. When, I asked, does a dream become a challenge you have to lock into whatever the cost?

This line of thinking was buying me teary eyes from Danielle. Shallow breathing. Headache lines. I reined in, but not much.

"Look, Danielle, I don't want us to drive off a cliff here, either. I'm not going to do that," I said, wondering how I could say that so confidently. "But I think we've got an opportunity to make something great happen here. I think we've come a long way toward making it happen. And I think our family has the resources to hang in there a little longer before we pull the plug."

The cicadas had already started their drone. Fall was coming. I looked at Danielle and the strain in her face, and I wanted desperately to make everything perfect for her. I wanted the business to be booming and me to have lots of time to enjoy life with her and the kids. I wanted to tell her she could give up work anytime she wanted to, raise her daughter, be at home with her last young child. I wanted to get the house painted and spend an autumn weekend in New Hampshire with her and kiss all the worry away from her eyes. But I couldn't. Lauren was growing out of her crib, and I couldn't even afford to buy her a little girl's bed.

"Tom," Danielle said, as if she were trying to speak to someone far away over a bad phone line. "I want to do what we can to blunt the worst of the trauma for the family. I don't want you to drop a sledgehammer on us. You are going to have to be reasonable."

Reasonable. Nothing seemed reasonable anymore. When I was at the office, in the thick of our effort, I wanted to push to the absolute limit, to give it every reserve I could call on, to fight with no regard for anything else until we broke through to success. Sitting here with Danielle, studying the pain and worry in her eyes, I wondered if I had already gone much too far.

Danielle listened, and her eyes brimmed with tears. I think she thought I was losing my mind. Perhaps I was. But I couldn't quit now.

The bank balance: $21,900. Add Danielle's salary and we had four months. God help us.

I wondered if birth and death felt similar somehow. And if they did, which was this? Pain. Turmoil. Light and dark and light. We'd be born soon or dead soon.

"The gold rush fever is over," Jeff Nixon told us on a hot late summer day. VCs were swamped with Internet business proposals, he said. Investors were growing more wary and skeptical by the month. "The world has turned very tough."

But within a week Intel was calling. At four-nineteen in the afternoon, according to the answering machine.

"Hi, Rolly, this is Stephanie Schear calling from Intel Corporation.

Your business plan has been passed around here and finally ended in the hands that I think make sense here, since I'm focused on e-commerce. I've got a letter here from Jeff Nixon. I'm not sure what the relationship between Jeff and your company is. I appreciate the fact that he passed this on to us. I am very interested in learning more about your company . . ."

Intel? Calling us? We must have listened to that message ten times. We knew Intel was investing in young companies. We had also learned to temper our expectations. But on that afternoon, that little message sounded like the voice of God, like a validation from the heavens that we were not crazy after all. We had started out so raw, and now Intel was calling us. If there was a God, he was a jealous cuss who seemed to relent only when we were ready to sacrifice everything. We got on our knees, laughing and bowing to the phone like it was Mecca. We would go to California to see Intel.

And there was more.

"My God, this is so real!"

Susan Clancy had been sent to us by Tom Aley and Matt Lindley at Ziff Davis. She was a strawberry blond B-school hotshot, a whiz in finance and planning with a gold-plated résumé of real-world accomplishment. She was at a career turning point, didn't need a paycheck right away, and had just spent two hours getting our whole perilous, promising story.

"This is not some stupid grousing about a department head or slogging through some brain-dead corporate stuff," she exclaimed, wide-eyed at our mad push, our no-safety-net struggle. "This is very real. I think I need a martini!"

Two weeks later she was coming onboard, ready to help whip our planning documents into shape, to add real heft to our little crew.

"The question for me is, do I want to be part of the revolution or not?" she said. "I want to be part of the revolution."

And Larry D'Onofrio was back, banging on our door with his *This Old House* experience and his major sales credentials.

"You've got the crowbar under me very strong," he said. Larry had a handsome, impish face with deep brown eyes and tons of warmth. A substantial guy. He had spent a lot of time thinking about

BuildingBlocks. He had checked out our backgrounds with people who knew us well and come back for more conversations. And, almost to our dismay, he was ready to jump in.

"I believe you are really onto something here," he said. "I'm thinking things like this happen with leaps of faith. I realize I have a lot of faith in you guys. You're guys I could do something great or crazy with. If need be, I could go down the tubes with you guys."

You know we don't have a dime, we said, moved by his embrace. Be sure.

"We are living in a time of miracles," I said to Rolly that night. "There's this go-for-broke attitude out there. Leap off the dock. Get your fingers locked onto the big boat. The worst that can happen is, you fall off and swim back to shore. But to be on that boat! It shines like paradise. It defies old gravity. On that big boat, anything can happen!"

Larry introduced us to Joe Doherty. Joe was a marketing legend from another generation. He had made the Pink Panther the ubiquitous representative of Owens Corning Fiberglas insulation, winning the company an eighty percent market share in what was essentially a commodity product. He had been executive vice-president at Burson Marsteller, the world's largest public relations firm, and chairman of the Association of National Advertisers. He had saved *This Old House* in its very early days, Larry said, before the show was an institution, when it was still dying for industry support. Joe brought Owens Corning in big behind it. He was a wizard.

"I've read your materials and I like what you're doing," said Joe on the first day he walked in. "Why am I here?"

"You're here because Larry says you're a living god of marketing in this industry, and that's just about what we need," I said.

"And you know that in terms of marketing, this industry is in the dark ages?"

"We know. Stone age. But that's the opportunity, if they buy what we're building for them online. We think we can create an explosion of new consumer awareness and market growth for this industry — if the industry will come online with us. That's the issue, Joe," I said. "If we build it, will they come?"

Joe was a big, robust Irishman with a puckish grin and thick, grizzled gray eyebrows. He had been through many battles. He had always loved discovering the great new thing, Larry had said. Now he was weighing us. He ran his eye over the white board filled with Shawn's technical sketches and the bookshelves filled with books on architecture and home design and the Web. He looked us up and down and patted the stapled packet we had sent him in advance.

"Yes, I think they'll come," he finally said. "It will take some work, but yes, I do think they'll come." And he would be delighted to help us. It looked like fun.

Caroline Vanderlip called. Bob Lessin, the vice-chairman of Smith Barney and a major investor in the Internet, was interested in BuildingBlocks. He wanted to meet us.

Rick Segal put in another fifty thousand. God bless him! He wasn't giving up on us yet. BuildingBlocks gulped it down.

Danielle left a withdrawal slip from our own account on the bedroom dresser, the balance of our remaining cash circled in bright red: $14,632.

E-mail from Danielle at MIT:

Tom — I just vomited in the bathroom. I have been crying all morning. This just cannot go on. You have been pushing deadlines back and changing the story for so long. You have been able to work excessively over the past year without much complaint from me. Maybe other people who do this have other financial resources. We do not. Something definitive has to happen. I am astounded that we are weeks away from being completely broke. This was never part of the plan. I'm really in trouble here, Tom. I'm freaking out. Please help me. Please convince me that you still know what you are doing, at a personal level. I'm sorry to resort to e-mail, but I'm afraid I will just be an emotional blob via phone. Danielle.

Responding e-mail:

Danielle — Sweetheart, I am sorry for your distress. I know this is a very difficult patch. But as you know, I am not panicked. Here's why: In the next week, we have meetings with three and maybe four investors who represent the richest concentration of interest yet in this current round of funding. Each of them represents money that could do this entire next round alone. All understand that we are looking to close the deal quickly. I understand how hard it is for you to watch this process and maintain faith over so many months, and so close to the bottom of the barrel. But I believe we are about to clear this hurdle, which will bring a margin of relief. You have been a trooper, and I am grateful beyond words. I wish this had all happened with more breathing room. But nobody can script these things perfectly. Please hang in there for this next couple of weeks and I am confident we will reach the shore. Let's talk tonight. Your challenging but loving husband, Tom.

I'm on the big field at the end of the block with Lauren, walking Sadie. It's early and Lauren has scrambled to come out with me. Anything for time together. She's wearing her pajamas and a torn old Nantucket sweatshirt and, for some reason, Dylan's old checkered painting smock from kindergarten over everything. Quite a sight.

It's a big field, big enough for four soccer games at once, and this morning there's a playful wind dancing across it, ruffling the tree-tops, skittering in the grass. Lauren spots a bright white plastic gro-cery bag puffing across the grass in front of her and leans to pick it up. The wind puffs it away. She follows, stooping, grabbing, missing, as the white bag dances just out of reach.

I throw a stick for Sadie and turn around and Lauren is still chas-ing, almost in the middle of the field now, believing at every step that she is about to grab that bag, not knowing how easily the wind can keep it out in front of her all morning. She just turned three. She doesn't know. And the bag goes on billowing and tumbling, three steps ahead of her. I'm watching and starting to worry at how far away she is running, how tired she must be getting, how frustrated she must be.

"Let it go, sweetie," I yell across the wide grass. "It's okay, let it go."

But it's too windy. She can't hear me. Or maybe she can, just barely, and doesn't want to listen. She believes that if she just keeps chasing this bag — just an old plastic bag! — she will get it. And she runs and runs, and leans over to grab it and falls, and gets up and chases some more. Until she's just a speck on the other side of the field, running and running with those little legs.

For me these days, everything is metaphor. And this one is hurting me. I'm full of admiration for her sticking to it, but this is my craziness that she is acting out. This is my kind of obsession. And I don't want her to be stuck with it. Not this race, again and again. It's too painful to watch.

There's a fine old school building by the field, converted into housing for seniors now, but with four or five subsidized apartments for low-income families. Last week Ben asked me if we could move in there if we had to sell the house. He didn't want to have to leave his school.

"Who said anything about selling the house?" I asked.

"Oh, nobody," he said. "I was just thinking about it."

Right. It's bleeding into everything. The week before, I filed homesteading papers with the state that would protect the house if we go bankrupt. It was Gene Barton's suggestion. Just in case. But I hadn't even mentioned it to Danielle. How did Ben feel our house shaking?

"We're not moving anywhere, buddy," I told him, and gave him a hug. "We're staying right here, at home."

But what did I know?

Far across the field now, my girl is running. And the bag is full of mischief and twists and puffs that keep it just always ahead of her, just out of reach. She has fallen again. And she's up again, in her crazy clothes and flying hair. And now she turns and lunges in her sprouting toddler way, and suddenly she's got it. She's got it!

I cheer and shout across the field. She turns in triumph, holding her little arms out like a bird against the wind and runs back toward me, bag in hand. Sadie runs alongside her, leaping and turning. It is a perfect picture. I jump and howl and clap in big swings of my arms. She got it! She didn't give up. She never gave up. And I am hollering in the morning light and running to her, holding my arms out across the broad field, and I realize I am crying like a fool.

Chapter 13

www.homeportfolio.com

Now, *this* was the new economy.

Dinner for four at Caroline Vanderlip's excellent new apartment on Manhattan's Upper East Side. A block from Park Avenue. A block and a half from Central Park. Almost no furniture yet, but a vase of beautiful cut flowers on the sideboard. A table strewn with cartons of Chinese takeout. Eight days before Christmas. And not one of us had the slightest idea what we would be doing in six weeks. High road to glory? Busted and starting over? We had no idea. Only gripping possibilities.

Caroline was now CEO of Softbank Interactive Marketing, a prominent New York firm selling banner advertising on the Internet, and the firm was hugely in play. It would be sold within days. Caroline was working the deal herself but had no idea if she'd be staying on. New owners, new strategies, new considerations. No guarantees. Zero. Maybe they'd want her out. Maybe she'd be gone before they could even decide. And who would *they* be, anyway? Who knew?

Mark was on the phone eight hours a day raising money for an Internet startup in New Jersey where he had signed on. They had a great concept, putting the Web to work in the field for big insurance companies. But they needed just a few million more to really get going. Just five or ten million. And it might be there for them! He was so close! And it might not be there for them! What then?

Who knew?

Then there were the juice guys, Rolly and I, just into the city for yet another manic rush at money. We had not a certainty in the world as we stabbed dumplings at Caroline's warm table, twirling chopsticks and laughing and slurping soup like Shanghai boatmen. Only a plan and possibilities. A vision and a gun to our heads. The end was near. And so was the dream.

"Hey everybody, we're home!" we would sing out these days as we tumbled into their apartment, eyes bleary and rear ends sore from yet another four-hour push down the highway from Boston. Danny and Linnae's suburban place wasn't central enough for the do-or-die crusade we were on now. Caroline and Mark's was perfectly located and perfectly attuned to the high-wire atmospherics. All limos and jewels on the street outside. All keen apprehension and sympathy for our quest inside. The place was battle-ready: phone lines, fax lines, Internet on, cabs right outside. When opportunity knocked, we would be at its throat. We slept in the "green room." The color of money, I thought. And life, and envy, and traffic lights when they're saying go. Go, go!

"Welcome home, kids!" Mark would call back from the den or kitchen, in his best post–Partridge family allusion to slippers and pipes and hearthside ease. There were still trappings. Their doorman knew us well by now. So did their little Park Avenue dogs with their little pink Park Avenue bows and sparkly collars. And there were the flowers.

"Come on in!" Caroline would say, sweeping through the foyer, grand as always, wise blue eyes taking an instant reading on our health, posture, and morale. "Chef Dragon is on the table."

The weeks since Caroline hooked us up with Bob Lessin had been a light-speed introduction to the top echelon of American wealth and New York scheduling. In Boston we were struggling to hold our families together, juggling new talent and near-empty coffers, crunching night and day with Shawn to get up the first fully functioning Web site version of HomePortfolio. It was cool. It was sophisticated. It was a lot of work for one tech guy and a thimbleful of help.

In New York we were running. Always running, from meeting to meeting with our shoulder bags and laptops and business plan. Running from posh office to posher office. Running for cabs when it was too far to sprint. Running through Manhattan's glossy, Christmas-decked canyons to five and six investor meetings a day. Running for money. Running for our lives.

Lessin had given us his thumbs-up in November. He was a legendary Wall Street dealmaker, fabled for starting his days at Morgan Stanley at four in the morning and keeping a whole platoon of lieutenants racing in his wake to wrap up the deals he spun off in waves. Everything about him said speed. Even phone calls were double-pumped, with his secretary, Michelle, hovering in the background on the line, always ready to execute on Lessin's shower of instructions, ideas, simultaneous interlocking phone conversations. Go, go.

He had been knocked down by a crippling stroke when he was thirty-nine, but fought his way back to health, jumped to the top tier of Smith Barney, and now, at forty-two, lived like a man who didn't assume he had forever. We had not met anyone who cut to the heart of things so quickly. Lessin had become a huge believer in the transforming power of the Internet. He was in the middle of a major personal investment push, sinking millions of his own money into promising Web startups and encouraging his circle of wealthy business friends to do the same.

We had taken Jeff Nixon's advice and were focused on raising just enough money to get the full HomePortfolio Web site up and into the market. We wanted to be raising more, enough to really push ahead, but one million would cover us for now if it had to. Just one million.

We met Lessin twice, the second time with Joe Doherty along. Bob grilled us upside and down, tapping notes nonstop into his pocket computer. He was a high-gigabyte combination of numbers whiz and instinct player. He had already dug into the beta desktop version of HomePortfolio. He had done his homework on Rolly and me. Now he ran us through our business assumptions and projections again, turning the model this way and that, and began to nod.

"I like you guys," he said suddenly, slapping his computer shut. "And I like this opportunity."

Two days later he was back to us. He would come in at a pre-money valuation of BuildingBlocks that was flat with our first round. He knew we'd prefer a bump, but that wasn't where the market was today, he said. He would invest $250,000, contingent on our

WWW.HOMEPORTFOLIO.COM / 263

raising at least a million beyond that, to leave us with a million free and clear in the fuel tank after the company's outstanding debts were paid. He would commit his chunk on those terms and would put us in touch with a group of his high-flying tycoon friends to raise the rest.

"You will be exposed to an incredible pool of capital and an incredible community of support," he said, and he was off, working his next deal. Three days later our new patron-in-waiting, the fabled vice-chairman of Smith Barney, e-mailed an introduction to his golden horde:

> The more I've analyzed BuildingBlocks, the more interested I've become in the company. Simplistically, the company develops software and services that allow consumers and trade professionals to select home design products more efficiently via the Internet. There are a number of aspects that particularly intrigue me about this company, including:
>
> 1. The quality of the management in its business acumen, maturity and honesty;
> 2. The technological skills of the company, which have been confirmed to me by knowledgeable third parties;
> 3. The fragmented nature of the industry, with 20,000 manufacturers and no national upscale retailers;
> 4. The nature of the purchase decision, which is both large and infrequent (thereby resulting in an uninformed market);
> 5. The nature of the decision maker, who is most likely upscale and female, a highly attractive demographic profile; and
> 6. The enormous upside potential in latter years. . . .

Suddenly, finally, we had a big friend in very high places.

What we didn't have was time.

The plastic was stretched to the limit. Rolly and I had drawn no salary for ten months. Rick's last dollop of cash for the company was almost gone, and there was no more coming. Our personal resources were almost tapped out.

Meanwhile, the economy was booming all around us. It was hard some days not to feel like idiots. We had turned ourselves into paupers in the middle of the hottest economy of the century. The stock market was beyond sky-high. Manhattan was rippling with money. There were flocks of well-dressed skaters skimming under the glittering Christmas tree at Rockefeller Center. Why had I ever read that damned *New York Times* series on the downsizing of America? What a joke! Even the *Times*'s own stock, the currency of my old *Globe* stock options, had soared since I was required to cash out. I started to do a quick calculation as we drove down from Boston, and it looked as though I might have walked away from almost a million dollars. Danielle would kill me if she knew. Prosperity absolutely ruled. My God, even the snowman was probably rich! And here we were, on the freaking brink of bankruptcy.

It's still the right thing, I told myself. Breathe slowly. Don't panic. Keep going. You're on the right wave. Eyes on the prize, now. Don't get confused. Grab the future. Keep the faith, baby.

But I was almost flat broke. Only my brother Todd's bailing me out with $10,000 just before Christmas kept the furnace running and put a little fringe of presents for the kids under our tree. God only knew how long that ten thousand would have to last.

"Our daughters will travel with steamer trunks!" Rolly would say with his crazed confidence when I would look down from the high wire and start to moan.

"We can't eat moonbeams, Tom!" Danielle said when I came home late and she was wrapping the little mound of presents by the tree.

"It's not moonbeams." I sighed, standing weary and wondering in the twinkling light. "It's our future."

She eyed me now with the look of a wary animal trying to figure the exact strength of another. I had taken us to the very edge. Did I have the strength to make it? Did she have the strength to somehow stop me if I started pulling the whole family over the brink? If it hadn't been the Internet, it probably would have been something else. I had come to feel in some unspoken way that the best way ahead was not more but less. Less security. Less comfort. Less practiced ways and habits. I had wanted to be vulnerable. I had wanted to struggle at the cliff's edge, to feel the adrenaline flow. Now it was flowing. But what a monumentally self-absorbed urge! An absolute affront to her priorities of family, bread, and wine. I will take a wild leap, I was saying. And I will take you with me. But she was no passive hostage. In the end — and the end was close — she would make her own decision.

And so she looked at me with the close, steady gaze of a jungle cat whose turf was being seriously threatened by some large, crazed animal. It was an unnerving look. Frightening, even though I was almost twice her weight. I didn't know how to read it. And for a moment, she knew she had me scared.

"Are you going to leave me?" I asked, lunging for the bottom line, hoping to break the spell.

She kept me hanging, turning a pair of scissors slowly in her hand, then released me nice and slow. And I knew she would hang in.

"Not until you make your millions," she said evenly, with the one arched brow and deep glimmer that told me she would stay. She would stay on her own terms, with her own values, her own view. And her own humor.

"If I divorced you now," she said, "I'd be the one paying you support."

And so we ran. Rehearsing our first pitch for the Lessin gang in the back of a battered cab hurtling down to Wall Street. Me fumbling the pitch at a breakfast meeting high above the J. P. Morgan building, where the silver was perfect and crystal was spotless and the orange juice was freshly squeezed. Never mind. Go, go. To a pile of German money managed out of offices with a bigger view of Central Park than Landsat's. To Hollywood money and high-tech money and real estate money and even Venezuelan money. And hey, that was Cindy Crawford we just ran by! Right there, by the Plaza Hotel! Never mind. Go. To Olaf Olafsson, the cool Icelandic mogul up off Fifth Avenue. To Joe Flom, the biggest media attorney in New York. To Kohlberg Kravis Roberts, as in KKR itself, and Mark Lipshultz, the gatekeeper for Henry Kravis. And we stood in the lobby of KKR's astonishingly lavish offices with holes in our shoes, the last meeting of that day, sweating in December, trying to catch our breath as we stared out over a view of New York that looked bigger than the world. Was this really us? Here? The crazed bedroom guys with their wild idea and not a pot to piss in?

It was. It was us. And the commitments started to come in. Fifty thousand here. Two hundred and fifty thousand there. A nod from one of the original investors in Home Depot. But the holidays were rushing down on us. Not everyone was as quick on the trigger as Bob Lessin. None of the money turned to cash anyway until we hit Lessin's requirement of a million dollars free and clear. And the rich started to leave town, for Park City, Utah, and Tahiti and Patagonia. Or they wanted us to come out and visit, in L.A. and Caracas.

Caracas!

There wasn't time!

Greetings from Planet Ashbrook. We wish you holly berry, pine bough, fire and snow, or whatever sweet totems your hemisphere adores. . . .

The Chinese curse says, "May you live in interesting times." Well, my dears, we are there. Tom's midlife outburst of Internet entrepreneurship has reacquainted the family with seven-day work weeks, spine-tingling financial adventure, and some serious Gs on the nuclear contract. We remain upright, united, and amazed by the journey. But whether this sudden pilgrimage is burnishing our souls or just punching them up is the subject of considerable household debate.

Danielle, while loving and supportive way beyond the call of duty, thinks Tom is nuts. It would have been so much easier if he had just gone bungee jumping. She agrees that opportunity is a wonderful thing, but prefers opportunities that do not begin with a capital "O." Like getting bulbs planted or the house painted. Or having Dad around to put his three-year-old to bed at least once a month. Danielle did not sign up to be a struggling single parent, but has nearly been awarded that status anyway. This escapade would not work without her, but it is not what she would have chosen from the menu of life just now. "I knew when I married you that you would probably do something crazy in the middle of your life," she said the other night, on a rare occasion when Tom got home before 11 and they fell asleep together. "I just never expected this kind of crazy."

Tom, meanwhile, is a man on a mission, with all the charming eccentricities of that fevered state. He works all the time and is distracted when he's not working. He hates to talk about bank balances. His idea of fun is good chemistry in a meeting with venture capitalists in New York. He saw Cindy Crawford on the sidewalk in Manhattan last week, but was in such a rush he didn't even look twice. This is serious. He says he feels fine, but his dentist recently recommended a nighttime "appliance" that would stop him from grinding his teeth in his sleep. Tom likes to see this passage as a transformative test that will yield to a bright new dawn of insight, life mastery, and family ease. But transformative test results are hard to predict. Most days, this test feels like driving a loaded car — make that a minivan — along a sheer cliff at 110 mph. Can this be good? He prays for God's mercy.

Blessedly, the younger passengers are thriving. Lauren, 3, is a fabulous pistol, into ruby slippers and group hugs. Ben, 11, is in the groove, with his guitar and sports and observant streak that will serve him well in middle school. Dylan, 15, is a man, holding down his job at Johnny's Diner, hefting a load of honors courses, and hitting the river every day this fall for crew. Together, they keep the house full of music and mischief and smelly socks and hordes of friends of many ages. Their sweet, earnest energy challenges and uplifts and supports us every day. Some days, it is our main fuel. . . .

So, life is wild. We'll take it. We send our love and wish you joy.

Tom, Danielle, Dylan, Ben & Lauren — Christmas, 1997

"We loved your Christmas letter," my friend Jonathan said when I met him on the street. "Barb read it and was full of admiration for your honesty. She said she couldn't remember a more honest conversation with anybody in Newton. Everybody here is supposed to be winning all the time. Nobody talks about failing. She just loved it."

And I laughed and said thanks, yes, things had been a little crazy. But I preferred to think of it as striving, not failing, thank you. Striving that flirted with failing. Striving marbled with setbacks. But not failure. Please.

Behind the fund-raising storm and fury, a quiet, beautiful thing was happening. The fully functioning HomePortfolio Web site was finally coming together. We'd been told to simplify, and the Web was great for that. It demanded simplicity. Elegance. Forget the bells and whistles. Focus on the main thing.

And the main thing was finding wonderful home design products. Premium products, not in the sense of snobbish or slathered in gold, but in the sense of truly excellent quality. Products that would serve and last, with top-tier design and materials and workmanship. People were tired of junk that broke. When they could have it, they wanted the top-of-the-line. People were tired of mass-produced homes. When they could manage, they wanted unique home design products that expressed their personal tastes and aspirations. And people didn't want to have to search forever for the right products for their homes. Women, especially, with everything else they were juggling, didn't have the time. But women were often the ones with the most demanding eye, the ones who took responsibility for making their personal living environment a place of comfort and wonder.

Month by month, gasping along on our shoestring finances, we had pulled the pieces together. We had designed a service that had never existed before the Web — that could never exist without the Web. From a thousand trade shows and showrooms and catalogues and architects' and designers' suggestions, we had built the core of a great database of the world's best home design products. They were beautiful. And the software Shawn had woven around them would help people easily find exactly what they wanted. And if users found something they liked and wanted to see more products like that one — whether it was a carved mantelpiece, or a copper sink, or an off-beat Windsor chair, or a leaded window — HomePortfolio would scan the database and pull up their options. Seung Park, a terrific young graphic artist, was working with us now, producing the highest-quality photo scans anywhere on the Web. Images that were up-to-date, luscious, detailed, almost tactile. And when people found the things they wanted to make their house their home, they could save those images and product information to a personal online portfolio with the click of a button. They could learn where the nearest retail showrooms for that product were. And soon, we knew, they would be able to order right there, on the Web, if that's what they wanted to do.

It wasn't our full vision. The Web couldn't handle that yet. But it would, in time. For now, we would offer all the Web could deliver. And it was a lot. To a lot of people. Month by month the number of Americans online was soaring. And we would soar with them.

Night after night we worked, tweaking, coding, honing, refining. We were hardworking churchmice. And in January, when the snow was deep and the cupboards were bare, and we had tested and tested our creation, the new HomePortfolio site went live. Shawn poked his head through my door, grinning and twinkling.

"The whole world can see it now," he said.

"You mean it's up?"

"It's up!"

I turned to my keyboard, brought up the Web browser, and for the first time ever typed in our electronic address to the world, watching it grow letter by letter across the screen: www.homeportfolio.com.

And there it was. Clean, beautiful, and working. The Internet would change the world in a million categories. We had just changed it in ours.

At last.

"This is beeeeeeauuuuutiful! Gorgeous! It's incredible. You guys should be very, very proud."

Art Bardige had come for show-and-tell. He had HomePortfolio up on Shawn's monitor and was putting it through its paces, poking and prodding, asking exactly how we had pulled off its different features. And he loved it. Top to bottom.

"This is plum gorgeous," he kept saying under his breath. "Plum gorgeous."

We couldn't hear it enough. He played and played until he had explored every feature. He asked about the desktop version and its CD-ROM starter kit. Coming, we said. Right, he said. Good priorities. Web first. The Web's the thing. Let's go to lunch, he said. He had an agenda.

It took two cars to hold us all that day. Joe Doherty was in. Susan Clancy was not. Her brother-in-law was sick and she was helping the family. Jim Tobey was there. Jim had spent most of his life designing and building high-end houses in Vermont. He had helped launch a successful medical information company. He was looking for something new. A friend of Jeff Nixon's had put him in touch with us, and he had dug into BuildingBlocks with a vengeance, all pay deferred until we were funded. What a time we lived in, when talented people like this were free agents, ready to be snagged and employed by a tiny startup stuffed into an old church.

Art got straight to his point. HomePortfolio was fantastic. But until we had paying customers, we were not a real business. And until we were a real business, investment money was never going to come as fast as we needed it. Not everyone would invest in a dream.

He knew we had been stretched to the limit. He knew it had been tough. But what were we waiting for now? Scott Smith and Rick had asked for proof of concept a year ago. It was time to stand and deliver.

We were mildly defensive. We had been talking to manufacturers all over the country, we said, showing them early versions of the product, getting their feedback, using it to guide our work, to shape the product.

Art didn't want to hear it. His money was in this company. And his brother-in-law's money, and his brother-in-law's friend's money. And he had never said it, but we knew he was out on a limb for us. A $650,000 limb now.

"Okay, okay," he said sharply, suddenly animated, pushing his face into ours, wagging a big finger at our chests. "That's good. That's great. But forget about feedback for a minute here, guys. You've created something of real value to them. Tremendous value. These manufacturers should be ready to pay for it. So go get the money! Go sell. Go sell it right now!"

He was almost shouting. Bertucci's was not a quiet restaurant, but Art's voice had steadily risen above the din until the tables around us were beginning to hush and turn and listen. People stared. Art was oblivious. He had come with a message. He was going to be sure we got it. Rolly and I, right between the eyes. We were the ones who would have to make the first sales. And he wasn't sure yet that we really, really got it. We weren't yet nodding with enough gusto.

"What?" he flat-out shouted now, challenging, hands opened wide and pumping the air over his plate like he was shaking us. "You think it's going to be easy? Excuse me? You are selling something brand-new here! Brand-new! It won't be easy! But you . . . are . . . ready! Got it? You're ready! So get . . . out . . . there . . . and . . . sell!"

We nodded hard now. Real hard. Shoulders and everything. So did half the restaurant, peering at us like we were dim and shiftless bums who needed a swift kick in the ass. And we'd just got it.

Five days later, Rolly and I landed at O'Hare airport in a blinding snowstorm. The American headquarters of Grohe, the giant German faucet maker, was just outside Chicago. Our little rental car could barely move in the drifts and howling wind. Street signs were plastered, unreadable. We got lost, wandered, and finally found Grohe America's big plant in the swirling snow. This was it. Proof of concept time.

Grohe made beautiful, finely engineered faucets. Their marketing staff was not afraid of technology. They had their own Web site up and had already learned both the advantages and limitations of their corporate site. Al DeGenova and Jeff Carney had been avidly watching HomePortfolio evolve for two years. They had worked with us to see how we built electronic brochures for our beta version. They were smart, open-minded marketers trying to peer into the electronic future. And there we were. They took us upstairs to an enormous boardroom. I pictured a planeload of sturdy German executives showing up here once a year to sit in splendor and look over their shoulders.

We opened the laptop and began again to tell the HomePortfolio story. We had told it so many times now, it was distilled almost into scripture. What we were doing, why we were doing it, what it would do for them. The snow muffled everything outside. Our whole world shrank to this one room, this one table. At that moment, Al and Jeff were our best-informed potential customers anywhere. They were our single best chance in the world at landing this first sale. They could have no idea how much was riding on their decision this morning. And we could not tell them. If they came in, the odds of BuildingBlocks thriving, of my marriage thriving, of my children having college tuition money, of Louise and our parents and my brother and sister and Art and Rick and Scott seeing their money again, all soared. And if they said no, you could just flip all those odds right around.

We showed them the electronic brochures we had created for Grohe in HomePortfolio. They looked fabulous. The big clear images of their beautiful faucets looked almost real enough to touch. HomePortfolio users, we reminded them, would be able to see all the best faucets on the market, including those of their competitors. We would show all the best for free, editorially. That's what people needed. That's what they would come for. But if Grohe was a client, users could click right through the smaller editorial presentation and into these luscious electronic brochures. Right at the moment of their greatest interest. And the brochures would tell them everything they needed to know about the faucet that had caught their eye. And they would direct them to the nearest showroom or, when they were ready, take an order right there online. They could fill the order themselves or let the nearest showroom have the sale. It would all be the same to us. Either way, this was the future. This was the emerging main line to the minds of their very best customers.

Please, please, please believe that, I was thinking, praying, beaming across the table. Please feel the power of the dream, of the new frontier, of everything we've slaved over. And most of all, pleeeeease don't send us home empty-handed!

They didn't. They liked it, they said. They liked it a lot. In fact, it looked really great.

And we walked out with a handshake on a contract for $27,000 and stood in the parking lot just breathing, with snow in our shoes and snow in our hair and snow in our eyes. And for a long minute, I thought I might faint dead away.

We had proof of concept.

I had been dialing for dollars for so long, I felt like a telemarketer. Hello, Mrs. Yablinsky? I hope I didn't interrupt your dinner. I'm calling from BuildingBlocks Interactive and we're looking to raise three and a half million dollars, and I wondered if you and your husband might consider a small . . .

But now we had something to talk about. We had a sale. Grohe's $27,000 check had come in, as promised. When I deposited it, the BuildingBlocks balance came to $29,000. We had been down to $2,000. That, I thought, definitely qualified as cutting it close.

And soon we had another sale, from Gaggenau, the German manufacturer of fabulous ranges, cooktops, and ovens. What was with these Germans? I told Shawn they must like his precision software engineering. Wolfram Pabst von Ohain, the grandly named marketing head of Gaggenau USA, said he was looking for good value and we offered it. Simple. Then Du Pont Corian was in. Carol Gee gave the green light. This was good. The people who knew us best were beginning to vote with their feet, with their dollars. Thank God.

But we were still teetering at the edge of the cliff. We were making our little payroll with pennies to spare. We were tapping out Uncle Visa. The credit card companies had finally begun to notice the huge bump under the rug of this guy named Rolly Rouse. They could pull the cards, call the loans, bring the whole tent crashing down.

So I was on the phone again to VC land, scouring our lists for the firms that had left an open door. Maybe, just maybe, we could bypass the million-dollar round and go straight to three million, our ideal target — not so big that we had to sell too much of the company before we could build its value, not so small that we would run out of gas again.

Who to call? Intel had been vague when we got there. We couldn't get a fix on their real interest. None of the Boston VCs seemed to go for this kind of play, except for one maybe. We had talked several times in the fall with Joe Tischler at the Still River Fund. Still River was a relatively new venture capital fund, but they had already had some remarkable successes and they weren't afraid of consumer-oriented businesses. Best of all, they knew our category very well. Joe had a strong background in retailing, including mail order and a stint as head of Bloomingdale's furniture division. He knew our neck of the woods intimately. He had always told us to call him when we made our first sale. Rolly called him. Let's catch up, he said.

Who else had we talked to who really understood the market we were in? I ran up and down the list, asking myself why on earth we had dug into such a complicated industry. Why hadn't we just put up a site for books or music CDs? Something easily shipped. An industry with big, existing databases that had already catalogued all the available products. An industry with simple, single-product purchases. You want a book, you buy a book. You don't have to sit on it first. And it doesn't matter if it goes with your wallpaper. Amazon.com was already a phenom; we were still building the deep architecture required to handle the huge, hairy home improvement industry. I asked myself the question, but I knew the answer already. We had dug into this industry because it excited our passion, and we wanted to work with passion. And we had dug into this industry precisely because it was so complex. Even getting simple information was difficult, let alone selecting whole rooms of products that had to work together. And the Internet made available, for the very first time, a medium that could cut through that complexity. All it took was a company wild enough to tackle the challenge. Like ours.

Who would understand that? Oh, yeah, Scripps Ventures. We may have been zombies the day we met with Benjy Burditt, but he had liked what he heard. Their parent company, E. W. Scripps, owned HGTV, so they knew the industry. And they were a major investor in Garden Escape, at garden.com, already the leading gardening e-commerce site on the Web. I called Benjy in New York. We had started to make sales, I said. He bored in on the details and seemed to like what he heard. I'll get back to you, he said.

I hoped he meant soon. BuildingBlocks was bumping the bottom every day. Running on traces of fumes. What could we do? Sell! Sell more!

Jim Tobey and I hit the road. Down to Philadelphia, where old John Ashbrook came ashore, and into Pennsylvania. We met with Baldwin Brass, one of Masco's big companies. They loved Home-Portfolio. And they were huge! Make us a proposal, they said. We drove deep into Pennsylvania Dutch country, weaving around the old clip-clop carts of the Amish and through miles of dairy farms to see Rutt, the fine cabinetmaker, and Plain & Fancy, whose lovely cabinetry was riding a wave of consumer enthusiasm.

We almost had to jam our foot in the door to talk to Plain & Fancy. Their head of marketing, Vince Achey, was just back from Europe and couldn't be bothered with some unknown Internet site. But Tobey was unstoppable. He talked us in and kept talking while we fired up the laptop, and before we were five minutes into our presentation, Vince was on the phone to his advertising agency in Bethlehem.

"You've got to see this," he was saying on the phone while we clicked on through the presentation. "This is not like the other stuff. Can you see these guys today?"

So there we were, in a grand old mansion that had been converted into an ad agency in Bethlehem, Pennsylvania, the home of the once-great U.S. steel industry, the mythical heart and soul of brick-

and-mortar America. And the steel mills were empty. And the mansion of some great captain of industry was now the funky office of White, Good & Company. And we were sitting at their big conference table selling something even less material than traditional advertising, selling electrical impulses that would travel over an invisible Internet. Fancy that, Andrew Carnegie!

And they loved it.

We kept rolling through coal country and, by evening, were into the Delaware Gap, on a truck stop pay phone effusing to Rolly about the reception we were getting. It was awesome! He was subdued on the other end of the line. There was no money left, he said. Zip. And no credit. And he didn't know where to turn. And I didn't know what to tell him. We had lightning in a bottle here, and the bottle was falling toward the floor.

We rolled on north. In Greenwich, Connecticut, we sat with Christopher Peacock, the classy English cabinetry manufacturer who in only a few years had made his name into a vaunted American brand. And Christopher wanted into HomePortfolio, too. We talked to the head of Country Floors' Greenwich showroom, with its amazing tiles, and showed him our stuff, and he insisted we get in touch, and soon, with their head office in Los Angeles. But would we still be around?

Should we believe in miracles? Two days later, we were sitting in the old church with Alan Steinert. Alan was on the board of Boston's biggest homeless shelter with Carole, Rolly had told me, and I'm thinking, great, maybe he can get us a bed. But that wasn't it. Alan was interested in investing in BuildingBlocks. He had for years been the New England distributor for Whirlpool and KitchenAid. He knew the business inside and out. He saw the opportunity. And he was crazy about Carole.

He was ready to put in $50,000. Right away.

"I'm doing this because of you two guys," he said when we had told him the story and laid out our circumstances in unvarnished detail. "I'm doing this because I trust you to work hard and to work smart."

And another angel was born. Just in time.

* * *

We were getting very familiar with near-death experiences. Now Rolly had his own. We were booked to present BuildingBlocks at the Harvard Business School's Cyberposium, an annual gathering of many of the biggest names in the Internet world. Jerry Yang, co-founder of Yahoo!, was the keynote speaker. The program was jammed with Internet heavyweights, top executives from E*Trade and AOL and ONSALE and iVillage and Trilogy and Ziff Davis and the Motley Fool and ABCnews.com. And us. BuildingBlocks Interactive. Tom Ashbrook and Rolly Rouse, right there in the program as representatives of the next wave of promising Internet startups.

The only problem was, Rolly's body decided not to go along with the program. He had been feeling poorly, and just before the conference had checked in with his doctor. The doctor stopped everything. Rolly's appendix was swollen to the size of a plump California grapefruit. It could burst any second. It had to come out immediately.

And so I stood that night in front of a packed B-school hall alone, with laptop and digital projector, walking once again through the basics of the BuildingBlocks business model and showing off HomePortfolio. It looked like the same hall where I had listened to Amar Bhide instruct his class of would-be entrepreneurs to find good models, and learn the right lessons, and be good observers, and be ready for lifelong change. The hall was standing room only, and the questions came fast and hard. These people were trained to pick apart business proposals. But I had been picked apart a hundred times before and had listened and observed and changed. And when the lights came up, there was applause. Not just polite clapping, but real, rippling applause. And a mob of students being very complimentary and handing over their business cards and asking about jobs.

It was too surreal. BuildingBlocks was being applauded at the Harvard Business School. HomePortfolio was selling like hotcakes in Chicago and the Amish country and Greenwich. My wife thought I was borderline insane. My partner was going nip and tuck under the surgeon's knife. My personal bank account was rattling down to its last few coins again. And even with Alan Steinert's marvelous $50,000, we were only weeks away from flaming out.

I drove to Rolly's house and got him on the phone in his hospital bed and danced in the kitchen with Carole while I relayed our B-school triumph. And his voice was so weak and pained and small on the other end that it felt once more that even now it could all be a cruel mirage. We could have dragged our families across the rugged foothills of this thrilling, punishing new economy for all this time only to see the whole glittering dream go *poof!*

The envelope was addressed in her familiar hand and mailed to the office so Danielle wouldn't see it and be worried. Rolly was still in the hospital. Shawn had worked all night and was snoring in a sleeping bag at the back of the office. Tobey was on the road. Katherine, who had suffered the weight of keeping our nightmarish books through this trial, had finally found it all too much and left to weave birch and willow. I sat at my desk with a stack of bills and a plain little envelope from my mother.

"Dear Tom," she wrote, with the hand that had sent me a thousand encouraging notes over the years. She had never had money, but she was a river of love.

"Enclosed is a little present. Don't even dream of not taking it. It makes my working worthwhile to do something like this. Somehow we thought there might be some bills that this could help with a wee bit. You've given us so much pleasure. This is just a 'little repayment.' We love you all. Love, Mom & Dad."

And a check for $1,000.

It was not a small sum to my mother, not a small gift to me. She was right. We did need it. But so did they. And I stood alone on the top floor of the old church and cried. Again. What kind of journey was this? Were we finally winning here or just plain losing it? And what did I do to deserve parents like this? A wife like mine? Kids who didn't mind moving to subsidized housing but just hoped we could stay in the neighborhood?

I didn't know. But we were way past the exits now. We were naked and lashed to the mast. And I could smell redemption out there. Somewhere.

I clutched that check like a good luck charm, like a totem of powers that were bottomless and beyond all this. And ran to the bank.

* * *

Benjy Burditt called, from Scripps Ventures. He had talked with HGTV in Knoxville, he said, and the home and garden cable television powerhouse owned by E. W. Scripps had said it saw no conflict if Scripps Ventures considered an investment in BuildingBlocks. HGTV would be active on the Internet, but in its own way. He had a green light to talk with us, he said. And what's more, he had been hearing good word-of-mouth reports on BuildingBlocks.

Cool!

"So we should get together," Benjy said. "Send us your most recent business plan, and let's make a date to meet in New York."

Yes!

Rolly was back on his feet. The business plan factory was back in business. FedEx was there, right on time. Joe Tischler from Still River was calling. Between Alan Steinert's money and our first few sales, we were covering the rent. Bob Lessin was still onboard, with his gang in the wings. We were on the dance card with Scripps. Maybe this was the wave that would get us to the other side. I prayed it was. I didn't know if we had the resources to wait for another one.

So don't wait. Push now. Keep moving. Keep selling. One chance. This chance. Right now.

I was on the plane to Memphis and driving south across Mississippi, to Greenwood, on the Yazoo River, deep in the Mississippi Delta. Greenwood was the home of the Viking Range Corporation, and Viking wanted to talk about HomePortfolio.

Next to Corian, this was the biggest name we had talked with yet. Viking was a phenomenon. Its powerful, commercial-style ovens and ranges had become such a hit that people tended to assume the company had been around forever. Not so. Viking was the brainchild of a Greenwood native, Fred Carl, Jr., who wanted a commercial range that would work in his kitchen and couldn't find one, so he started a company and became the first manufacturer to offer an oven with a commercial look and quality for the home. It was a wild success, but for all Viking's stature and name recognition, the company was little more than a decade old. It was a lesson in how a smart bricks-and-mortar company could still turn out a smart, well-made product and hit it big in a hurry.

The drive down from Memphis was a journey through time. Mississippi's red clay and swampland and scrub forests still looked to my eye like a setting for William Faulkner and misty tales of the Old South. The radio was all country music and fierce gospel. The bare fields of early spring were ready for cotton. They made me think of my grandfather, Evar, and our long days working in the fields together, and the old glass water jug we would carry with us, wrapped in ancient rags and deep dust to keep it cool by the fencerow. I loved those days with him and that cool, deep jug and the smell of earth that would fill us when we drank. And Mississippi brought all that back. There were some things that the Web would never do.

Viking had a big factory on the edge of town, but its corporate headquarters was in the middle of Greenwood's historic cotton trading district, in a wonderful restored opera house right on the banks of the Yazoo. Where riverboats had loaded cotton and delivered Dixie dandies to the opera, Viking was now designing high-style, high-tech cooking and cooling appliances that had made it world-famous.

Bob Gregory, the company's easygoing advertising manager, took me into the old opera house, and I laid out in detail what Home-Portfolio could do for Viking. His company had a deep line of wonderful products that most people never got to see. HomePortfolio could help them communicate their full line to serious shoppers and direct those shoppers to showrooms where they could touch and feel and buy.

With their deep line, I said, Viking ought to consider a big presence in HomePortfolio. Maybe a $45,000 contract. And Bob liked it. The whole thing. He even liked being on a Web site where people could see all his top-tier competitors' products, too. That would draw the crowd, he said. And Viking would stand up just fine to the competition. More than fine. He expected they'd like to do this. I'd know in a few days.

This was really getting to be fun. I drove back up to Oxford, Mississippi, to spend the night before my flight the next day from Memphis. Oxford was Faulkner's hometown, not to mention John Grisham's. I slept in a bed-and-breakfast that dated from before the Civil War and rose at dawn to walk the grounds of Rowan Oaks, Faulkner's famous home. It was easy to feel his mystic rhythms there, in the quiet first daylight. Me, a heat seeker. Pushing Internet dreams. Longing for a dusty old water jug. Walking happy with Faulkner's ghost. This life could be all right if it would just pull together. I'm not crazy. I'm just looking for air.

The flight out of Memphis was delayed. I worked the phone for two hours from the airport, until I ran out of numbers to call. There was a message on my office phone from the *New York Times,* the House & Home section. They were interested in HomePortfolio. Cool. I still had hours to wait.

I took a cab to Graceland.

I laughed in the Jungle Room.

I marveled at the amazing face of the American dream. His face. My face. All our faces.

I put a flower on Elvis's grave. It couldn't hurt.

Be with me, Elvis, I prayed. Be with me now. It's my last train to Memphis, brother. Get me on it.

Chapter 14

The Real McCoy

THERE IS A LIMIT to what anybody can ask from their family, themselves, their colleagues.

We were at that limit. A ways beyond it, even. We were marching in free fall. Rolly added up the company's bills. The BuildingBlocks account was $800 short, and the hole was growing every day. I had four weeks' worth of my own cash left to support the family. We'd be bankrupt just in time for the boys' birthdays. The dining room ceiling at home was falling in, from a hidden leak upstairs. I couldn't afford the plumbers to get it repaired. Lauren was still sleeping in her crib, jammed in corner to corner now. We were making the minimum possible payment on every overdue bill. This could not last.

I had started rambling on to Danielle about living in the moment. We couldn't change the path that had brought us to this point, I said. And we couldn't know the future. So let's just try to live in the moment. Let's look for joy second by second.

She looked at me now as if I was truly a dangerous lunatic.

When Danielle went out one Saturday morning to carefully shop for groceries, I crept to the upstairs phone and quietly inquired of some polite young woman at an 800 number exactly how to cash out our last cupful of dollars, the humble little retirement savings that we had worked for years to put aside. What would the penalties be for early withdrawal? How quickly could I get the money? I mean, exactly how many days would it take?

When I wasn't looking for joy second by second, I was feeling like a criminal. I never imagined it would come to this. I believed this venture would work, but I never expected to have to back up that belief with so much faith. It wasn't rational. It was way beyond rational. I imagined there were people out there who were somehow much better at playing this game, but I didn't know how they did it. I only knew we needed to win. I only knew that if we didn't win now, the consequences for my family would be very real. I had never imagined exposing them to this much turmoil. Where would we go if it all fell apart? Back to the farm, like my parents, to scrape by? Would we be as resilient as my parents had been? Would I be bitter? When would we really laugh again and be lighthearted? When would Danielle smile?

I had no idea.

And then, only then, the phone began to ring.

First, it was Joe Tischler. He had been following our progress. He was impressed. It was time for his Still River Fund to take a serious look at investing. No guarantees. He had warmed and walked before. But he was interested. One thing he knew he would want us to do was to bring on a proven operations guy. Someone with strong hands-on experience with the day-to-day management of a business operation. He had a great candidate, he said. Alan Klein. Alan had made companies work on the East and West Coasts. He knew how to scale up an organization, how to drive sales, how to push to profit. Joe respected him enormously. If he would agree to join us, it would mean a lot in Still River's consideration of an investment. Would we see him?

Oh, we guessed so.

We called Alan instantly. There was not one extra day here to fool around.

Then Scripps called, Benjy Burditt. We had his attention. He was ready to come up with his colleague Sean Foote to dig into Building-Blocks. How soon could they come?

Never look too hungry, Rolly and I always reminded ourselves. But we were starving.

"How about next week?" I suggested, wishing they would just take the next shuttle up from La Guardia. Right now. Today.

"Good," he said. It was set.

Then the *New York Times* called again. They were doing a story on HomePortfolio. They wanted photographs. Several. One for the cover of the House & Home section.

This was getting to be too much.

Caroline called. She had a major publishing company, a global operation, interested in BuildingBlocks. They were looking for good new media investment opportunities. They wanted to talk as soon as possible.

My God. We were broke. And we were hot.

Alan Klein came in, rolled up his sleeves, and spent two weeks exploring BuildingBlocks in detail. He was being courted by major national firms in New York and Chicago. He chose us.

"Those I can do anytime," he said. "But this is special. This is exciting."

"You understand that we're broke?" I asked. I was sick of having to ask that.

"I think that's going to change," Alan said. He was ready to join.

Benjy and Sean came up from New York. Benjy was as electric as ever. He came out of investment banking and McKinsey, the consulting powerhouse. He had an M.B.A. from Yale. He was an avid pilot, and I guessed he flew fast. I had to strain to keep up with his mental leaps. But he listened, too. Very carefully. Sean had been with Scripps less than three weeks. He was a young engineer and M.B.A. out of Missouri, Bell Labs, and Boston Consulting Group, with a mile-high forehead, piercing boyish eyes, and a quick, sharp laugh. Benjy and Sean told us again about E. W. Scripps, their parent company, and how an entrepreneur within the company had started HGTV, which was now two years old with a market value headed toward perhaps a billion dollars. They told us about their other venture investments and how well they were doing. They grilled us for a full day on BuildingBlocks.

They announced they were ready to move to due diligence.

Due diligence. We had waited so long to hear those words. When a VC really gets serious about an investment opportunity, it has to go through a process of turning the company and its plans and target market and resources and background and projected revenues absolutely inside out. This probing is the diligent investigation a venture capital team is obligated to perform on behalf of the backers whose capital they are investing. Scripps looked at maybe a thousand investment opportunities a year, they told us. Only a handful made it to due diligence. Due diligence is a lot of work. In our case, they wanted to move fast. They would throw all their resources at dissecting BuildingBlocks. If we would cooperate, they would condense a process that normally took a month or more into just two weeks.

Oh, we would cooperate, said Rolly.

I drove them to the airport for their flight back to New York. On the way, they probed at how Rolly and I worked together, at our roles and individual strengths.

"We're so woven together at this point that it's hard to pull apart," I said. "If I absolutely had to do it, I guess I'd say I'm the gut and Rolly's the brains. But it's not nearly that simple. All I know is that it works."

Jeff Nixon called the next morning. Scripps had already begun showering us with questions, with requests for detailed reports on every aspect of the business, the market, our personal references. And Jeff had been taking their temperature.

"They're pumped," he said, noting that Scripps was fully aware of the other interest we were drawing and was accelerating its efforts partly in response.

"Guys," he said, "they see it as a breathless run for the roses."

Rolly and I stared at the speakerphone. A breathless run for the roses? A horse race to invest in BuildingBlocks? Were we hallucinating? A year earlier, just the attention would have had us somersaulting through the office. But we had been slapped sober. This was our last shot. If one of these three potential investors didn't come through, it looked to me like it was all over. We never said that out loud. Not even to each other. Rolly would probably dig up yet one more scheme for going on. But the way I saw it, this was do-or-die time. For two years, we had spent far more time with each other than with our wives and children. I had come to a profound respect for his vision and resourcefulness and refuse-to-lose determination. But it had to come together now. At some point, Danielle had to be right. We had learned we could eat moonbeams for a while, but we could not eat them forever.

Day after day we pumped documents and data down to Scripps. And they combed through and critiqued and called around the country, doing reality checks with every sector we were touching. And the responses came back strong. They wanted another meeting. Full summit. Our offices. Their full team.

"And by the way," Benjy asked the day before they came back up, "how are you on bridge financing for the next two weeks?"

Bridge financing! More magic words. Bridge financing meant survival money advanced ahead of a major investment. He wasn't offering it yet, but he was raising it. They must have been stunned by what they saw in our books. We were defying gravity.

But we could never look hungry.

"Oh, we're fine, Benjy," I said, but the maw was too obvious to deny. "Just sucking blood from our wrists. No problem."

He laughed.

That night I drove home late and numb. It was the end of March. I had spotted crocuses on the way to work that morning, pushing up purple and white. I had wanted the life of vivid intensity. I got it. It had pulled everything down to one white-hot flame. I saw it like the tip of a welder's torch. I needed that torch to do its work and set me free. I needed to spread out again, to be tendriled and gangly, to daydream for five minutes sometime.

Dylan was finishing his homework in the living room. Everyone else was asleep. I sat next to him on the couch, loving his nearness, his lanky physical presence. This was my boy, grown into a man. We used to have such amazing conversations. Now he spoke in grunts. But I still felt the connection. And on this night I was depleted and he nourished me. We sat in silence, shoulder to shoulder, as he studied. This was rare. I think he felt my need, and he generously gave me access to our deep, shared place. I was a near-zombie.

"It's time for bed, Dad," he finally said.

"Okay, good idea," I said, and we climbed the stairs.

Sadie and I went out at dawn. The sky was oddly dappled, brass and rose across a tall ridge of clouds headed out to sea. Sadie foraged for sticks, the bigger the better, in the little woods by the field. I got centered with John Peng. I imagined him turning, on the other side of the globe, along the Sunghua River, turning focused and free, combing the mane of the wild horse, grasping the peacock's tail. And for a sacred moment I was his silent mirror, beyond all cares and longing. Beyond all desire. Focused. Free.

Then came the rush. First the summit with Scripps. Benjy and Sean were back, along with Bobby Chowdury, their brilliant technical guy, and Doug Stern, the CEO of Scripps Ventures. We already felt terrific chemistry with Benjy and Sean. They were smart and intuitive, irreverent and funny. Doug was all that plus something more embracing. He was a Ph.D. in psychology who had moved into the business world via Hollywood, publishing, and heavy lifting in corporate turnaround work. Doug was an empath type, with huge sparkling green eyes under a thick gray thatch of hair. Those eyes patted down the room, the dynamics, the heart of things. You got the feeling he looked first at the numbers in a business plan, then right to the souls of the people presenting them. In this case, those were our souls. The Scripps team had chewed through every document and business assumption we had dumped on them in minute detail. Now they were here to take our measure.

Bobby Chowdury hunkered down for the morning with Shawn, combing through our technology. By lunchtime he was pronouncing Shawn "a gem." We knew that. Rolly and I were the rougher-cut stones. Our references had come back well. "They're wonderful references," Sean Foote said. "They say you're honest and smart and determined and creative. All the right stuff." But still, we hadn't done this before. We hadn't built a company from nothing to enormous size. And nothing less than enormous would do for Scripps or any other venture investor. They were in the game for big returns or they were not in at all. That's why they called it venture capital.

We had Alan onboard now. That helped. We had proven we could walk through fire. That was big. But could we execute our plans at high speed on a grand scale? There we were untested.

"Let's have you give it to us from the top," Doug said over lunch. "We've banged on all the numbers. I'd appreciate it if you would tell us your story again. Your backgrounds. Why you got into this. Your vision. Your way so far. How you see it going forward. The whole thing."

And so we told him. Lunch went long. It was a saga. But this was the audience we had always looked for. This group knew, from its connection with HGTV, the ground we were working. They appreciated the power of vision. They understood what we had built on a shoestring. They were not put off by passion.

Doug was listening closely. Cocking his head this way and that. Looking under our skin. Weighing our heft, our attitudes, our understanding. Then exhaling big with a smile.

"There's a saying in the movie business," he said, chuckling. "They say, 'Movies aren't made, they're forced into existence.' I guess you could relate to that."

And we dove back in on the business model. Midafternoon, we all crowded into my van, piled on top of the kids' soccer cleats and basketball and crayons, and headed to the airport for their flight back to New York. A warm spring sun was shining. The mood in the van was buoyant. We joked and laughed all the way. Nobody was saying so yet, but this was looking very good. I didn't dare look at Rolly. I didn't have to. I knew we both wanted to work with this team. And I believed they wanted to work with us. We wanted to raise $3 million. Doug was on his cell phone in the backseat, checking in with HGTV. Scripps would call to give us a strong signal within twenty-four hours, he said. Not a promise yet, but a signal. And the call came, and the signal was good. If nothing blew up, we would have a term sheet from Scripps by the end of the week, they said, which would lay out their offer to invest.

But one thing. They would prefer we raised $5 million, not $3 million.

"It's a land grab." Benjy's voice came over the speakerphone. "You want to have plenty of ammunition. You want a war chest."

Rolly began to protest that we didn't really need $5 million yet. I thought I would have a heart attack. I gripped my chest and silently bulged my eyes at him, staggering across the office for effect. But we would be happy to hear their offer, he said. Thank God.

Things just got faster. We were in Joe Tischler's Boston office, making the pitch again. We couldn't stop until we had a signed term sheet from somebody, and we didn't actually have one yet. Joe was heating up. We were in Manhattan, talking with the big publishing company. They were enthusiastic. But our hearts weren't in it. We had fallen hard for Scripps and their brains and their verve. We wanted them in. Once, it was just Rolly who didn't breathe. Now, we were all holding our breath.

On Thursday, April 2, we were featured in the *New York Times*, with a photograph right on the cover of the House & Home section and a great article inside. RENOVATION STYLE, NOW JUST A CLICK AWAY, said the headline, and the article effused about Home-Portfolio. It was a long way from Rwanda and China and affairs of state. But when I looked at the *Times*'s front page that day, I couldn't muster up any envy. The leading headline was on the dismissal of the Paula Jones sexual harassment case. We would hear no more about whether the president dropped his trousers in Arkansas. Monica Lewinsky was emerging as the next big story. There was a page 1 teaser on Howard Stern's getting a new TV show. It wasn't so obvious to me anymore which events were really moving the world. HomePortfolio was lauded in the *New York Times*. That moved my world. Traffic on the Web site went soaring.

On Friday, Scripps gave us a heads-up call, and our fax machine under the eaves of the old church began to whir. We watched the term sheet come up, line by line. They were putting a $5.5 million value on the company, pre-money, about the same as our seed-round valuation. We could live with that. They wanted us to raise $5 million. Rolly frowned. They would put in three. I was ecstatic. Jeff Nixon was on the phone.

"We have until five o'clock Monday to respond to their offer," he said. "That's a short fuse."

Scripps was calling any minute. We raced through the details, point by point, marking our questions and objections. I knew Rolly would be dogged to the end on every detail. I was ready to sing. Jeff had a list of issues to raise, but I didn't hear any dealbreakers.

"I'm not getting much heartburn here," said Jeff. And the phone rang.

It was Benjy and Sean, with Doug patched in from the airport in Austin, Texas, about to board a plane. The connection was terrible. Rolly and I were practically laying our heads on the speakerphone to hear. It was Doug, proposing.

"We've got a credo," he was saying. "We've got to all really like and feel compatible with the people we invest in. If we don't, we don't do a deal, even if we love the opportunity. To us, this relationship is like a marriage, and marriages can go through really difficult times. So if we don't come in feeling very, very good about it, it's never worth it. Life is too short."

The phone echoed and crackled wildly. This was modern technology? I was thinking about Danielle. He was right. Life was too short.

"We feel tremendously good about you guys," he was saying. "We would love to be partners with you and go forward. We've put an enormous amount of energy into this in a short time. We're prepared to fly you down Monday morning to work through the issues. If you need it, we'll pay for the tickets. We understand your circumstances. We look forward to being a team and doing whatever it takes to put this thing into orbit. I really hope we end up being partners with you."

We shouted back something about feeling the same, hoping he could hear us, and he was on his plane, gone. We leapt up.

"Jesus!" I shouted. "I don't care if it sounded like it came from the moon, that was a hell of a marriage proposal!"

"It was," said Rolly, holding his face in his hands. "It was pretty darned impressive."

"Like down on one knee, but with all that strength and sense of purpose."

"It was awesome."

"Let's do this deal, Rolly."

"I think we'll do it."

And then we were roaring with joy. Riffing our air guitars. Leaping.

It was Monday, and we were running late, rushing onto the eight-thirty shuttle to La Guardia. On the flight down, we slept, talked little. It was a day for doing. Rolly read the *Wall Street Journal*. My old newspaper colleague David Wessel had his new book excerpted there. *Prosperity*, it was called, and it ran with Rolly's favorite idea, that we were living in a time that paralleled the beginnings of the electric age, a century earlier, and the vast economic gains that flowed from that technology. Not right away at its inception, but inexorably and then, suddenly, very quickly. Our timing was perfect, I thought, nodding sleepily on the plane. The hockey stick was coming. The fast, screaming updraft. It was coming on us now. It would be huge. And our little boat was pushing out into the jetstream just as the lines went north. Straight up. And we would be there. Ready to ride that millennial tide.

There was sweet young April sunlight streaming down everywhere. This would be a good day. A pure Manhattan day: fast, intense, golden. We piled into a conference room next to Doug's office with the Scripps team and Jeff Nixon, above Madison Avenue a block from the Empire State Building. Talking, negotiating, pushing, giving, patching in their attorney from Ohio and ours, Gene Barton, from Boston. Caucusing. Returning. Nailing down a deal. Gene was our rock. He had carried tens of thousands of dollars in our legal bills to keep us going. Always with a light heart and good humor. And now it was turning around. Just before dark we signed the term sheet. Scripps would put in three million. Bob Lessin and his gang would put in half a million. We had insisted they be kept in the deal. And we agreed to accept another two million as part of the round, from investors not yet named, to bring the total to $5.5 million. Scripps would throw in $200,000 immediately so we could make the office rent and payroll. The rest would be in by June.

We were paupers with despairing wives. But we were paupers who had caught the wave. We were in the new world.

"Do you understand, you could be worth twenty million in a year and a half?" Jeff asked.

No, I didn't really feel that. All I could think about was getting Lauren a new bed. Ben his guitar lessons. Dylan a fighting chance at college tuition.

"What a great day for Yale." Benjy laughed on the way out into Manhattan's evening streets. "We'll all build libraries with the money we'll make!"

And that was the very last thing on my mind. All I could think about was kissing Danielle's eyes, and stroking her hair, and breathing again. Really breathing.

I wasn't a failure! I wasn't bankrupt! I wasn't a damned fool!

Hallelujah!

We were on the pay phones at the Delta Shuttle lounge at La Guardia until the last boarding call. Calling Caroline. Art. Danny and Linnae. Louise. Our families.

"You're on your way," said Caroline. "Now go make up with your wives."

"I am thrilled," said Art. "You've suffered and pained. You've made it happen. This is a story you can tell your grandchildren."

My mother cried. It was that Swedish blood.

"Oh, Tom, oh, Tom," she said. "Now go home."

"I am, Mom. I'm going," I said when I had thanked them again and again, and my father had laughed and sighed with relief, and I felt the beginnings of some balance in the family ledger.

"But promise me one thing," I said. "People have always said I'm lucky, that things come easily to me. And I know they're right. But I want you to bear witness that this was not easy. I want you to tell anybody who asks that for this I crawled on my bloody knees. That for this, I paid."

I was getting delirious.

"Just go home to your family, Tom," my mother said gently. "There's been enough paying. We know. Now go home."

And there was Danielle. First, last, always.

"Come home," she said.

Nothing was over. It was all about beginning. Beginners' eyes. Beginning again. Now there was a company to build, and we would build it. But I had come first for the passage. For a new skin and tang. For the vivid life. I got it. The gods had a laugh with my naiveté. They made it a rough way. But the old skin was gone. I had survived the passage. I was alive. I felt redeemed, and maybe that could spread.

I had promised Carole we would dance in her kitchen when the money came. We would dance like in the first days, when every new idea was a thrill and we celebrated brainstorms like great days on Wall Street. So we danced. Across Rolly's soft pine floor, up on the benches of the breakfast nook, around her braided rug. It was joyful, but it was not the dance we expected. It was not the high-fiving cha-cha of our vision days, full of fortune fever and easy bravado. It was slower. It was more knowing. We called it a tango.

The dance with Danielle was even slower and more measured. Touching lightly before a full embrace. Circling closer, palm to palm, forehead to forehead, we slowly found each other's eyes again in careful, unspoken acknowledgments of wonder and relief. We were like battered swimmers staggering from a flood, a flood that I had brought through our door.

"That was almost too much, Tom," she said.

"It was too much," I said. "But we did it."

There were so many people who had helped make this miracle. We had to have a party. We faxed out invitations with our bold, new face. The tango would be private. The public face would be sweet roaring glory.

"We're fit. We're funded. We're ready to rock," the invitations announced. "Let's celebrate!"

We gathered at Gwen's house, with our new staff that was pouring in now and with the whole tribe of dreamers and saviors who had helped make it happen. Nick d'Arbeloff was there, and the incomparable Louise, and Jim Righter and Joe Doherty and more than we could count, all over the house and spilling out onto the back porch.

The Scripps guys were there from New York. They had been sorting through the debt the company had carried at the cliff's edge and Rolly's monster embrace of Uncle Visa. Six hundred and fifty thousand dollars, all told. It still made me shudder. Benjy rolled his eyes.

"Were we crazy, Benjy?" I asked, and it was a serious question.

"No," he said, shaking his head, looking over the crowd of backers and believers and friends, watching Rolly raise a glass to Shawn. "No, you weren't crazy," he said. "You're entrepreneurs. A little nuts, maybe, but not crazy. You guys are the real McCoy."

God, I loved that. Take me now, Jesus, I thought. I'm ready to go.

Danielle and I put Lauren to bed — in her new bed! — after the party and took a walk. It had rained. The night sky was dark and clear. We held hands. I didn't know what to say to her. We sat on a big rock by the field and looked at the stars. I remembered sitting all night like that in Illinois when we were sixteen, by a lake near the little zoo, of all places. And the lions had roared in the night and thrilled us, and I had roared back to them, and they responded again and again and again. Danielle and I had laughed until we cried. And then she had really cried. Softly, all those years ago. And I had watched the moonlight in her tears, confused, and hadn't known why she cried. And she wouldn't say. We fell in love, and she stuck with me, even when I was crazed, and more crazed. Even when I took us down a path that stripped our relationship to its foundation and made us start over. And I owed her, but that didn't begin to capture it.

I could feel her breathing next to me. Not in unison, but in alternating breaths. Always that yin and yang. Those opposites attracting, terrifying, gripping. We had held. We would hold. We were on the other side.

Epilogue

WITHIN A YEAR of our celebration at Gwen's house, the company had raised nearly $25 million from some of the top venture capital firms in the country. HomePortfolio.com had become the leading destination on the Web for premium home design products, with millions of visits to our online pages each month. The company's name was changed from BuildingBlocks to HomePortfolio Inc., to match the Web site's name. We had nearly one hundred employees, with offices in Chicago, Los Angeles, and Charlotte, North Carolina. A long list of top manufacturers were paying to offer complete information on their products at the site, and hundreds more were cooperating to have their products shown editorially. We were committed to directing our users to the nearest showrooms where they could touch and buy the products they found online, but many manufacturers also wanted to make their products available for sale online, and we had begun to oblige them. We described HomePortfolio.com as the first "portfolio" site, using the Internet to reorganize an entire industry around the interests of the individual consumer. Big-time investment banks from New York and San Francisco were pounding down our door to help pour more millions into the company. Their limousines lined up outside the old church while the bankers and their analysts excitedly told us what a huge opportunity we were riding. Internet fever was sky high, but even so, this was an amazing turn of events. We were running full-page ads in the *Wall Street Journal* and the *New York Times*. Our phones were ringing off the hook. Some days Rolly and I would pause in the whirlwind and stare at each other in astonishment. All this from the little third bedroom? We really had not been crazy after all. Or maybe we had. But what did it matter? The thing was born and real and beautiful. There were still no guarantees. There never would be now. But it was working.

We were seeing our families again. They had survived and flourished. Danielle was still holding down her job, but with a sense of new possibilities close at hand. She was laughing easily again, with a certain rolling of her eyes that I thought was new. Maybe we lived with permanent amazement and relief.

In the summer of his sixteenth year, Dylan went to Africa to work on the Web site of a newspaper in Namibia. A new realm was emerging online, and I was thankful to be part of it. But the whole world, old realms and new, was still our home, and we were glad to be in it.